A DEMOCRACY OF DISTINCTION

A DEMOCRACY OF DISTINCTION

Aristotle and the Work of Politics

JILL FRANK

The University of Chicago Press

CHICAGO AND LONDON

The University of Chicago Press, Chicago 60637
The University of Chicago Press, Ltd., London
© 2005 by The University of Chicago
All rights reserved. Published 2005
Printed in the United States of America
14 13 12 11 10 09 08 07 06 05   1 2 3 4 5

ISBN-13: 978-0-226-26018-1 (cloth)
ISBN-13: 978-0-226-26019-8 (paper)

Library of Congress Cataloging-in-Publication Data

Frank, Jill.
A democracy of distinction : Aristotle and the work of politics / Jill Frank.
p.   cm.
Includes bibliographical references and index.
ISBN 0-226-26018-6 (cloth : alk. paper) — ISBN 0-226-26019-4 (pbk. : alk. paper)
1. Constitutional history.   2. Democracy.   3. Aristotle—Contributions in political science.
4. Political science—Philosophy.   I. Title.
JF51.F695 2005
320′.01—dc22
2004010905

♾ This paper meets the requirements of ANSI/NISO Z39.48-1992 (Permanence of Paper).

To the memory of
Anya Tannenbaum Kisilevsky Puterman

All human happiness or misery takes the form of action;
the end for which we live is a certain kind of activity, not a quality.

ARISTOTLE, *Poetics*

It is the activity of the present that really counts.

ARISTOTLE, *Nicomachean Ethics*

CONTENTS

ACKNOWLEDGMENTS xi

LIST OF ABBREVIATIONS xiii

INTRODUCTION 1

ONE The Nature of Identity 17

The Force of Nature 21
The Nature of Nature 38
The Work of Man 49

TWO The Use of Property 54

The Activity of Use 57
The Virtue of Property 69
The Politics of Property 74

THREE The Virtue of Justice 81

Reciprocity 85
Good Judgment 95
Justice and Virtue 101

FOUR The Rule of Law 112

The Laws of Citizens 115
The Laws of Polities 126
Constitution 135

FIVE The Polity of Friendship 138

Unity and Difference 143
Friendship and Faction 147
The Middle Class 163
The Work of Politics 178

WORKS CITED 181

INDEX 193

ACKNOWLEDGMENTS

> The philosopher, even when by himself, can contemplate truth, and the better the wiser he is; he can perhaps do so better if he has fellow workers.
> ARISTOTLE, *Nicomachean Ethics*

This philosophical project owes much more than I can say to the participation of many fellow workers, to their generosity, friendship, critical good judgment, and enthusiastic support.

For conversations and contributions to particular chapters, my thanks go to Amittai Aviram, Marianne Constable, Jeremy Elkins, Peter Euben, Michaele Ferguson, Bryan Garsten, Bonnie Honig, Nancy Kokaz, Richard Kraut, Allen Miller, Joshua Mitchell, Sara Monoson, Ed Munn, Alfred Nordmann, Jennifer Pitts, Dan Sabia, Steve Salkever, Jerry Wallulis, and Bernie Yack. Danielle Allen, Steve Salkever, Arlene Saxonhouse, and an anonymous reader read the whole manuscript and provided, at a crucial point, exacting and generous comments that improved it tremendously. I am grateful to have in Marianne Constable, Marcie Frank, Bonnie Honig, and Nina Levine longstanding and invaluable interlocutors on the themes of this project as well as on others that have influenced my writing. For their unflagging interest and steadfast confidence in my work, their willingness to read early versions of every chapter and often middle and late versions as well, and for their inordinately helpful comments along the way, I thank Larry Glickman, Gerry Mara, and Gary Shiffman. Amittai Aviram, late in the game and at short notice, read the whole manuscript, homed in on what was still missing, and, in his inimitable gentleness, offered penetrating and important suggestions. For doing all of the above, over many years, again and again, and with overwhelming generosity, my very deep thanks go to Patchen Markell.

For inspiring my interest in thinking philosophically about matters political and for shaping my thinking about Aristotle on property, in particular, I thank my graduate school teachers and peers, especially Philippe Nonet, Hanna Pitkin, Jeremy Waldron, Dan Avnon, Marianne Constable, Jeremy Elkins, Jackie Stevens, and the members of the Heidegger reading group, led by Philippe Nonet. After graduate school, generous fellowship support from the Canadian government provided the distance I needed to substantially reformulate the project that was my dissertation into this one. A supportive and stimulating community broadened my appreciation of the ways in which political philosophy and political science can work together and contributed fundamentally to the structure of this project. Eva Bellin, Keith Bybee, Danny Goldhagen, Bonnie Honig, Michael Jones-Correa, and Deborah Yashar gave me this community. While completing this project at the University of South Carolina, I have been surrounded by congenial colleagues, students, and friends. The Department of Political Science, its chair, Harvey Starr, the Philosophy Department, and the College of Liberal Arts provided much-appreciated academic and financial support. For their intellectual generosity and bountiful goodwill, I am especially grateful to Amittai Aviram, Nina Levine, Esther Richey, the late Bill Richey, and Brian Roots. Corey Garriott, Glenn Prince, and Elisha Savchak were exceptionally able research assistants.

I presented early versions and parts of chapters to audiences at Harvard University, Hebrew University, Northwestern University, Yale University, the University of Alberta, and the University of South Carolina, as well as at meetings of the American Political Science Association, the Midwest Political Science Association, the Western Political Science Association, and the Northeastern Political Science Association, where I received extremely helpful feedback. An earlier version of chapter 1 was published as "Citizens, Slaves, and Foreigners: Aristotle on Human Nature" in the *American Political Science Review* 98, no. 1 (February 2004). Parts of chapter 4 appeared in "Aristotle's Theramenes at Athens: A Poetic History" in *Parallax* 9, no. 4 (2003), co-authored with Sara Monoson. I am grateful to the American Political Science Association and to the Taylor & Francis Group for permission to reprint this material. For his commitment to and confidence in this project I thank John Tryneski at University of Chicago Press. I am grateful as well to Jane Zanichkowsky for copyediting, Ashley Cave for promotions, Leslie Keros for production editing, and Barbara Jellow for my book's design. I owe special thanks to Kevin Glowacki for permission to use his photograph on the cover of this book and to Nina Levine for finding the photograph.

For teaching me early and often to appreciate the ways in which the work of life involves generosity and friendship, two Aristotelian themes that appear again and again in the pages of this book and that I have had the great good fortune to experience in abundance, I am most grateful to Esther and Hershey Frank, Adam Frank, Marcie Frank and Kevin Pask, Emma and Violet. And for cultivating my appreciation of the ways in which pleasure perfects—another critical Aristotelian theme that appears only from time to time in the pages of this book—my deepest thanks go to Larry Glickman and to our children, Alexander and Abigail.

ABBREVIATIONS

AP	*Constitution of Athens (Athenaion Politeia)*
DA	*De Anima*
EE	*Eudemian Ethics*
HA	*History of Animals*
MM	*Magna Moralia*
Meta.	*Metaphysics*
NE	*Nicomachean Ethics*
PA	*Parts of Animals*
Po.	*Poetics*
Pol.	*Politics*
Rhet.	*Rhetoric*

INTRODUCTION

> Where one man rules and another is ruled,
> they may be said to have a work.
>
> ARISTOTLE, *Politics*

Politics has been described as work ever since its birth in ancient Greece. Where there is ruling and being ruled, Aristotle says, there is "a work."[1] Hannah Arendt rightly adds that Aristotle was "well aware" that what is at stake in politics is "no less than . . . the work of man."[2] This book is about the work of politics and about the work of man. It is about how constitutions work to form citizens and how citizens work to actualize themselves and the political institutions that guide their formation. It is about how the work of building political structures and that of establishing individual character—the work of what the Greeks called city and soul—coexist in a dynamic and reciprocal relationship. And above all, it is about the activity, *energeia,* at work in making city and soul.

It may seem obvious to claim that the constitution of a polity and the institutions it sets up to administer security, healthcare, education, employment, and housing, the tax burdens it levies, and the familial structures it promotes all affect its citizens, shaping not simply the courses of their lives but the formation of their self-understandings and subjectivities as well.[3] And it may seem equally obvious to claim that the character of citizens and the individual choices they make, especially at the ballot box but also in their daily lives, shape the policies that preserve their constitution and produce the institutions that affect the courses of their lives. And yet any number of recent debates attest to how difficult it is to keep simultaneously in mind these modes of work and their interrelation.

---

1. This quotation appears in Aristotle's discussion of the relation between master and slave, but I am using it to broader purpose. I use Rackham, trans., *Nicomachean Ethics,* and Ross, *Nicomachean Ethics,* rev. Ackrill and Urmson; and Rackham, trans., *Politics,* and Jowett, trans., *Politics,* at times modified. In all English translations from Aristotle, the Greek terms have been added by me.

2. Arendt, *Human Condition,* pp. 206–7.

3. This is not to say that citizenship exhausts identity. There are institutions and practices that contribute to and are constituted by one's activities but do not have an obvious or direct relation to one's political regime.

Consider the popular and congressional debates about welfare reform in the mid-1990s. Supporting the Republican-backed Personal Responsibility and Work Opportunity Act of 1996, conservatives favored stopping welfare payments or replacing welfare with "workfare" so as to force welfare recipients to fulfill their personal responsibilities and to meet their obligations to contribute to society. Insofar as welfare was blamed for trapping people in a "hopeless cycle of dependency" and making those living in poverty poor citizens, there was, to be sure, the implicit recognition that governmental institutions contribute to the shaping of individual character. The virtues of good citizenship, it was nonetheless argued, require not governmental intervention but "tough love" to encourage individuals to make of themselves responsible citizens by achieving independence from government.[4] Agreeing about the dangers of dependency and its threats to political life, liberals, by contrast, argued that, although development is a matter of individual character, the state has an obligation to provide those living in poverty with the resources they need (in the form of, say, education, healthcare, and freedom from drudgery) to become independent citizens.[5] To them, this responsibility lay, in large part, with governmental institutions.

Recent debates in political science about the role of social capital in "making democracy work" similarly tend to set apart and oppose the roles of individual character and political institutions. Robert Putnam argues that the creation of social capital and civic responsibility depends on the presence of voluntary associations and charity, which themselves depend on the characters of individual citizens.[6] Theda Skocpol counters that social capital may be the product of voluntary associations but that these associations are guided not by the characters of citizens but by governmental incentives.[7] Consider as well debates in the United States about affirmative action. One side argues that distributive justice mandates allotting slots at a university only to those whose individual talents—usually determined by grade point averages or standardized test scores—merit them. The other side counters that just decisions about allotments must compensate for the bias of standardized tests, the history of exclusionary institutions, and the ongoing

---

4. For the adoption of this approach by Republican speaker of the house Newt Gingrich and Senator Phil Gramm, see Kinsley, "Ultimate Block Grant."

5. See, e.g., Moon, "Moral Basis of the Democratic Welfare State"; King and Waldron, "Citizenship, Social Citizenship, and the Defence of Welfare Provision"; Goodin, *Reasons for Welfare.*

6. Putnam, "Bowling Alone"; Putnam, "Strange Disappearance of Civic America."

7. Skocpol, "Unravelling from Above."

institutionalized oppression of women, African Americans, and other minorities. Individuals or institutions? This opposition structures not only debates about the distribution of social benefits but those about the distribution of social burdens as well. Think of debates about punishment. When criminal acts are performed in environments of oppression, deprivation, and violence, should these acts count as voluntary and so inculpate the individual actor? Or does responsibility lie instead with the structures and institutions (or their absence) that nurtured these acts? Should women who have suffered abuse at the hands of their partners, for example, be subject to the same homicide laws as others when they kill their tormentors, or ought inadequate safeguards against domestic abuse bear the real blame?

These opposing approaches produce significantly different outcomes. When individual character, talents, and virtues are credited with or blamed for making someone the citizen she is, these entitle her to benefits or burdens regardless of how or whether distribution in her favor affects others.[8] When, on the other hand, governmental institutions are treated as responsible for the formation of citizenship, capability, and character, the social goods or evils produced by exercises of individual agency will be viewed as collective benefits or burdens. And they will be distributed as such, which is to say, without particular attention to the talents and virtues or disabilities and vices of specified citizens.[9] Although it may seem obvious to insist that institutions *and* individual character jointly do the work of politics, these ongoing debates demonstrate that there is a substantial lack of clarity about what this insight means. They also demonstrate that, in the face of complex social and political phenomena, the content and force of this insight are all too often lost. By insisting on the (partial) truth of each side's claims and thus moderating both sides, this insight changes the structure of these political debates and also how we think about political life itself.

To explore the political work of constitutions, institutions, and character and their interrelation, my primary guide is Aristotle. This is because Aristotle refuses to choose between political structures and individual character or, to put it another way, between politics and ethics. He insists, instead, on both. Aristotle is an especially productive resource owing to his unique understanding of activity—which includes the doings of daily life, along with the practice and administration of property, justice, and law—and to the key role he assigns to activity, *energeia*, in

---

8. See, e.g., Nozick, *Anarchy, State, and Utopia.*

9. In John Rawls's famous formulation, individual talents ought to be considered "arbitrary from a moral point of view" and therefore should play no role in the determination of a just distribution of social and political goods. See *Theory of Justice,* p. 312.

4   INTRODUCTION

the formation of individual character and political structures. I return to this claim below. First, a few words about what relevance Aristotle might have for contemporary politics, broadly construed, to lay the ground for the discussion of activity.

Some writers claim that pre-modern polities are irrelevant for our times given considerations of size. Many ancient Greek cities, however, had populations of up to four hundred thousand. That is, to be sure, not the 27 million of Canada or the 270 million of the United States, but it is also not the face-to-face community many imagine when they think nostalgically of the Greeks. If at first glance Aristotle's advocacy of what, by current standards, would be called a politics of exclusion suggests that he has little to contribute to contemporary political theory and practice, a closer look at his ethical, political, psychological, physical, and metaphysical writings opens possibilities that he is usually seen to be foreclosing, both for his political science and for our own. Indeed, although his time and place and vocabulary are different from ours in crucial ways, Aristotle addresses what Stephen White, drawing on dominant strains in contemporary theory, describes as the three challenges facing late modern democracies: social and material inequality, tendencies toward variants of fundamentalism, and the need to recognize and accommodate the pivotal political role of relatively stable middle classes.[10]

Putting the question of equality at the center of his political philosophy, Aristotle discusses property, justice, and law in terms of the inevitable conflicts that arise owing to differing perceptions and treatments of equality. Insisting that the unity proper to a political community is one that respects and safeguards difference or plurality, Aristotle seeks ways to discipline the overreaching characteristic of fundamentalisms of all kinds and, understanding difference to be a matter of differentiated individuality, he effects a shift away from debates about the politics of identity *or* difference. Finally, in his advocacy of mixed and middling regimes, Aristotle translates the mean—as that which aims at "what is intermediate" (*NE* 1106b28–29)—from an ethical attitude to a political mandate, making him perhaps the first supporter of a strong middle class.

Aristotle's celebration of the mean is probably his most familiar doctrine. In a time when lives, practices, and theories are structured and informed by extremes (Left versus Right, friends versus foes, high versus low, universalism versus relativism, nature versus nurture, community versus individual, rich versus poor), it provides a welcome and much-needed reminder that a middle exists and that it is

10. White, "Three Conceptions of the Political."

a viable course to choose. His is a stronger point, however, namely, that the middle is the only course to choose if our ethical and political associations are to be sustained. To many, it may seem that Aristotle's call to the middle has already and all too eagerly been heeded. The American Left has moved right. In foreign and domestic policy, erstwhile foes are friends (and vice versa). Hollywood celebrities win presidencies and governorships. Politicians write educational books about virtue. We live, some say, in a culture of mediocrity, where the middle, as the common denominator, contributes not to a vitalization but to a "dumbing down" of our associations.

Aristotle's mean, positioned between excess and deficit, is not a middle ground in any usual sense, however. It is not achieved simply by combining excess and deficit. As we will see, a middle class cannot emerge from a combination of rich and poor. Good policy is not produced by practicing bipartisanship. Acting well is not a matter of combining slavishness and mastery. Aristotle's middle, instead, combines both extremes and neither to come up with a common term that, as such, is not reducible to its component parts. A middle class emerges when, on the basis of their self-interests, the few and the many cooperate to their mutual advantage to produce a common good that is something more than an aggregation of their discrete self-interests. Good policy recognizes ideological extremes but produces nonpartisan outcomes. Acting well is a matter of obeying (as do slaves) and ruling (as do masters), but in a way that is characteristic of neither—freely. This orientation to the middle is not in any sense an orientation to mediocrity. On the contrary, requiring, as we will see, hard work over time, particularly in the form of the practice of virtue, it is, rather, a call to an ethics and politics of distinction, one that is no less urgent today than it was in fourth-century Athens.

Testifying to Aristotle's continued relevance, the past decades have seen a renewed and vigorous interest in his writings. Scholars with varying and often opposing political commitments claim that Aristotle's writings offer rich resources for contemporary politics, although they disagree about what sorts of resources and what sorts of politics his work promotes. Some see in Aristotle, particularly in what they understand as his commitment to the central place of excellence or virtue in political life, a call to governance by the aristocratic few who are properly educated to virtue.[11] Others read Aristotle's emphasis on nurturing by means of education the individual capacities of citizens as a call for a well-functioning lib-

---

11. See, e.g., L. Strauss, *City and Man,* chap. 1; Winthrop, "Aristotle and Political Responsibility"; E. Miller, "Prudence and the Rule of Law."

6   INTRODUCTION

eral or social democratic regime.[12] Although their political commitments are at odds, these commentators all read Aristotle with the aim of extracting a prescriptive model for contemporary politics or as a point of departure for developing political institutions for our times.

With the aristocratic interpretations, this book argues for the central place of virtue in a political life. And with the democratic readings, it sees in Aristotle's writings resources for contemporary democratic theory and practice.[13] At the same time, it challenges both interpretive approaches and their conclusions. Aristotle's writings, in my view, do not offer prescriptions or blueprints either for ethical behavior or for how to organize political institutions. The crucial question, I believe, is not whether Aristotle's politics is democratic or aristocratic. It is, rather, what his philosophical theory and practice may teach about ethics and politics. Focusing on his practice of philosophy, a number of scholars have argued that Aristotle's "endoxic" method—whereby he canvasses the particular, different, and conflicting opinions of the many and the wise to arrive at philosophical truths—"may be a model of what is supposed to go on when the many act and deliberate collectively."[14] Aristotle's endoxic method is said, in this way, to model democratic sovereignty even if Aristotle did not himself profess to be a democrat.[15] But unlike democratic sovereignty as it is usually practiced, in which differences among conflicting opinions are resolved by the rule of the majority, truth, to Aristotle, is very rarely a matter of majority rule (*Meta.* 1009b2). Aristotle's endoxic method, rather, seeks answers to hard questions by bringing conflicting opinions into conversation with one another to come up with a middle

---

12. See, e.g., Nussbaum, "Aristotelian Social Democracy"; Nussbaum, "Nature, Function, and Capability."

13. Nichols, *Citizens and Statesmen,* pp. 1–12, takes up the competing democratic and aristocratic interpretations of Aristotle's politics and, situating her book at their juncture, describes her interpretation of Aristotle as offering an understanding of politics that retains the emphasis on political participation and community from the democratic interpretation, thereby correcting and resisting the authoritarian impulses of the aristocratic one while simultaneously retaining the aristocratic commitment to excellence and to the respect of individual merit and contribution, thereby correcting what she calls the arbitrary character of popular rule and of an undifferentiated populace espoused by advocates of democracy. My readings are in line with Nichols on these fronts.

14. Waldron, "Wisdom of the Multitude," p. 570.

15. For similar treatments of the politics of Aristotle's philosophic practice, see Nussbaum, "Saving Aristotle's Appearances"; Barnes, "Aristotle and the Methods of Ethics." For accounts that challenge this view, see Schofield, "Ideology and Philosophy"; Nichols, *Citizens and Statesmen,* pp. 8–9.

that, as an Aristotelian mean, draws on both sets of opinions but represents neither.

Indeed, Aristotle's signal methodological contribution to contemporary debates lies in his commitment to bringing together to produce something new ideas and practices that are usually set in opposition.[16] These include not only the ideas of the many and the wise but also institutions and popular action, individual and community, and unity and difference. Aristotle's political philosophical method thus resists the binarisms that inform and stymie much of contemporary political thought.[17] The dialectical quality of Aristotle's political philosophy, its open-endedness and, indeed, its circularity are evident not only in his endoxic method but more subtly in his substantive teachings about fundamental ethical and political concepts and practices. For him, the constituent parts of each of these unities are in a dynamic and reflexive tension: virtue is constituted by habits and actions (*NE* 1098b31–1099a4); property is a mode of holding things as one's own for common use (*Pol.* 1263a25–26); the soul is composed of potentiality and actuality (*DA* II.1); and the polity is a unity of the different (*Pol.* 1261a24, 30). Aristotle does not set out to obviate these tensions but, as I show in the following chapters, he takes them and their irreducible combination to be of the essence of virtue, property, soul, and city.

Understood in this way, his accounts of virtue, property, soul, and city, along with his treatments of justice and law, look different from our own. They are nonetheless available to us and are especially productive sources for expanding the horizons of some of political philosophy's perennially difficult questions. If we generally treat identity as either natural or constructed, Aristotle's insistence on tying identity to activity makes such a choice unnecessary. If property is generally thought of as private or communal, Aristotle's "holding as one's own for common use" bridges that opposition. If the rule of law is generally opposed to the rule of men, Aristotle's rule of law is not. Aristotle, in other words, confronts head-on the fundamental conundrum of unity and difference for each of us as individual citi-

---

16. Here and in the rest of this book, I depend on an account of practices not unlike that of Alasdair MacIntyre, according to whom a practice is "any coherent and complex form of socially established cooperative human activity through which goods internal to that form of activity are realized in the course of trying to achieve those standards of excellence which are appropriate to, and partially definitive of, that form of activity, with the result that human powers to achieve excellence, and human conceptions of the ends and goods involved, are systematically extended" (*After Virtue,* p. 187).

17. *Contra* Paul Cartledge, for example, who takes Aristotle's primary mode of analysis to be "binary and polar." See *The Greeks,* pp. 11–16.

zens as well as for regimes and their constituent institutions. And he aims not to resolve the *aporia* attendant on this conundrum but rather to set it out in its depth and breadth as the crucial matter for ethics and therefore for politics, for politics and therefore for ethics. It is Aristotle's activity-centered philosophy that produces these complex and convincing accounts of character, constitution, property, justice, and law. Seen through its lens, these crucial constituents of a political life become not set structures and frameworks, as many moderns would have it, but everyday practices. Such practices gel into habits and customs and institutions, to be sure, but ones that may be altered by the activities of those who, in the first place, help make them.

In offering these readings, my primary aim is not to produce a definitive Aristotle but to bring to light elements of his political philosophy that have been underexplored and that are of interest today, particularly for contemporary democratic politics. It may seem odd to argue for making this philosophy available for democratic political practice. As is well known, Aristotle was largely critical of the democracies of his time. Ruled by the many who are free, democracies, he says, tend to be immoderately liberal. With too much liberty, people live as they like rather than as they ought (*Pol.* 1317b10–15). As the exclusions from citizenship under his preferred constitutions make plain (masters are citizens, not slaves; heads of households, not women, working farmers, shopkeepers, or craftsmen; Greeks, not foreigners), Aristotle is also critical of democracy's treatment of everyone as equals without regard to their distinction. He criticized, then, not only democratic liberty but democratic equality as well.

If Aristotle makes no secret of his hostility to democracy, I argue that his activity-oriented philosophy nonetheless harbors democratic possibilities. Indeed, it opens the way to a particularly dynamic form of democracy that can accommodate the reciprocal relation between institutions and citizens. For some scholars, democracy is best understood from the top down, which is to say, as a formal institutional and constitutional phenomenon that emphasizes the rule of law, regime formation (and formalization), and regime change.[18] For others,

---

18. For top-down approaches, see Hansen, *Athenian Assembly;* Hansen, *Athenian Democracy;* Ostwald, *From Popular Sovereignty to the Sovereignty of Law.* For versions of this top-down approach applicable to contemporary politics, see such deliberative democrats as Jürgen Habermas and Seyla Benhabib, who, while emphasizing the activity of politics, nonetheless seek to derive transcendent ethical norms for this activity or to guide it by rational dialogue made possible by rules or laws or a constitution.

democracy is better understood from below as an "*a*constitutional" phenomenon associated with popular action and sporadic revolutionary moments.[19] Working from the top down and from the bottom up, Aristotle, in my view, invites an understanding of democracy as constituted by what Josiah Ober calls "dynamic tensions" between institutionalization and popular action.[20] But this use of *democracy* is controversial when applied to Aristotle. For, notwithstanding scholarly disagreements about democracy, classical and contemporary scholars broadly agree that as the inventor of the rule of law and of constitutionalism, Aristotle is primarily responsible for the "rule-centeredness" and formalism of Greek political theory and, some would add, of Western political theory.[21] To many scholars who take popular action, alone or in combination with institutions, to be the hallmark of democracy, he can be no friend of democracy.

Focusing on the premium Aristotle places on activity in his treatments of all aspects of politics, from its definition to its constituent parts, allows for a more complex appreciation. Unlike the other branches of philosophy, Aristotle says, politics, like ethics, has a "practical aim," which is to say that it invites an "inquiry into the region of action, *praxis*" (*NE* 1103b26–30). Such an inquiry requires taking seriously the ways in which action is its own end (*NE* 1140b6), the way in which the subject matter of politics—action—governs itself. And so Aristotle's political philosophy, suited to its subject matter, avoids the theorization and formalization characteristic of much political philosophy. Rejecting certainty as a standard for ethics and politics, Aristotle maintains that "we must . . . be content if, in dealing with subjects and starting from premises thus uncertain . . . we seek the degree of precision which belongs to its subject matter" (*NE* 1104a4, 1094b21–30). This is not to suggest that his approach is not normative. But recognizing the centrality of activity to his ethical and political philosophy and taking seriously the ways in which action is self-governing challenges the dominant interpretation of Aristotle's poli-

19. For arguments "from below," see Wolin, "Norm and Form," p. 37; Wolin, "Transgression, Equality, and Voice"; Wolin, "Fugitive Democracy." See Barber, "Foundationalism and Democracy," and Lummis, *Radical Democracy,* who advocate this approach to contemporary democratic theory.

20. Ober advocates this way of understanding democracy in his studies of democratic Athens, although he does not attribute it to Aristotle: see *Athenian Revolution,* p. 31; Ober and Hedrick, introduction to *Demokratia,* pp. 3–16. For his reading of Aristotle, see Ober, *Political Dissent in Democratic Athens,* chap. 6.

21. Wolin, "Transgression, Equality, and Voice," pp. 63, 85; Wolin, "Norm and Form," p. 44; Ober, *Political Dissent in Democratic Athens,* p. 295.

10   INTRODUCTION

tics as rule-centered and formalistic. It challenges as well interpretations that take his teleological commitments to presuppose an "authoritarian" standard—a *telos*—that governs action from without.[22] And it calls into question the very possibility of using Aristotle's ethical and political writings as a blueprint for our time. In those interpretations, action is the means to some end determined by a rule, set either in the past or in the future. This denies the *activity* of action, the way it takes place in a present between past and future.

To treat action as self-governing is not, however, to say that there is no "doer behind the deed." It is not to say that action is a kind of spontaneous generation, for this is to treat action as appearing in the world from nowhere, that is, as without a past. Instead, to Aristotle, because actions have "nothing fixed or invariable about them," they depend on actors who must consider "what is suited to the circumstances on each occasion" (*NE* 1104a4–9). This means that Aristotle's ethical and political philosophy is not only activity-oriented but agent-centered as well. Action, thus understood, is neither ex nihilo nor fully determined from its inception. Instead, actions emerge from individual habits or dispositions, what is generally called character, and so are bound to their author. This neither erases the boundlessness of actions nor renders them determinate because Aristotle understands agency itself in terms of activity. Who the doer of a deed is, is not set once and for all but is continually being determined by the activities the doer performs.

To see how action can be both determinate or stable *and* contingent or unpredictable requires looking more closely at the activity of action itself, and this calls for understanding action not simply as a deed but rather as including what gave rise to the deed in the first place, the conditions of its possibility. These cannot be reduced to a rule—past or future—but depend on an agent, her character, and the stable dispositions that generate the activity that produces the deed. Activity, *energeia,* is, for Aristotle, the more inclusive term.[23] If the deed or action is a product of activity, it is not activity's sole product. For even as activities emerge from a stable character, activities themselves are formative of character. The more courageously I act, the more courageous I become. Activities produce actions and activities produce character. They also produce institutions and, indeed, constitutions. It is the repeated practice of law, for example, in this particular way, that produces this institution of law. It is that institution of law that preserves and produces this

---

22. See, e.g., Villa, *Arendt and Heidegger,* pp. 42–52.

23. For discussion of the relation between action, *praxis,* and activity, *energeia,* see chapter 1, pp. 34–36.

constitution. Activity thus operates as a bridge between individual character and political structures. The activities performed by citizens produce political institutions and structures, and these structures, produced by individual activities, guide the activities that are formative of individual character.

Which comes first, then, character or institutions? Jean-Jacques Rousseau's famous answer is: neither. Rather, "the legislator," the godlike lawgiver who appears from outside the regime and remains always outside, comes first. It is the legislator who sets up the regime's offices and institutions and also persuades the citizens that they should follow the dictates of this constitution.[24] Rousseau thus resolves the circularity of the relation between character and institutions by recourse to a deus ex machina, something foreign to the regime. Modern and contemporary political philosophy are replete with this sort of solution to the problem of circularity: for the social contractarians, there is the founding moment; for Adam Smith or John Stuart Mill, there is the impartial spectator; for Immanuel Kant, the categorical imperative; for John Rawls, the original position. These mechanisms may solve the problem of circularity. In so doing, however, they remove from politics the work that I claim is its substance.

Aristotle, in my reading, seeks not to resolve the circularity but to exploit it, staying within the relation between individuals and political structures by way of the in-between of activity. In this way, the resources for regulation are to be found in the practices of citizens. Self-regulation, so understood, does not require recourse to a part of the self that is outside its usual activity or an alienation of one part of the self from another, and self-governance does not require a framework of laws or institutions immune to challenge. Instead, citizens of a polity participate in the activities of politics, and regulatory standards emerge from these activities, even as they, as activities of politics, presuppose institutional fora for their practice and a constitution for their guidance. This means that there is no causal arrow in Aristotle's story about character and politics or, if there is one, it points in both directions.

When they are understood in terms of activity, individual character and political structures become less static and are able to accommodate the dynamism that is key to political analysis and that, as we have seen, is, in theory and practice, too often missing: a person's character will change if and when the activities she performs change; the institution of law will change if and when the activity or practice of law changes; a constitution will change when its institutions and practices

---

24. Rousseau, *On the Social Contract,* pp. 162–65 (bk. 2, chap. 7).

12   INTRODUCTION

of citizenship change. Were distributive determinations of property and offices, the art of legislation, and citizen identity all and only regime-dependent and fixed, or all and only pre-politically character-dependent and fixed, or dependent on a deus ex machina and thereby fixed, changes and reversals of fortune affecting citizens, institutions, and regimes would be hard to explain. Changes are possible and explicable only with due emphasis on the site of these changes, namely, activity. When they are understood in terms of activity, character and political structures may be seen in their proper light, namely, in accordance with the initial and obvious insight that they are mutually constituting. It is activity that turns the work of politics—institutions, character, and regime itself—into works in progress.

A person's activities belong to no one but the person. The site of activity is, thus, irreducibly singular. Activities, in this way, distinguish one person from another. At the same time, because activities emerge from habits and dispositions that are products of education and socialization, a person's activities are influenced by a plurality of people and in multiple ways. Because activities produce actions and institutions in a world, activities throw each actor into a plurality. Insofar as activity is singular in its doing and plural in its origin and effect, it is integral to understanding the simultaneously unifying and differentiating work of politics. Indeed, by insisting, via activity, on a dynamic and reciprocal interrelation between individual character and political structures, this book rejects the terms of one of the leading debates in late twentieth-century political theory: the debate between liberalism and communitarianism.[25] Communitarians in varying guises (including civic republicans and virtue theorists) tend to emphasize community rather than individuality and unity rather than difference, and liberals in varying guises (including rights theorists and utilitarians) tend to stress individualism and difference instead of community. This book, by contrast, is about how political orders require a nontotalizing commonality, one whose pursuit safeguards plurality and individual interests. Rejecting the priority of either individual or community produces a polity that is neither a homogeneous unity nor a simple aggregation of differentiated individuals but, rather, both and neither, that is, a unity of the different (*Pol.* 1261a24, 30).

---

25. Yack, *Problems of a Political Animal,* pp. 1–23, also addresses the ways in which Aristotle's politics, although cited as authority by advocates of liberalism and communitarianism alike, offers an alternative to both. Stressing the ways in which Aristotle's political theory refuses liberalism's commitment to a pre-political state of affairs and resists communitarianism's romantic attachment to an ideal of social harmony, Yack develops what he calls a communitarian account of political conflict and competition.

Not all activity is unifying, of course. When I hit you, or refuse to allow you to walk across my property to get to the beachfront, or evict you from my rental unit owing to your sexual orientation or religion, these activities—everyday occurrences in any political life—generate not unity but conflict. Two factors mitigate conflicts such as these: the regulation of activity by laws prohibiting such conduct and punishing it when it occurs, and the regulation of activity by the practice of virtue on the part of citizens. The first mode of regulation—the rule of law—is an integral part of the work of politics and plays a key role in unifying a political order. Insofar as law operates impartially and generally, however, treating all citizens equally or without distinction, the unity it achieves will compromise individual difference, unless, that is, it is paired with the second mode, namely, the practice of virtue.

The practice of virtue and, indeed, its opposite—the practice of vice—are brought into play by Aristotle's emphasis on individual agency, not rules. For some scholars, Aristotelian virtue lies somehow outside and beyond politics. It functions as a master concept by which to judge political regimes and their citizens or acts as a doctrine that produces prescriptions.[26] Virtue, as I understand it, plays both a more limited and a more expansive role in Aristotle's political philosophy. It is more limited in that, unlike law, virtue regulates conduct by being partial and agent-specific. That no two people are courageous or liberal or moderate in exactly the same way—some need to be more daring to act courageously, others need to exhibit greater reserve—attests to the singularity of the practice of virtue and to the differences among its practitioners. Although self-ish, virtue unavoidably involves other people. Virtue thus regulates our activity in relation to others as a mode of self-regulation. So understood, as a self-governing *activity,* Aristotelian virtue (no less than vice) is acquired and maintained, or lost, by practice. Not a static trait of character, something one has or lacks, it is better understood not simply as a noun but also as a verb.[27] As the practice of self-governance, virtue, at the individual level, models the bidirectional work of politics, functioning simultaneously to form individual character and to shape, by interactions with others, political structures. As the proper use and cultivation of one's habits in activity, virtue is equally an individual aim and a communal aim. It is, thus, the aim not only of ethics but of politics as well.

26. See, e.g., F. Miller, *Nature, Justice, and Rights.*

27. In my reading, Aristotle would find Bernard Williams's distinction between something being a problem in moral philosophy and something being a problem in the philosophy of action to be a distinction without a difference: see *Ethics and the Limits of Philosophy,* p. 44.

14   INTRODUCTION

Virtue plays an expansive role in my reading of Aristotle, then, insofar as it makes manifest the ways in which politics and ethics belong together and depend on one another. As a reading of Aristotle and as a claim about politics, this is controversial. Stephen Salkever argues, by contrast, that Aristotle treats human happiness, *eudaimonia,* as the most comprehensive end, or *telos,* subjecting even his most preferred or virtuous regimes to critique from the standpoint of happiness, thus calling attention not to the possibilities but rather to the limits of political practice as a project for the constitution of virtue.[28] Driven by somewhat different concerns, contemporary liberal political theorists tend to argue that politics must not be joined to ethics because only by keeping them apart may both identity and difference in modern life be respected: we can agree about justice but not about the good life, and so to say that politics and ethics belong together is to subject ethics, as a space of difference and disagreement, to the unifying force of politics. Communitarians, by contrast, tend to argue that politics must be joined to ethics, but, paradoxically, they offer the same reason as do liberals: because that is the only way to respect both identity and difference in modern life. Politics, on its own, is a space of difference and disagreement where strangers act strategically in the pursuit of self-interest; ethics is the site of thicker attachments that counterbalance the centrifugal tendencies of politics. Liberals and communitarians thus assign "identity" to one sphere and "difference" to the other (but in different ways) and then relate them to one another either by establishing a firm barrier between them (the liberal insistence on the distinction between private and public, for example) or by insisting on the permeability of that barrier (the communitarian insistence on the situated self).

Aristotle, in my view, takes none of these positions regarding the relation of ethics and politics. For him, there is no question of making politics into either a site of identity (only) or a site of difference (only). It is not a site of public rather than private. It is both. The skills needed for dealing with this are "ethical," which means also that ethics is not a site of difference or identity only.[29] It, too, is both. Political life opens spaces for the practices of human excellence by simultaneously cultivating those practices and also by depending on them. If, insofar as politics depends on virtue, politics points beyond itself to ethics, this does not make ethics prior to politics, nor does ethics provide an external critique of politics. Neither,

---

28. Salkever, "Women, Soldiers, Citizens," pp. 165–90.

29. Thinking of the ethical, as liberals and communitarians both do, in terms of community or culture or a religious tradition or a set of personal beliefs or a conception of the good that you might or might not share with others is, in other words, part of the problem.

however, does politics transcend criticism. Instead, insofar as a political life is also ethical, it will have the resources for *self*-criticism available within it.

The practice of virtue is central to any adequate account of a political life. As self-governing activity, it models the practice of politics, in particular, the practice of a distinctively democratic, that is, self-regulating, politics. Accordingly, this book is about the work of democracy, and specifically about the work of making what I call a democracy of distinction, a democracy that requires the practice of virtue by differentiated citizens in order to actualize itself. The following chapters move from a discussion of identity to analyses of property, justice, and law to an exploration of regime, which is to say, from the citizen to institutions or practices to the constitution. Because, as I argue, character, institutions, and regime all depend on one another in reciprocal, dynamic, and recursive ways, the order of the chapters could have been reversed. To show how our thinking changes when attention is paid to the interactive relation between individual character and political structures by way of activity, the titles of the middle chapters of this book pair an individual activity with a political institution by way of the genitive "of": "The Use of Property," "The Virtue of Justice," "The Rule of Law." As in "the work of politics," these titles are meant to invite understandings of these institutions as practices that accommodate and insist on the simultaneity of individual character and political structures and on their dynamic interrelation.[30]

Chapter 1 investigates the nature of the identity of those who make up a polity and condition its possibility, specifically, citizens and slaves. Against those who construe Aristotle's treatment of nature as establishing the pre-political conditions of political life and the grounds for membership in that life, I draw on Aristotle's philosophical accounts of nature to reinterpret his treatments of slavery and citizenship. I argue that there is nothing immutable or necessary about human nature and that personal identity, as stable *and* changeable by virtue of human activity, is nonessentialist and internally plural. Chapters 2, 3, and 4 examine Aristotle's treatments of property, justice, and the rule of law to show how these political practices function as sites of excellence, that is, how they simultaneously require

---

30. The work of politics involves not only the dynamic and reciprocal relation between individual human beings, political structures, and constitutions within particular polities but also relations among polities. This is because a polity's foreign relations are in a dynamic and reciprocal relation with its constitution, domestic policies and infrastructure and, accordingly, individual agency as well. My discussion of Sparta's warlike virtue in chapter 4 touches on this issue. A fuller treatment is beyond the scope of this project. For Kenneth Waltz's classic treatment, see *Man, the State and War.*

16 INTRODUCTION

that their practitioners exhibit virtue and educate to virtue and, hence, how they require self-governance even as they teach citizens to practice it. More specifically, chapter 2 argues that property, rethought as the activity of "holding things as one's own for common use," functions not only to circumscribe a private sphere of individual liberty, as most moderns would have it, or only to provide occasions for ostentatious self-display to consolidate class interests, as many scholars of the ancient world maintain. As first and foremost a practice of proper use, Aristotelian property also and perhaps paradoxically engages its holders with others and facilitates the redistribution of wealth toward the growth of a middle class. Foregrounding Aristotle's treatment of reciprocal justice, chapter 3 shows how the centrality it accords to the practice of good judgment on the part of exchanging citizens and other members of a polity makes it the bond of a polity whose justice is determined by the judgments of citizens themselves. Chapter 4 explores Aristotle's dual commitment to law as, on one hand, a general and regime-dependent guide of citizen activity and, on the other, a product of that activity. Chapter 5 explains Aristotle's distinctive treatment of the polity as a unity of the different to argue that a well-constituted polity, like musical harmony and like friendship, requires not sameness but difference. Offering a new interpretation of Aristotle's account of "use friendship" as the best model of friendship for a well-constituted polity, this chapter concludes with a discussion of the mixed regime that best embodies the dual commitment—individually, institutionally, and constitutionally—to unity and difference. Aristotle calls this regime the so-called aristocracy. I call it a democracy of distinction.

In what sense, then, is this book about contemporary political theory and practice? Not in any conventional sense. It does not treat Aristotle as a conceptual forerunner of contemporary theorists of politics, justice, and rights. It does not apply his work to contemporary political problems, at least not in their specifics. It does not use him to criticize or commend any particular contemporary political practices. Instead, it seeks to make available his appreciation of the tensions and complexities of the world of politics so that we might rethink and reorganize our own political ideas and practices. In this way, this book offers an ancient education for our time.

CHAPTER ONE

The Nature of Identity

This is a matter of nature: what a thing is potentially, that its work reveals in actuality.
ARISTOTLE, *Nicomachean Ethics*

Man is by nature a political being.
ARISTOTLE, *Politics*

To most readers, Aristotle's introduction of natural slavery, along with his many references to "nature," *phusis,* throughout *Politics* I implies a foundational role for nature outside and prior to politics.[1] *Politics* I is important, they say, because it pairs nature with necessity and sets nature, including human nature, as a standard that fixes the boundaries of inclusion and exclusion in a political life.[2] Among these readers, some find Aristotle's science of nature, which they take to underpin his ethics and politics, to be outdated, discredited, and altogether unacceptable and so reject his account of nature and the politics and ethics to which it is linked.[3] Others reject Aristotle's science of nature but remain committed to his ethics and politics, severing the latter from the former.[4] Still others see in it rich resources for his political and ethical philosophy. Of these, some endorse what they take to be his elitist exclusion of all but a few aristocratic men from participation in a political life.[5] Others argue the opposite, namely, that Aristotle's understanding of hu-

---

1. Ambler, "Aristotle on Acquisition," p. 487, counts eighty-six references in book I to "words based on the root 'nature.'"
2. In *Morality of Happiness,* p. 136, Julia Annas writes: "The ancient appeal to nature is an appeal to what *human* nature is" (emphasis in original).
3. See Williams, "Replies," pp. 199, 201; Habermas, "Discourse Ethics." For a number of recent accounts which argue that "modern and Aristotelian science, when both are rightly understood, are not opposed but complementary to one another," see Bolotin, *Approach to Aristotle's* Physics, p. 2; Arnhart, *Darwinian Natural Right;* Park, *Fire within the Eye.*
4. For example, Stephen G. Salkever rejects Aristotle's physics but thinks his teleological biology makes sense. See *Finding the Mean,* chap. 1.
5. For justification of political inequality on the basis of natural inequality, see L. Strauss,*City and Man,* chap. 1; Winthrop, "Aristotle and Political Responsibility"; E. Miller, "Prudence and the Rule of Law."

18   CHAPTER ONE

man nature is less hostile than is generally thought to women or slaves.[6] Yet others split the difference, endorsing his philosophical account of human nature while deploring some of his political applications of it.[7]

These are not merely abstract arguments about nature and politics. One reading justifies elite social hierarchy formation and its perpetuation on the ground that some people are inferior by nature and therefore should be excluded from the practices of citizenship and from the distribution of political goods. Other readings call for expansive political distribution on the ground that human nature yields a set of basic needs and desires, essential to well-being, that any good polity must meet. The differences among these interpretations are deep, and it is no small wonder that Aristotle's texts invite all of them.[8] Despite their differences, these interpretations all claim that human nature determines the ends and purposes of politics. With *Politics* I thus devoted to establishing the boundaries of politics, Aristotle can move on, in the rest of the *Politics*, to engage the real business of politics, including citizenship, regime formation and change, and revolution. Where nature appears later in the work, as it does, for example, in Aristotle's identification of certain foreigners as natural slaves (*Pol.* 1285a19–24, 1327b27–28), it simply serves to confirm the lesson of book I, namely, that nature secures the distinction between free and unfree.[9] This reading of *Politics* I is powerful. It explains why Aristotle begins his treatise on politics with an account of nature, and it vests nature with a normative force that justifies the political exclusions that follow.

By understanding Aristotle's account of nature in this way, however, Aristotle's readers assimilate his appreciation of the relation between nature and politics to

---

6. On women and slaves, see Nichols, *Citizens and Statesmen,* chap. 1. On women, see Saxonhouse, *Women in the History of Political Thought,* chap. 4; Salkever, "Women, Soldiers, Citizens." On slaves, see Booth, *Households,* chap. 2.

7. See Nussbaum, "Aristotle on Human Nature." In her writings concerning Aristotle's ethics and science Nussbaum offers a nuanced treatment of Aristotle on nature, and there are key points of convergence between her reading of Aristotle on nature and my own. See her *Fragility of Goodness,* pt. 3. It is when Nussbaum turns to what this mandates for politics that her Aristotle emerges as essentialist and objectivist, a reading I reject. See Nussbaum, "Human Functioning and Social Justice"; Nussbaum, "Aristotelian Social Democracy"; Nussbaum, "Nature, Function, and Capability."

8. Wallach's "Contemporary Aristotelianism" gives a good sense of the plurality of interpretations. See also Schofield, "Equality and Hierarchy," and, for the direction of more recent scholarship, Mara, "*Logos* of the Wise."

9. See N. Smith, "Aristotle's Theory of Natural Slavery"; Kraut, *Aristotle: Political Philosophy.*

that of the moderns. Modern political philosophers tend to treat nature as a mark of the absence of political life and, simultaneously, as a threat to it. They see nature as the domain of necessity; politics, the domain of freedom. Political life, they argue, requires leaving states of nature behind, and political agency calls for man's mastery of nature (his own or that of the natural world) as necessary to personal identity formation, the first step toward political life. Although they oppose nature to politics in these ways, modern political theorists also take nature, specifically human nature, to fix the boundaries and content of a political life. It is because Hobbes takes the state of nature to be a state of war among beings who are by nature solitary, mean, nasty, brutish, short(-lived), (and not sufficiently fearful) that the Leviathan must be a punishing and terrorizing artifice. It is because Locke takes the state of nature to be more or less peaceable, peopled by human beings who are more or less trustworthy and naturally disposed not only to preserve themselves but to preserve others as well (except when self- and mutual preservation conflict), that Locke's legislature holds and exercises the powers given to it by the people in trust for them. Both thinkers set up regimes to fit their presuppositions about human nature. Sharing their methodological assumptions but thinking poorly of their execution, Rousseau criticizes Hobbes and Locke for producing beings who are not natural enough but already too political. Rousseau's natural beings—without language, morality, law, property, and so forth—are, by contrast, designed to be so truly natural that they will be able, unlike the political beings described by Hobbes and Locke, to set the appropriate hypothetical standard for actual political institutions to meet.

I read Aristotle's account of nature differently. Unlike the moderns, Aristotle, in my view, does not use nature to establish the pre-political and necessary conditions of politics. He treats human nature, instead, as both a measure of polity and as itself a question for politics. He thereby divests nature of the moral authority usually granted to it, subjects to scrutiny the exclusions said to be secured by that authority, and, placing authority in those who establish the hierarchies of politics, namely, rulers and citizens, renders them accountable for those hierarchies. To see this, consider that in *Politics* I, Aristotle uses language that works not only to secure nature's ability to underwrite politics but also, simultaneously, to call this ability into question: what nature wants, he says at least twice in the course of his discussion of slavery, it may fail to achieve (*Pol.* 1254b26–32, 1255b3). Nature, Aristotle implies, cannot stand as a guarantee. This is because nature as *phusis*, how a thing grows, unlike nature from *natura*, how a thing is born, connotes no prior determi-

20   CHAPTER ONE

nation, fixed destiny, or even congenital tendency.[10] Not already there from birth and unable to sustain itself, nature, *phusis,* must be sustained instead by something else. In the case of human beings, this something else, as the context of Aristotle's discussion suggests, is politics. This is not to make politics prior to or more fundamental than nature or to say that nature is wholly political. It is, rather, to call attention to the complex relation Aristotle sets up between politics and nature. Human nature may be a measure of politics, but the fact that we are, in Aristotle's terminology, naturally political beings (*NE* 1097b12, 1169b20; *Pol.* 1253a2, 1253a7–8, 1278b19) suggests that human nature is also, at least in part, constituted politically. Nature is, thus, not immutable but changeable, and this means that the boundaries it underwrites and the hierarchies it secures, although necessary to politics, will be changeable, too.[11]

That hierarchy is necessary to politics is clear enough. Politics depends on rule, *arche,* which is to say, on ruling and being ruled. Without hierarchy, there can be no political association. Political association also depends on the freedom of its members, and so a second hierarchy is necessary, one that distinguishes free from unfree (*Pol.* 1255b18–19). In Aristotle's account, this second hierarchy is secured by slavery, which is necessary to free masters from meeting their daily needs so that they can, as rulers or citizens, practice politics (and philosophy) (*Pol.* 1255b35–38). To those who pair nature with necessity, *Politics* I is about this second hierarchy only; the rest of the *Politics* is concerned with the first hierarchy, the one within a political association, between rulers and ruled. A brief look at the dangers of hierarchy, brought to light in Aristotle's discussion of slavery, suggests a more complex picture. That hierarchy can be dangerous to slaves goes without saying. This is why Aristotle is centrally concerned in *Politics* I with the justice of slavery (*Pol.* I.5–6). At least as important to Aristotle, however, is that slavery can also be dangerous to those who stand most to benefit from it: rulers and citizens. When rulers or citizens act only as masters, Aristotle notes, hierarchy ceases to be properly political

---

10. For phusis, see Liddell and Scott, *Greek-English Lexicon,* s.v. "phusis"; for natura, see *Oxford English Dictionary,* s.v. "nature."

11. Swanson, "Aristotle on Nature," also argues that Aristotle understands nature to be changeable but claims that he presents his conclusions dogmatically for two reasons: first, because only the few philosophers can properly appreciate nature's changeability; and second, to discourage "political challenges to the natural order in the name of progress or freedom" (p. 225). I argue, by contrast, that Aristotle presents his conclusions imprecisely. I therefore disagree with Swanson's assessment and explanation of Aristotle's rhetorical approach to nature.

and becomes, instead, despotic (*Pol.* 1292a14–38, 1295b20–24).[12] This is why Aristotle makes a point of distinguishing the rule of masters from political rule (*Pol.* 1252a7–17). Dangerous, too, is when rulers or citizens act as slaves, for then there ceases to be a distinction between free and unfree, and hierarchy collapses (*Pol.* 1277b5–7). Where there is no hierarchy, as where hierarchy is all and only despotic, political association ceases. This suggests that Aristotle's account of slavery is not only about the necessity of slavery, nor only about securing the hierarchy between slaves and masters. It is also about the dangers of slavery to citizens and rulers, that is, about the dangers of a politics of slavery.

Politics I, concerned with the nature of hierarchy and its justice is, then, hardly a false start to Aristotle's engagement with politics. On the contrary, he raises fundamental questions of politics in his discussions of nature. Against those who take Aristotle's account of nature in his ethical and political writings to be static and straightforward, and also against those who take it to be equivocal and questionable, I demonstrate that it is, rather, dynamic and complex, unified, and continuous with his scientific, metaphysical, and psychological writings about nature.[13] Aristotle's discussion of the nature of slaves may be filled with inconsistencies but, as we will see, this is no reason to dismiss it as incoherent or to resolve it into "clear and uncontroversial" propositions.[14] His imprecisions there as elsewhere in his ethical, political, and natural scientific writings are, I argue, better read as accurate reflections of the nature of beings who act in and change over time. What is the nature of these beings? To explore this question, I turn first to Aristotle's discussions of citizenship and slavery and then to his philosophical treatment of nature itself.

The Force of Nature

CITIZENS

To ask who is a citizen, as Aristotle does at the start of *Politics* III, is to ask about the identity or nature of a citizen.[15] In Aristotle's hands, this is to ask who deserves to

12. See Davis, *Politics of Philosophy,* pp. 23–24, for what he calls the "tragic implications of [hierarchy's] unlimited extension."

13. For interpretations of Aristotle's account of nature as equivocal and questionable, see Annas, *Morality of Happiness,* p. 146; Irwin, trans., *Aristotle:* Nicomachean Ethics, p. 416–17.

14. For claims that Aristotle's account of slavery is incoherent, see Garnsey, *Ideas of Slavery,* pp. 107, 125; N. Smith, "Aristotle's Theory of Natural Slavery." See Kraut, *Aristotle: Political Philosophy,* p. 282, who resolves it into "clear and uncontroversial" propositions.

15. "The general question about the nature of 'what is' . . . is equivalent to the question about . . . *ousia* . . . a question of identity": Nussbaum, "Aristotle," p. 386. That the "who is"

22   CHAPTER ONE

be a citizen or who merits the political good of citizenship.[16] He answers by saying what will not qualify someone for citizenship: not place, location, or the capacity to sue and be sued (*Pol.* 1275a7–11); not birth, ancestry, or blood (*Pol.* 1275b23–34). Rather, a citizen is one who participates in ruling and judging (*Pol.* 1275a22–23); one who rules and is ruled in turn (*Pol.* 1277b13–16); one who shares in the judicial and deliberative offices of a polity (*Pol.* 1275b18–20).[17] Place, legal capacity, birth, and parentage—as static qualities or markers of status—do not demonstrate merit, in Aristotle's view. Although there may be subtle differences among the formulations Aristotle approves, they share an emphasis on activity: "sharing in a constitution," in Malcolm Schofield's phrase, qualifies one for citizenship.[18]

Aristotle's emphasis on activity has a curiously tautological or self-contained quality. Practicing citizenship, Aristotle seems to be saying, makes someone a citizen: a "citizen is a citizen in being a citizen."[19] This circularity is a feature not only of Aristotle's understanding of citizenship but of all human activity. In doing, he says, "the end cannot be other than the act itself" (*NE* 1140b6). Activity, *energeia* or *entelecheia,* is that which has, *echei,* what is aimed at—an end, or *telos*—in, *en,* itself (*Meta.* 1050a23–24). Although self-contained, human activity is not invulnerable to external influences. There is no carrying out one's citizenship in a vacuum. Indeed, there can be no citizen *qua* citizen prior to the regime of which that citizen is a part (*Pol.* 1275b4–5). For this reason, Aristotle pursues his investigation of citizenship by asking who is a citizen *of a democracy* or *of an oligarchy* (*Pol.* III.3). Being a citizen is regime-dependent not least because what it means to share in a constitution largely depends on the laws, education, and other social and political institutions of that particular constitution.[20] These institutions all contribute to

---

question is one about nature and identity is evident from the translations of the *Politics.* The translations of Rackham, *Aristotle: Politics,* p. 173, and Barker, *The Politics of Aristotle,* p. 92, ask about the "nature" of the citizen; those of Jowett, *The Politics,* p. 51, Reeve, *Aristotle: Politics,* p. 65, and Robinson, *Aristotle, Politics: Books III and IV,* p. 3. ask "who is a citizen?"; and Lord, *The Politics,* p. 86, asks "what the citizen is."

16. This means that the question of citizenship is a question of distributive justice. The parallels between Aristotle's discussion of citizenship in *Pol.* III.1 and his discussion of distributive justice in *Pol.* III.9–12 are noteworthy.

17. These are not all the same, but the differences do not matter for my purposes. For discussion of the differences, see Nichols, *Citizens and Statesmen,* pp. 55–61.

18. See his "Sharing in the Constitution."

19. For this formulation, see Winthrop, "Aristotle and Political Responsibility," p. 407.

20. This is not always the case. As I discuss in chapter 4, Aristotle calls Theramenes a model citizen in the *Constitution of Athens* for refusing to follow the laws of the polity. Being

the making of citizens. This suggests that being a citizen is a combination of doing on the part of citizen practitioners and making on the part of social and political institutions.[21]

At the start of his inquiry into citizenship, however, Aristotle says that it is important to leave to one side "those who have been made citizens and those who have obtained the name citizen in any other accidental way" (*Pol.* 1275a5–7). This sentence is key. It carves out what, for philosophical reasons, Aristotle thinks ought not to be included in an inquiry into the identity or nature of a citizen. To be excluded, as already noted, are those who are "made" citizens by the accidents of birth, ancestry, parentage, or location. That is clear enough. But, against the backdrop of Aristotle's ready acknowledgment of the role of social and political institutions in the making of citizens, how are we to understand his apparently sweeping exclusion of all "made citizens"? He offers the following examples. To be excluded from consideration of the nature of a citizen are those who have been made citizens "by the magistrates," a kind of making he analogizes to the production of artefacts, specifically, kettles (*Pol.* 1275b29–30), and those who have been made citizens "after a revolution" (*Pol.* 1275b35–36).[22] As with the granting of legal rights under a treaty, these are examples of citizens having been made citizens, one might say, ex nihilo: by being so named by a magistrate, by fiat after a revolution, or by the force of legal treaty alone. Aristotle does not identify those who are made citizens in any of these ways *as* citizens for the same reason he excludes those who are made citizens by accident: their citizenship does not come about by virtue of their own activity. It is, rather, granted to them.

Aristotle includes laws, education, and other social and political institutions in the proper making of citizens because, unlike treaty, revolution, or magisterial edict, which, like accident or force, make irrelevant the activity of a citizen, a

---

a good citizen calls for disobeying the laws when there ceases to be a difference between the polity's laws and force, when *nomos* becomes *bia*.

21. I have more to say below about why this is not in conflict with Aristotle's insistence on distinguishing doing and making (*Pol.* 1254a5–7; *NE* VI.4). For an excellent discussion of the relation between the two in the context of Aristotle's *Poetics,* see Davis, *Poetry of Philosophy,* chap. 8.

22. Winthrop, "Aristotle and Political Responsibility," p. 410, explains the pun on Larissaeans, which names both the people and the artefact. Aristotle's example is the foreigners and alien slaves supposedly enrolled by the Athenian reformer Cleisthenes and so made citizens "in one stroke" after the expulsion of the tyrant Hippias in 510 B.C.E. For discussion of the interpretative controversies regarding this example, see Manville, *Origins of Citizenship,* pp. 173–209, esp. p. 191. See also *Constitution of Athens* 20.1, 21.2; *Politics* 1319b19–27.

polity's institutions do not make that activity irrelevant but rather supervene upon or guide it (*Pol.* 1258a22–23). Indeed, it is impossible to understand a citizen's identity without taking into account the ways in which it has been shaped by these institutions.[23] Citizen identity is, then, a product of making and doing, where doing is a kind of self-making (by sharing in the constitution, I make myself a citizen) and making, as guided shaping by laws, education, and other institutions, entails citizen doing. Accident and force must be pushed to one side when investigating the nature of the citizen because they make irrelevant what is at the heart of both formations of citizen identity: the dynamic and reciprocal relation between identity and action, between doers and their deeds.

Citizens are made not only by their particular or individual activities but also by sharing in a constitution, in other words, by their collective activity (*Pol.* 1275b4–6). At the same time, collective activity produces the social and political institutions that contribute to the making of citizens in the first place. If, to be citizens, citizens must act as such, they do so not only individually but also in the collective action by which they make for themselves the social and political institutions that also help make them. There is an interdependence between polity and citizen identity. Aristotle models this interdependence on the relation between a whole and its parts (*Pol.* 1274b39–40). A polity, as a unity, is a whole; a whole, to be a whole, must consist of parts; a part, to be a part, must be a part of something other than itself to which it belongs.[24] Parts presuppose the whole of which they are parts, and the whole presupposes the parts that constitute it. Unlike contemporary liberal and communitarian writers for whom either the individual citizen or the political community must be prior and foundational (at least in principle),[25] Aristotle denies to either the polity or the individual citizen a foundational status. It is because he analyzes the polity and its citizens in terms of the relation between a whole and its parts that he unpacks the identity of the polity by reference to the identity of citizens, and citizen identity by reference to the polity. Against this backdrop we can make sense of Aristotle's otherwise confusing claims. He says that, in order to answer the question "what is a polity," it is "evident that we must

---

23. For discussion see Salkever, "'Lopp'd and Bound,'" esp. p. 176; T. Smith, *Revaluing Ethics*, pp. 23–26.

24. "A whole is that which so contains its contents that they form a unity . . . in the sense that the unity is composed of them": *Meta.* 1023b28–29.

25. I say "in principle" because strictly speaking there are very few liberals or communitarians anymore. A recognition of the inadequacy of the original oppositional formulation has produced instead liberal-communitarians and communitarian-liberals.

begin by asking who is the citizen and what is the meaning of the term" (*Pol.* 1274b32–1275a3). He calls the question of citizen identity the first question of politics (*Pol.* 1274b42), for, as we have just seen, it is citizens who, in carrying out their citizenship, make the social and political institutions that determine the identity of the polity.[26] At the same time, Aristotle can insist that it is the polity that takes precedence (*Pol.* 1253a19–27) because it is the polity, via its institutions, that produces citizens as the citizens they are.

Taking democracy, with Josiah Ober, to be constituted neither by institutions alone nor by popular action alone but rather by "dynamic tensions" between institutionalization and participation, we find something nicely democratic about Aristotle's understanding of citizen identity, read in this way.[27] Citizenship is a matter of individual self-determining activity, and it is participatory. By acting in concert, sharing in their constitution, citizens make the institutions that, in turn, guide but do not fully determine their individual activity.

A full treatment of Aristotle's writings concerning citizenship and political participation calls for attending not only to those he includes but also to those he excludes, not because of what they do (run shops, create crafts) but, ostensibly, because of who they are: women, foreigners, and slaves. For most readers, it is because Aristotle takes the nature of these individuals to be essentially and necessarily different from the nature of citizens that they must be excluded from political participation.[28] I disagree. To explain why, I turn next to an extended treatment of Aristotle's account of natural slavery in *Politics* I and of foreigners as natural slaves there and elsewhere in the *Politics*.[29]

26. By defining the polity's identity in terms of its citizens, Aristotle effectively denies to the polity a nature independent of the natures of those who constitute it. For discussion, see Nichols, *Citizens and Statesmen,* chap. 1; Yack, *Problems of a Political Animal,* chap. 3; F. Miller, *Nature, Justice, and Rights,* chap. 2. For a different understanding of the nature of the polity, see J. Lear, *Aristotle,* pp. 192–208; Keyt, "Three Basic Theorems in Aristotle's *Politics*."

27. Ober, *Athenian Revolution,* p. 31. In Ober's view, however, Aristotle is no friend of democracy. See also Ober, *Political Dissent in Democratic Athens,* chap. 6.

28. They are excluded even as they condition its possibility for others: *Pol.* 1328a34–36, 1328b19–22, 1329a35–38.

29. Scholars who argue that Aristotle's treatment of the nature of women is more complex than is usually appreciated also nicely problematize the usual appreciations of Aristotle's view of the nature of slaves. See Nichols, *Citizens and Statesmen,* pp. 19–24; Saxonhouse, *Women in the History of Political Thought,* pp. 68–71; Salkever, "Women, Soldiers, Citizens."

26   CHAPTER ONE

SLAVES

Aristotle opens his treatment of slavery with the question, who is a slave? As he does in the case of citizenship, he analyzes this as a question of justice, that is, in terms of desert or qualification. Rejecting parentage or ancestry (*Pol.* 1255b1–3) and convention (which he calls *nomos* and equates with violence or force, *bia, Pol.* 1255b15) as inadequate justifications of slavery, Aristotle pushes to one side, as he does when he discusses citizen identity, those who have been made slaves by accident or by force. The significance of these moves should not be underestimated. That Aristotle parses slavery as a question of justice, which he treats as the key question for politics (*Pol.* 1255a7–17) and "a question for political philosophy" (*Pol.* 1282b23), signals that he intends to give it careful political and philosophical consideration. That he rejects as unjust all forms of enslavement by force shows that he is prepared to challenge the predominant form of slavery in ancient Greece, which was the enslavement of foreigners captured in war or kidnapped by pirates and the foreigners' descendants.[30] For these reasons, those who read Aristotle as simply a product of his times or as merely an apologist for the institutions of his regime are mistaken.[31]

In the light of the structural similarities between his accounts of slave and citizen identity, one might expect Aristotle to draw the same conclusion in the case of slavery that he draws in the case of citizenship. If being a citizen is to be understood in terms of citizen activity, then being a slave is to be understood in terms of slave activity. If citizen activity (including the way this activity is guided by a polity's social and political institutions but nothing accidental, forced, or necessary) defines the nature of a citizen, then slave activity (similarly understood) should define the natural slave.

These are exactly Aristotle's conclusions. He says, "The good man and the statesman and the good citizen ought not to learn the crafts of inferiors except for their own occasional use; if they habitually practice them, there will cease to be a distinction between master and slave" (*Pol.* 1277b5–7). He warns against including

---

30. MacDowell, *Law in Classical Athens,* p. 79; Kraut, *Aristotle: Political Philosophy,* p. 280.

31. For accounts that treat Aristotle as an embarrassed apologist of slavery, see Williams, *Shame and Necessity,* pp. 103–29; Waldron, "On the Objectivity of Morals." For accounts that treat Aristotle as a product of his times, see Annas, *Morality of Happiness,* pp. 153, 155; Annas, "Aristotle on Human Nature and Political Virtue"; the commentary by Saunders in *Aristotle, Politics: Books I and II,* pp. 79–83; Brunt, "Aristotle and Slavery." For an excellent challenge to the common views that take Aristotle's teaching regarding natural slavery to support actual slavery, see Ambler, "Aristotle on Nature and Politics."

in the art of household management knowledge on the part of the master of how to do the tasks of slaves (*Pol.* 1255b23–38), and he warns his audience of free citizens in the *Nicomachean Ethics* against engaging in slavish kinds of activities (*NE* 1118a23–b4, 1118b21, 1128a22).[32] Aristotle demands this sort of vigilance on the part of masters, citizens, and rulers because, as these examples suggest, performing the activities of a slave can make one a slave. The reverse seems to be true as well: presuming the capacity to cease being a slave, Aristotle maintains that it is appropriate to hold out to slaves the promise of their freedom (*Pol.* 1330a33–34). Insisting that friendship is not possible with a slave as a slave but that it is with the slave as a person (*NE* 1161b5–6), he holds out the possibility that a slave can become a person worthy of friendship, his model for free politics.

All of this suggests that there is nothing immutable that singles out any particular person as a slave. Instead, slave identity, like citizen identity, is determined by activity. If this is right, then there is no "permanent and complete" difference between slave and citizen.[33] Aristotle's account of slavery in *Politics* I, accordingly, serves not to describe and set apart a domain that is pre- or nonpolitical but to warn his audience of free citizens of their vulnerability, not only to accident and force but, more important, to the power of acting in shaping their political destinies.[34] It follows that when I make myself a citizen or a slave by virtue of my own activity, it is just to so treat me.

There is, however, a fundamental difference between citizens and slaves in this regard: the social and political institutions that supervene on self-determining activity to produce citizens as citizens and slaves as slaves are the product of citizen activity alone. Insofar as I am produced as a slave by social and political institutions in whose making I have not myself participated, I am made a slave independent of my own activity. I am, therefore, by the terms of Aristotle's own account, made a slave by accident or, more likely, by force. As we have seen, Aristotle insists

32. Not, to my knowledge, noticed by scholars, Aristotle uses different words when referring to those who are slavish because of the practice of vice (*andrapodon* root) and those whom he calls naturally slavish (*doulos* root). Although this may be read as evidence that Aristotle assumes an essential and necessary difference between these two ways of being a slave, the first reversible, the second not, it might just as well be a symptom of Aristotle's worry that they are not different; hence the need to enforce, nominally at least, a strict boundary between them.

33. *Contra* Nichols, *Citizens and Statesmen,* p. 6, where she claims that the distinction between slaves and masters is absolute, although, at p. 184 n. 21, she also says that the distinction is a matter of degree.

34. See Mara, "Near Made Far Away," pp. 286, 296; Davis, *Politics of Philosophy,* p. 22.

28   CHAPTER ONE

that the effects of accident and force are to be left out when considering the nature of identity. A study of slaves produced as slaves by coercive social and political institutions, then, reveals little about the nature of slaves. It does, however, reveal something about those who create such institutions, namely, that they confuse political rule with mastery, a science Aristotle refers to as servile (*Pol.* 1255b30–35).[35] Showing that they are prepared to rule despotically, citizens or rulers who act as masters participate in the unmaking of their polity (*Pol.* 1292a14–38, 1295b20–24). The practice of slavery and its institution, though necessary to free citizens individually and collectively, are also, and at the same time, dangerous to the very freedom they secure.

Against the backdrop of this reading of *Politics* I, how might we understand Aristotle's defense of natural slavery? Appearing to carve out a category of nature whose definition is independent of activity, it seems to display a lack of parallelism with his treatment of citizenship. As I demonstrate next, this appearance is deceptive. Aristotle's discussion of who is by nature a slave imports into the *Politics* language he has introduced in the *Physics*. Parsing this question along two axes, he asks whether nature as matter, meaning physical bodies, will distinguish slaves from nonslaves, and he asks whether nature as form, meaning soul, will do the trick. In *Politics* I, Aristotle has insisted that nature makes nothing in vain (1253a9). On the contrary, nature makes things to particular uses and so should mark a slave in a way that shows him to be fit for use as an object of property by giving him a body suited to menial chores. Aristotle notes, however, that although "nature would like to distinguish" slaves from nonslaves on the basis of physical appearance, nature can fail to do so, giving slaves, instead, the bodies of freemen (*Pol.* 1254b26–32). Under its material aspect, as body, nature does not tell us who deserves to be a slave.

Most scholars agree that under its formal aspect, as the soul, nature does a better job of distinguishing slaves from nonslaves. They claim that, to Aristotle, it is the absence of the faculty of deliberation, a deficiency of the soul or, in the terminology of *De Anima*, a first-level incapacity, that makes natural slavery natural. Aristotle's examination of the soul of the slave is not so clear, however. He says that slaves lack the deliberative element (*Pol.* 1254b22–23, 1260a12–13) but also that if they did not participate in reason they would not be able to execute their masters'

---

35. For this reason, Aristotle recommends that those in a position to occupy themselves with philosophy or politics have stewards to attend to the management of their households (*Pol.* 1255b35–37).

orders (*Pol.* 1254a23−24). He says that slaves are not capable of self-rule (*Pol.* 1254b16−21) but also that they have the excellence necessary to prevent them from failing in their function because of lack of self-control (*Pol.* 1259b22−28, 1260a1−3, 1260a35−36). He distinguishes slaves from children on the ground that children possess the deliberative element (albeit in an immature form, *Pol.* 1260a13), but he also insists that the proper response to slaves, even more than to children, is admonition rather than command alone (*Pol.* 1260b5−7). He says that slaves are essentially not-form but simply matter or bodies waiting for minds as form to impose order on them (*Pol.* 1252a31−34, 1254b15−20) but also that, as human beings, they are constituted by matter and form (*Pol.* 1254a32−34) and share in the capacity to reason (*Pol.* 1259b29).[36] On the basis of these inconsistencies, some scholars dismiss Aristotle's account of natural slavery as incoherent.[37] Aristotle is not, however, unaware that his examination of the soul of the slave pulls in different directions. He maintains, by way of response, that "beauty of soul is not seen" (*Pol.* 1255a1). Because the soul is not visible to the eye, his answer to the question of who is a slave by nature in terms of soul can be no more conclusive than was his answer to the question of who is a slave by nature in terms of body.

Aristotle nonetheless concludes that "it is clear then that some men are by nature free and others slaves and for these latter slavery is both expedient and just" (*Pol.* 1255a1−2). If natural slavery is not determined by an immutable physical sign, and the soul's invisibility makes it impossible to know whether natural slaves suffer from an immutable psychological deficiency, what, then, makes slavery natural? Aristotle is usually read as treating certain foreigners as justly enslaved on the basis of an immutable inferiority he is said to associate with them.[38] If this is right, then understanding human nature in terms of activity would falter in the face of Aristotle's xenophobia. Its force would also become questionable because, as noted, most slaves in Athens were non-Greeks. Rather than posing a challenge to the account I have developed, however, the passages in the *Politics* about foreigners confirm it. Aristotle's distinction between Greeks and certain non-Greeks, it turns out, rests not on nature as something immutable, not on his conviction that

---

36. For a discussion of the virtues belonging to slaves, see Brunt, "Aristotle and Slavery," pp. 359−66.

37. See Garnsey, *Ideas of Slavery,* pp. 107, 125; N. Smith, "Aristotle's Theory of Natural Slavery." For tensions in Aristotle's account, see Davis, *Politics of Philosophy,* chap. 1; Barker, *Political Thought of Plato and Aristotle,* chap. 9; Schlaifer, "Greek Theories of Slavery."

38. Kraut, *Aristotle: Political Philosophy,* pp. 290−95.

30   CHAPTER ONE

Greeks were superior to foreigners, but on his observations about the (political and nonpolitical) behaviors of those foreigners.

FOREIGNERS

In *Politics* I, Aristotle maintains that "among foreigners no distinction is made between women and slaves, because there is no natural ruler among them: they are a community of slaves, male and female." Immediately following this statement, he quotes "the poets" as saying "'It is meet that Hellenes should rule over non-Greeks'; as if they thought that the foreigner and the slave were by nature one" (*Pol.* 1252b5–9). Aristotle first reports what he sees among foreigners, and then quotes the words of the poets, who proclaim the justice of Greek rule over non-Greeks on the ground that foreigners are natural slaves. If his observations are accurate, and the foreigners to whom he refers do, indeed, act as a community of slaves, then, in the terms of the analysis offered so far, he is justified in calling them natural slaves by virtue of that behavior. In light of the fact that he puts the identification of (all) foreigners as natural slaves into the mouths of "the poets," however, it is not clear, in this passage at least, whether he would endorse this identification.[39]

Also in *Politics* I, Aristotle says, "It must be admitted that some are slaves everywhere, others nowhere" (*Pol.* 1255a31–32). He is usually interpreted as maintaining that there are some, namely, certain foreigners, who (because they are natural slaves) are slaves everywhere and that there are others, namely, Greeks, who (because they are naturally free) are slaves nowhere. The rest of the passage, however, suggests a different reading. Aristotle is exploring the question of whether the enslavement of foreigners conquered in war is just. His answer, as we have seen, is that conquest, as a mode of force, cannot justify slavery. What can? Aristotle answers that worthiness determines one's qualification for slavery (*Pol.* 1255a25–26; see also 1255b21–23). When, just after this, he says that "it must be admitted that some are slaves everywhere, others nowhere," he should be read as saying that those who are ignoble are slaves everywhere, and those who are good, nowhere.[40]

39. For discussion, see Ambler, "Aristotle on Nature and Politics"; see also Davis, *Politics of Philosophy,* p. 17, arguing that Aristotle invokes the passage from Euripides with knowledge of its context to call into question any too-easy opposition between foreigners as natural slaves and Greeks as naturally free: "Iphigeneia, who is speaking, is about to be sacrificed by her father, Agamemnon, to propitiate the gods so that the Greeks can continue their expedition against Troy. Is this less barbaric than treating women as slaves? Iphigeneia is a living instrument used for the sake of an action."

40. See Saxonhouse, *Women in the History of Political Thought,* pp. 70–71.

He notes that there is a tendency among Greeks to regard foreigners as ignoble and themselves as good and, therefore, to treat foreigners as justly enslaved. In response, he reiterates that the proper determinant in regard to slavery is not foreignness but worthiness, or character (*Pol.* 1255b1), itself, we will see, a function of activity (*NE* II.1–2). In any case, even character, he continues, will not justify slavery in perpetuity: whereas nature intends that from good men a good man will spring (and from a slave a slave will spring), this desire is often thwarted (*Pol.* 1255b3). A person's character can therefore justify only his own enslavement, not that of his children.

Toward the end of the *Politics,* Aristotle uses spirit, *thumos,* the source of the love of freedom and the power of command (*Pol.* 1328a1–8), to distinguish free from unfree, calling Europeans comparatively free and Asians natural slaves (*Pol.* 1327b25–29).[41] He frames this discussion by reference to meteorological conditions: Europe is cold and Asia is hot. His attention to climate suggests right off that his distinction between free and unfree rests on something other than a fixture of foreign psychology. Aristotle seems, rather, to be saying something like, "Where it is often extremely hot, people act listlessly or without spirit." To say this is not to announce a necessary, immutable feature about the Asian soul, which, like any soul, is unobservable and hard to speculate about. Aristotle instead calls Asians natural slaves on the basis of what he sees as their lethargy, which is to say, their apparent tendency to forget how to act on their own initiative, or "inactivity."[42]

Discussing the fact that certain monarchies among foreigners sometimes resemble tyrannies, Aristotle claims that "such kingships have the nature of tyrannies because the people are by nature slaves" (*Pol.* 1285a22–23). He goes on to say that these tyrannies are in no danger of being overthrown because, unlike others,

41. Absence of thumos may be a sign of slavishness in Asians, but Aristotle also warns that the love of freedom and power of command that makes free politics possible can, like the art of mastery, orient its possessors toward despotism (*Pol.* 1324b19–26), thus rendering them no less unfree than those with no thumos at all. I return to this point in chapter 4. For treatments of thumos in Aristotle, see Koziak, *Retrieving Political Emotion;* Charney, "Spiritedness and Piety in Aristotle."

42. See *Oxford English Dictionary,* s.v. "inactivity." Unlike Hippocrates, for example, Aristotle does not, to my knowledge, invoke residency in the mother's womb or the quality or nature of the mother's conception in his account of the effects of climate on human psychology. In support of my argument about the key role of human activity in human nature, note that although Aristotle has a lot to say about the mechanics of reproduction, he does not seem to draw any clear causal lines between the biology of birth and reproduction, on one hand, and the psychology of the born person, on the other.

32   CHAPTER ONE

they are hereditary and legal, legal in that the subjects acquiesce voluntarily in the tyrannical rule (*Pol.* 1285a17–29). It is possible to read Aristotle, in this passage, as ascribing to certain foreigners, Asians once again, an immutable inferiority that explains their willing acquiescence in, and responsibility for, the despotic regime that governs them. The rest of the passage suggests another possibility. Aristotle stresses that the tyrannies of Asia are not only legal but hereditary. In the same discussion, he counterposes these to the elective tyrannies that, from time to time, governed the ancient Greeks (*Pol.* 1285a30–33). If an immutable inferiority is to be held responsible for the tyrannies governing the Asians, then he would have to conclude that the ancient Greeks were similarly inferior. Further, if the ancient Greeks were immutably inferior, then it would follow that Aristotle's contemporary Greeks were too, because, when nature is understood in terms of necessity, to be immutably inferior at one point in time is to be so always.

Aristotle does not, of course, ascribe to Greeks the status of natural slaves, and this suggests that explaining regime type by reference to an immutable inferiority is not his purpose. By focusing on regime, and, specifically, on the difference between the forms of the tyrannies governing Asians (hereditary) and those governing Greeks (elective), he seems, rather, to imply that human nature is as much a product of the regime under which one lives as it is a regime's cause. Insofar as they have long been habituated to living under tyrannies and acting according to the habits fostered by tyrannies, Asians are naturally slavish and so acquiesce in and thereby reproduce the regime that produced them. By contrast, it is because Greeks experienced tyrannies only sporadically, if willingly, that they did not become habituated to slavish behavior and so cannot be called natural slaves. This is not to say, however, that they cannot become natural slaves, and that seems to be at least part of Aristotle's point. Foreignness per se does not therefore qualify one for slavery, and the passages concerning foreigners, like Aristotle's early discussion of natural slavery, reinforce the idea that human nature is bound with activity and changeable.

PROHAIRETIC ACTIVITY

> The term "master" denotes the possession . . . of a certain character
> and similarly also the terms "slave" and "freeman."
>
> ARISTOTLE, *Politics*

How might we understand Aristotle's defense of natural slavery against this backdrop? He claims that the master-slave relation is natural when it benefits both individuals involved, when the interests of the slave and of the master are the same (*Pol.* 1255b13–14, 1252a34–b1). Under what sorts of circumstances might someone benefit from being a slave?[43] Aristotle says that a person whose soul is so disordered that it fails to guide his body might well be better off guided by someone else's soul than left wholly unguided (*Pol.* 1254b16–20). Because it is difficult to see and therefore to know whether a soul is well ordered, evidence of a disordered soul is provided by the activities in which the person engages. The inference that a person's soul is disordered is justified not when he acts, every now and then, "as most slaves act," because this would give the status of slavery too much weight. Nor is there a biological standard for determining when a soul is disordered, none, at least, in the sense of a necessary one. Rather, what might be called characteristically human activity itself provides a kind of internal standard sufficient to allow judgment about which activities and ways of living are more slavish than others.

What is characteristically human activity? At the start of the *Politics,* Aristotle distinguishes human beings from all other natural beings on the ground that humans alone possess *logos,* the capacity for articulate speech or reason (*Pol.* 1253a10). All humans, by virtue of being human, possess this first-level capacity, including slaves (*Pol.* 1259b29). It is by virtue of logos that humans make choices about the useful and the harmful, the just and the unjust, the good and the bad (*Pol.* 1253a14–18), and it is characteristic of humans that, in regard to these ethical and political matters, we act "according to thoughtful or deliberate choice," *kata prohairesin* (*Pol.* 1280a31–34).[44] Choice, *prohairesis,* charts the course of a human life. It is the act of choosing one action instead of (or before, *pro*) another, making a judgment about what to choose. It is, Aristotle says, the starting point or rule, *arche,* of action (*NE* 1113a4–9). As signaled by the prefix *pro-*, prohairesis, in the Greek understanding, has an embedded character: the choices that initiate the actions people undertake are determined by their habits, which reflect who they

---

43. Kraut, *Aristotle: Political Philosophy,* pp. 295–301, offers an excellent account of why slavery benefits slaves, which also, however, undermines his insistence that what distinguishes slaves by nature is the complete absence of the capacity to acquire practical wisdom. Insofar as Kraut agrees that a slave can develop sufficiently good habits and a sufficient measure of moderation to someday deserve his freedom (a position Kraut also rightly attributes to Aristotle), and insofar as, to Aristotle, there can be no moderation without practical wisdom (*NE* 1140b13–15), indeed no virtue without practical wisdom and vice versa (*NE* 1144b36–38), attributing to natural slaves even a "modicum of virtue" is, *eo ipso,* to attribute to them practical wisdom and thereby to call into question the naturalness of their slavery.

44. Salkever, "'Lopp'd and Bound,'" p. 195; Salkever, "Women, Soldiers, Citizens," p. 182; Saxonhouse, *Women in the History of Political Thought,* p. 66.

34   CHAPTER ONE

have been and therefore who they are.[45] Prohairetic activity is, thus, characteristically human activity insofar as it discloses the character, the soul, and thereby the nature of the one who acts, specifically by revealing the degree to which, in the actions he undertakes, the actor is using the capacity for logos he possesses by virtue of being human.

Prohairetic activity is not, however, distinguished by logos alone. It is not purely cognitive. Combining intelligence and desire (*NE* 1139b5–7), it involves what Aristotle calls intellectual and moral virtue. This is because, to him, human beings are most fully human when they engage in the practices of intellectual and moral virtue (*NE* 1098a14–16).[46] Intellectual and moral virtue are, in turn, linked in Aristotle's scheme of things: moral virtue depends on intellectual virtue insofar as acting well depends on properly discriminating what needs to be done, that is, on good judgment. And intellectual virtue depends on moral virtue insofar as such discrimination depends on being properly habituated (*NE* 1144b30–33).[47] It is because Aristotle understands prohairetic activity in this way that, in his investigations into slaves and citizens in *Politics* I and III, as in his inquiry into the work, *ergon*, of human beings more generally in *Nicomachean Ethics* I.7, he investigates their virtue.

Aristotelian virtue adds no new standard for measuring human nature not already present in the idea of prohairetic activity. As I argue next, Aristotle understands virtue as a product of habit-producing actions and action-altering habits. Thus, Aristotelian virtue is itself a mode of being by way of prohairetic activity, more a verb than a noun. Consider Aristotle's definition of virtue: "Of virtue, *arete,* there is the activity, *energeia,* according to it. But it makes no small difference whether we place the chief good in holding, *ktesis,* or in using, *chresis,* in habit, *hexis,* or in activity, *energeia.* For habit takes it in itself not to bring a good to completion, even when the habit lies there as a ruling principle, *arche.* But activity, *energeia,* not so; for the activity, *energeia,* will of necessity be acting and acting well,

---

45. For this reason, Aristotle distinguishes acting by choice and acting voluntarily: in the absence of external constraint, as we will see, all acts count as voluntary. That not all voluntary acts are, however, chosen (*NE* III.2) sets Aristotle's understanding of choice apart from more voluntarist and cognitive conceptions.

46. Included here are practical wisdom, *phronesis,* an intellectual virtue, and the moral virtues as well. The definition of excellence I discuss below is from the early part of the *Nicomachean Ethics,* before Aristotle has distinguished between moral and intellectual virtue, and so can be read to apply to both.

47. I have more to say about the relation between intellectual and moral virtue in chapters 3 and 4.

praxis" (*NE* 1098b31–1099a4, trans. modified). In this passage Aristotle contrasts *hexis*, habit, to energeia and praxis. *Energeia* and *praxis* are often rendered as "action" in translation, but they are not the same. Praxis is what lies before someone as a possibility, as something to be done. It is action in the sense of a deed. The deed to be done, *praxis,* once done, is something I have done and, as such, is something I "have" as my work, *ergon.* What do I keep having from this ergon? The hexis I have exercised in doing the praxis. This hexis is a capacity, *dunamis,* that I keep in store only to bring it to work in practice, in *energeia.* This energy or activity, *energeia,* brings what is had as one's own, dunamis, to work in action, *praxis.* Energeia thus works in two directions, allowing habits to show themselves in actions and actions to be the exercises from which habit is acquired. Both good action and good habits depend on the perpetual working of energeia. Virtue—intellectual and moral—consists of a hexis whose energeia does its work in praxis.

Being virtuous is a matter of energeia, of putting one's dunamis to work in praxis, for, however good his dispositions may be, man does not demonstrate excellence if he does not act well, and only by acting well can he come to have a good disposition in the first place (*NE* 1103b23). Were habit alone taken to be the mark of excellence, then excellence would simply be a matter of having certain capacities. It would not matter whether these capacities ever made their way into action and showed their work in action with other people. But if good habit alone does not amount to excellence, neither does action by itself. Actual deeds may or may not be evidence of the doer's character (*Rhet.* 1367b32), but it is not possible to act well without having the appropriate habits (*NE* 1103b24). Indeed, were action alone to be the mark of excellence, then no one could ever be said to have virtue, or skill, or anything like a capacity. If a person does something but does not do it from the appropriate habit or disposition, he may be acting in conformity with some principle or other, but the action is not freely his own. A stable disposition to act well is thus necessary for acting well to be preferred; acting well and preferring good acts both depend on good habit. Habits change as a result of action, and actions change with changes in habit. Habit as dunamis is a formation of one's possibilities from one's past actions, such that one "has" it in oneself to act a certain way: "We become just by doing just actions, and temperate by doing temperate actions and brave by brave actions . . . and in a word, habits are formed out of activities, *energeiai,* in like ways" (*NE* 1103b15–21). Activity thus seizes on a possibility opened up by habit. Acting justly, temperately, bravely, in short, acting well, depends on properly discriminating what needs to be done—good judgment—and such discrimination depends on being properly habituated. There is thus a reciprocal and

36   CHAPTER ONE

dynamic relationship between the actions and habits that constitute virtue: acting well depends on good habits, and good habits are formed by acting well. This means that the movement and change characteristic of activity inform not only human nature, and not only the soul, but intellectual and moral virtue as well.[48]

Virtue, Aristotle says, "will . . . on this view be very generally shared, for all who are not maimed as regards their potentiality for virtue may win it by a certain kind of study and care" (*NE* 1099b18). What do these preconditions of the practice of virtue amount to? Aristotle's example of a sick man who refused to follow his doctor's advice is instructive:

> In that case [when he was first diagnosed] it was then open to him not to be ill, but not now, when he has thrown away his chance, just as when you have let a stone go and it is too late to recover it; but yet it was in your power to throw it, since the moving principle was in you. So too to the unjust and self-indulgent man it was open at the beginning not to become men of this kind, and so they are unjust and self-indulgent voluntarily; but now that they have become so it is not possible for them not to be so. (*NE* 1114a17–22)

This example suggests that one is maimed to the extent to which not something external but rather one's own bad habits prevent one from acting well. This is an irrevocable maiming *now,* which means that it is not possible for one who is now unjust and self-indulgent not to be so (now). But being maimed because of one's own bad habits is not unalterable. Aristotle's understanding of virtue and, as we will see, his account of responsibility in *Nicomachean Ethics* III.1 and III.5 depend on it being always possible, in the absence of coercively constraining institutions, for a person to initiate actions that will over time change his habits and, along with them, his potential for virtue. Man, says Aristotle, is "a moving principle or begettor of his actions, as of children" (*NE* 1113b19). As the natality metaphor suggests, initiating actions to change ingrained habits, like giving birth, may be a difficult and arduous process involving doing and suffering (*NE* 1110a2–4). Although "as if" irrevocable, one's character may be changed nonetheless, by acting. There will always be those who choose to act badly (*NE* III.5), but the potential to act well lies

---

48. Williams, *Ethics and the Limits of Philosophy,* p. 51, claims that ethical "dispositions are part of the content of [an] actual self" and identifies them as the "ultimate supports of ethical value." By focusing on these alone rather than in conjunction with the actions that iteratively constitute them, Williams produces an account of the Aristotelian self that promises more fixity than it can sustain.

before each of us should we choose to win it. That potential, *dunamis,* is won by acting well, *energeia.*

If prohairetic activity defines characteristically human activity as a practice of intellectual and moral virtue, who, then, is a natural slave? The one who possesses the capacity, *dunamis,* for virtue but consistently does not use it, engaging instead in activity that falls short of prohairetic activity. Such a person can have no share in "a life based on choice" (*Pol.* 1280a34–35) but must have his choices made for him by someone who, by contrast, uses foresight to choose thoughtfully (*Pol.* 1252a32). Slavery thus benefits the person who consistently fails to engage in prohairetic activity by bringing that person into a relation that allows him to mirror or approximate it.[49] The deficiency of a natural slave is, then, his failure to actualize the first-level capacity for virtue that he possesses.[50] A natural slave thus lacks what Aristotle calls a second-level capability. To say this is not, however, to ascribe to natural slaves an immutable nature in the sense I have been challenging. A second-level capability is an actualization of a first-level capacity that comes about by virtue of the activity of its use (*DA* II.4–5): I actualize my first-level capacity for intellectual and moral virtue in prohairetic activity. Similarly, a second-level incapacity results from a failure to actualize the first-level capacity: my consistent failure to exercise my capacity for virtue produces my moral and deliberative deficiency.

Those who are morally and deliberatively deficient owing to their consistent failure to use what they have are, for that reason, worthy of slavery and are, therefore, in Aristotle's terms, natural slaves. By contrast, those who are prevented from using their virtues owing to conquest or coercive institutions, or those whose capacity for virtue is damaged from birth or incapacitated later in their lives (owing to no willing nonuse of their own), are made slaves by force or accident and are, therefore, to Aristotle, not natural slaves at all. Understood by way of prohairetic

49. On the importance of the relation between mimesis and logos for Aristotle, see Davis, *Poetry of Philosophy;* G. Lear, *Happy Lives,* chap. 4. This is not to impose on the master any obligation to teach the slave how to engage in prohairetic activity. In this I agree with Kraut, *Aristotle: Political Philosophy,* pp. 298–99.

50. Kraut argues that what distinguishes natural slaves from freemen is that the former can achieve only a low-level capacity for deliberation, a capacity that allows them to be skilled only at menial craftsmanship. Kraut cannot be arguing that this is a first-level incapacity (although he sometimes seems to, as when he argues that slaves "lack the faculty by which most people reason" from birth) because to have even a low-level capacity is to have a first-level capacity. If, by contrast, he is arguing that natural slaves lack the second-level capability to actualize their first-level capacity, this can change over time. As a practical deficiency rather than an immutable one, a second-level incapacity may be made capable by practice. Kraut, *Aristotle: Political Philosophy,* p. 282.

38   CHAPTER ONE

activity, nature thus distinguishes slaves from nonslaves but secures no absolute boundaries and offers no permanent foundations.[51] It is to preserve the prohairetic activity that he takes to be characteristic and also constitutive of a distinctively human way of living that Aristotle is especially keen, in his more explicitly philosophical treatments of nature, to safeguard nature's changeability. As I show next, this he does by guarding against the assimilation of nature to necessity and also to chance.

The Nature of Nature

> To enquire whether being is single and unchanging
> is no part of an enquiry into nature.
> ARISTOTLE, *Physics*

BETWEEN NECESSITY AND CHANCE

Aristotle understands the natural as what happens usually and for the most part, *epi to polu*. What happens usually and for the most part is a "modal" middle between what is always and what is rare.[52] If what is usually and for the most part corresponds to what is by nature, what is always corresponds to what is by necessity, and what is rare to what happens by accident. In an Aristotelian fashion, I begin my investigation of what is distinctive about the natural by looking first at what he counterposes to nature: the necessary and the accidental.

The primary signification of the necessary, *anagkaion*, or the sense from which "all others are somehow derived," is "that which cannot be otherwise" (*Meta.* 1015a34–b1). The necessary also includes the compulsory or forced, "that which is opposed to impulse or purpose" (*Meta.* 1015a27–28) and what is true by demonstration, the first principles of knowledge (*Meta.* 1015b7). The category of the necessary includes a range of significations across different fields of inquiry—ontology, epistemology, ethics—held together by a kind of family resemblance.[53] What

51. Insofar as all natural beings have souls, they are potentially human. This may open the possibility that animals, say, are potentially human. Where Aristotle stands on this question is not transparent. To him, the line between humans and nonhumans is not clear (*HA* 589a10–633b9; *PA* 648a6–8, 650b24–26, 686a24–687a23). For discussion, see Arnhart, *Darwinian Natural Right,* p. 53.

52. I take the word "modal" from Frede, "Necessity, Chance, and 'What Happens for the Most Part.'"

53. There are other significations that belong here as well: that without which life would be impossible, namely, respiration and food (*Meta.* 1015a20–22), and the "conditions with-

these significations share may be explored by looking at Aristotle's epistemological and ethical treatments of the necessary in *Nicomachean Ethics* VI.3 and III.1, respectively. Discussing the intellectual virtue of scientific knowledge, *episteme*, Aristotle says it studies what is eternal, ungenerated, and imperishable (*NE* 1139b24–25), numbers or figures, for example. Always and invariable, they are necessary in that they are out of time and, hence, without motion. As form without matter, numbers and figures may be precisely and scientifically studied by the intellectual virtues of science, *episteme*, and philosophic wisdom, *theoria*. Although they may be studied by human beings, what is necessary or always is independent of human being. Their independence, along with their invariability, distinguishes the necessary understood as the first principles of knowledge. This feature is present as well in Aristotle's understanding of necessity as compulsion or force: "actions are forced when the cause is in the external circumstances and the agent contributes nothing" (*NE* 1110b1).

The necessary, understood as that which cannot be otherwise, in its ontological, epistemological, and ethical senses, shares a kinship with the past. What is past, Aristotle says, "is not capable of not having taken place" (*NE* 1139b7–9). Once past, what has happened cannot be otherwise. People may study the past but, owing to its invariability, "no one deliberates about the past" (*NE* 1139b7–9). Likewise, no one deliberates about eternal things, for these cannot be brought about by our own efforts (*NE* 1112a20–22). The past, like the first principles of knowledge and like force or compulsion, is independent of human being; human agency cannot change it (*NE* 1140a32–34).

Counterpoised to the necessary and flanking the natural on the other side is the accidental or the rare. "Accident" is what applies to something "but neither necessarily or usually" (*Meta.* 1025a15). It is what can always be otherwise and so *is* never, at least not in the way the invariable is. The accidental is what may be and so is contingent. Aristotle associates the accidental with chance, *to tuchon*, "the thing that happened to happen," which he calls the indefinite, *aoriston*, and cites as the cause of accidents (*Meta.* 1025a25). If what is necessary can be studied precisely and sci-

---

out which good cannot be or come to be" (*Meta.* 1015a22–23). These are akin in the same way the different uses of the term *good* discussed by Aristotle in *Nicomachean Ethics* I.6 are akin: these uses are "one by analogy." Understanding *good* by analogy can accommodate its uses "in the category of substance and in that of quality and in that of relation" (*NE* 1096a20 ff.) without eliding the differences among these uses. Likewise, understanding the term *necessary* by analogy allows its application to these disparate domains and accommodates the ways in which these applications are the same and different.

40 CHAPTER ONE

entifically, what happens accidentally or by chance cannot be studied at all. Inexplicable, indeterminate, and random, chance or accidental events have no account of their own (*Physics* 197a18–19).[54] If there is a kinship between the necessary and the past, there is one as well between the accidental and the future: the accidental is the always possible, what lies uncertainly ahead. Although in most ways unlike the necessary, the accidental has one thing in common with it: what happens by accident is independent of human agency.

Between necessity and contingency, between what is always and what is never, between past and future, lies what is by nature: what happens usually and for the most part.[55] Unlike that which can never be otherwise and unlike that which may always be otherwise, that which is by nature is both variable and stable: it has within itself a principle of change and resistance to change (*Physics* 192b13–14). Neither motionless nor perpetually in motion, natural beings *are*. They can also be otherwise. Owing to their relative stability, what is by nature, unlike what is by accident, can be studied. Owing to their relative variability, studies of what is by nature, unlike studies of the necessary, will be imprecise. Hence it is no wonder that scholars have found tensions in Aristotle's account of nature. There is duality at its core.[56] It is because natural beings are stable and variable and because their possibilities may be actualized in any number of unpredictable ways that only by looking at what they do can anything be known about what they are.[57] Claims about the identity of natural beings will, therefore, be claims about their activities. This is why, in his inquiries into the natures of citizens and slaves, Aristotle, as we have seen, rejects status claims and focuses instead on what they do. It is also why, in his accounts of the natures of slaves and citizens, he is often imprecise. The imprecision arises because the nature of a natural being will change should its character-

54. There is a sense of *accident* which can be eternal that is not relevant for my purposes: see *Meta.* 1025a30–33.

55. The phrase "between necessity and contingency" belongs to Stuart Hampshire, *Justice Is Conflict*, p. 30. The phrase "between past and future" belongs to Hannah Arendt, *Between Past and Future.*

56. On the ways in which Aristotle's dualism differs from our more familiar contemporary dualisms, see McDowell, *Mind, Value, and Reality*, p. viii.

57. Aristotle uses this method to come to knowledge about nature in *De Anima,* where he explores the characteristic activities of the soul to investigate its nature, and in the *Nicomachean Ethics* as well, where he looks at the characteristic activities of human beings to explore their nature. For an excellent discussion of this method, see Salkever, *Finding the Mean,* chap. 3.

THE NATURE OF IDENTITY   41

istic activities change. There is thus an iterative quality to Aristotle's studies of natural beings that accommodates the revision of his own conclusions in cases of
change.[58] Recognizing this in the case of human nature, Aristotle rejects certainty
as a standard for ethics and politics, maintaining that "we must seek the degree of
precision which belongs to [their] subject matter" (*NE* 1098a26–29, 1103b34–
1104a5, 1165a13–14).

Even if the identity of a natural being is given by its characteristic activities and
is therefore variable, most commentators claim that Aristotle is nonetheless committed to there being something necessary about nature, something that somehow lurks behind or beyond a natural being's characteristic activities to disclose its
true identity.[59] As we have seen, this is not true of those whom Aristotle calls natural slaves. It is, indeed, not true of any natural beings, for to claim a necessity to
nature, especially in the case of human nature, is to undermine precisely what
Aristotle aims to preserve, namely, the characteristically human activities of prohairesis, accountability, and responsibility. To demonstrate this, I turn next to an
exploration of the boundaries of Aristotle's category of the natural.

Aristotle often includes in the category of the natural features that seem to belong more properly to the categories of the necessary and the accidental. He sometimes uses the phrase "what is always or for the most part" instead of "what is usually or for the most part" to refer to what is by nature (replacing "usually" with
"always," the term he associates with the necessary) (*Physics* 199b15–18). At other
times he seems to hold up as natural examples that are more rare than usual.[60]
Some commentators mistakenly take these to be signs that Aristotle adjusts his ac-

58. J. Lear, *Aristotle,* pp. 43–54, makes this point about Aristotle's treatment of the heart.
On the basis of his observations, Aristotle came to what we now know to be mistaken conclusions about the role of the heart and how it works. Stressing the bidirectional commitment of Aristotle's scientific approach, "from reality to its rationality and rationality back
to its reality" (p. 45), Lear makes the case that Aristotle's scientific method can revise its
own conclusions. See also Salkever, *Finding the Mean,* chap. 1; Mulgan, *Aristotle's Political
Theory,* chap. 7; Mulgan, "Aristotle's Analysis of Oligarchy and Democracy," p. 308: "Aristotle's approach is undogmatic and open-ended; he is ready to amend and supplement his
analysis if new evidence suggests itself even if this means disrupting the structure of his argument."

59. Swanson, "Aristotle on Nature," insists on there being an apodictic truth about nature
alongside nature's changeability. See also Annas, *Morality of Happiness,* pp. 144, 147, 158; Irwin, trans., *Aristotle:* Nicomachean Ethics, pp. 416–17.

60. He does this in the case of property acquisition and use, where Aristotle calls natural
not the more usual practices of exchange and retail trade but rather immediate use of things

42   CHAPTER ONE

count of the natural to fit circumstances that do not readily mold to his principles.[61] Starting first with the apparent elision of the distinction between nature and necessity, and looking next and more briefly at the relation between the natural and the accidental (because the tendency is to read nature as necessity, not as chance), I argue that although Aristotle takes necessity, or force, and accident, or chance, to affect natural beings—indeed, he sees natural beings as singularly vulnerable to both—neither has a part, and they must have no part in the definition of what is by nature. We have seen this already in Aristotle's exclusion of force and accident from consideration in his investigations of the natures of citizens and slaves. We must now look more carefully at what underlies these exclusions and his inclusion of what I call the "as if" necessary and accidental.

The nature of natural beings is discerned, we have seen, by looking at their activities. Although this is not to say that nature is determined by activity alone, these activities do form the patterns of the lives of natural beings. Because natural beings usually act thus and so, it is not hard to imagine patterns of activity becoming so ingrained as to be justifiably treated as predictable and precise, that is, as characteristic: a human being who *has* acted courageously when confronted with danger will always do so, we might say, for she *is* that sort of person. We often speak in this way, and it might be said that the stability and security of our daily lives depend on the trust in the world presupposed by this way of speaking. We think, speak, and act, in other words, *as if* usual patterns of activity were compelled, *as if* they were necessary. Aristotle's definition of "the usual" in the *Physics* makes this plain: what is by nature "always [tends] toward the same end, unless something intervenes" (199b18). Although we think, speak, and act as if the usual were necessary, we do so knowing that it is always possible that things will turn out otherwise. The courageous person may meet a danger she cannot face down. We speak of "the always" in the case of human and other natural beings only *as if* it were necessary. This is as it should be. Human beings are stable insofar as we have within ourselves a principle of staying the same, or rest. Insofar as we have within ourselves a principle of change, we are also changeable and in constant interaction with our circumstances. In different circumstances, human beings act differently. When na-

---

necessary to the end of living (*Pol.* I.3). Annas, "Aristotle on Human Nature," p. 733, treats this as evidence of Aristotle's inconsistent use of nature.

61. See Annas, *Morality of Happiness,* p. 146; Annas, "Aristotle on Human Nature"; Irwin, trans., *Aristotle:* Nicomachean Ethics, pp. 416–17.

ture is understood not in terms of stability but in terms of necessity, invariability controls beings who, for Aristotle at least, are defined as well by movement and possibility.[62]

Aristotle's vigilance against any more than an "as if" assimilation of nature to necessity is on display in his discussion of responsibility in *Nicomachean Ethics* III.1, where nature and necessity are brought into a confrontation. As noted above, Aristotle takes actions to be compelled when a person contributes nothing to the action; the cause of action is, rather, in external circumstances. Only two kinds of situations meet Aristotle's definition of compulsion: when an agent acts without knowledge of the circumstances of action (and his ignorance is honest or innocent) or when a third party physically effects the action in the agent's place by, to use an anachronistic example, putting his hand over the agent's when she is holding a gun and using his finger over hers to pull the trigger despite her efforts to resist. For all other actions, the agent, in Aristotle's view, is responsible, for, as he puts it, the origin of action is in the agent (*NE* 1111a23–30). In comparison to modern legal definitions, his account of force is exceedingly limited: it does not include actions taken under conditions of duress, debilitating drunkenness, pent-up rage, and the like, when these conditions are brought about by the agent himself. For Aristotle, an agent's actions are forced only when he is effectively prevented from acting voluntarily.

If Aristotle's understanding of force is narrow, his account of responsibility is remarkably expansive.[63] As the following passage from the *Nicomachean Ethics* indicates, people are responsible for all of their voluntary actions, vicious as well as virtuous:

> Virtue is up to us. And so also is vice. For where we are free to act we are also free to refrain from acting, and where we are able to say No we are also able to say Yes. If it is up to us to act when doing a thing is good or noble, not acting will be up to us when acting would be shameful or wrong; and, if not acting when inaction is good is up to us, so, too, acting when action is shameful is up to us. But if it is in

---

62. Frede's deterministic account of Aristotle on character, in "Necessity, Chance, and 'What Happens for the Most Part,'" p. 203, leaves out the key place of movement and possibility.

63. Some have argued that it is too expansive and too demanding because Aristotle does not consider duress, for example, as an excuse for bad action. He does, however, advocate taking justifications and other mitigating factors into account when determining how to respond to actions taken under difficult conditions (*Rhet.* 1374b13–16).

44   CHAPTER ONE

> our power to refrain from doing right and wrong, and if . . . being good or bad is
> doing right or wrong, it consequently depends on us whether we are good or bad.
> (*NE* 1113b6–14, trans. modified)

Prohairetic activity is at stake in Aristotle's vigilance against assimilating responsibility to force. Prohairetic activity is also at stake in his vigilance against assimilating nature to necessity. In the *Nicomachean Ethics,* necessity—as that to which the agent contributes nothing, because the cause of action lies altogether outside the agent—stands opposed to prohairetic agency as that which has within itself its own principle, *arche,* of action.[64] In the *Metaphysics,* the *Physics,* and elsewhere, necessity stands opposed to what is by nature as that which has within itself its own principle of motion and rest. Eliding the distinction between nature and necessity makes virtue and vice involuntary, a position Aristotle rejects (*NE* 1114b14). When nature and necessity are paired, prohairetic activity, responsibility, and self-determination disappear. What is by nature, then, may reach toward necessity, but it must remain distinct from the necessary so as to preserve the activity characteristic of human beings.

What is by nature also reaches toward but remains distinct from the accidental. Aristotle recognizes the role of chance or luck in the lives of natural beings and the ameliorative effects of contingent external goods throughout the *Nicomachean Ethics* and the *Politics.* As with necessity, however, Aristotle refuses to understand the identity of natural beings in terms of chance, luck, or accident. The stakes in keeping nature and chance distinct are no different from what they were in keeping nature and necessity distinct. Understanding the nature of natural beings in terms of chance, like understanding it in terms of necessity, makes prohairetic activity and responsibility irrelevant.

If, on the side of the necessary, Aristotle enfolds into the category of the natural what I called the "as if" necessary, on the side of the accidental he enfolds into the category of the natural the "as if" accidental, what, in the *Nicomachean Ethics,* he calls art, *techne.* Art is concerned neither with things that are or come into being by necessity nor with things that do so in accordance with nature. Art, rather, is "concerned with the same objects" as chance (*NE* 1140a14–20). Both are concerned with possibility, with how something may be or may come into being that is capable of being or not being (*NE* 1140a13). Moreover, in art, as in chance, the finished work is not completely governed by the activity of producing (*NE* 1140a18). Martin Heidegger puts it this

---

64. Note that the absence of force or necessity is a necessary but not a sufficient condition of choice, *prohairesis.*

way: "The essential characteristic of the accidental is that what emerges from it is out of its hands. The same occurs in the case of techne; it may be developed in the most minute detail, and yet it does not have at its disposal, with absolute certainty, the success of the work. In the end, the [work, or] ergon is out of the hands of techne."[65]

"Art loves chance and chance loves art," says Aristotle, quoting Agathon approvingly (*NE* 1140a20). But art is only "as if" accidental. Unlike chance, in which the cause is altogether indeterminate, in art, it is the blueprint, *eidos,* in the soul or mind of the maker, that is the cause of action (*Meta.* 1032b22–25). There is, in other words, prohairetic agency in art but not in chance. This is not to deny the difference Aristotle is at pains to underscore between the making of art and the doing that belongs to activity proper: in art, he says, the end is outside the activity of making, whereas doing is activity that has within itself its own end (*NE* 1140b4–6). Even if the end product in art is outside the agent's control, making, like doing, but unlike chance or necessity, involves activity and responsibility.

In keeping what is by nature distinct from necessity and also from accident, as Aristotle does in his discussions of the nature of citizens, slaves, and foreigners and in his account of the nature of nature itself, Aristotle preserves the prohairetic activity that characterizes and distinguishes human nature. In including the "as if" necessary and the "as if" accidental in his account of the natural, he reveals the expansiveness of his conception of prohairetic activity and the centrality of politics to its practice. For politics, like ethics, is the site of the as if necessary practices of human beings that inform their as if necessary natures (*NE* 1094a27–b11). Politics is also itself an art and so a product of human activity that produces as if by accident the institutions that also as if by accident help make citizens and slaves. It is because Aristotle understands prohairetic activity in these ways that he can, without inconsistency, treat human beings and, indeed, the polity itself as both natural and made (*Pol.* 1253a19–31, 1252b30).[66]

THE POWER OF ACTIVITY

Is human nature all and only activity? Aristotle's answer seems to be yes: yes, in that, as we have seen, there is nothing necessary lurking behind activity; yes, in that natural beings are distinguished by their activities; yes, in that even the stability characteristic of human nature is based on activity. Aristotle insists, however, that

---

65. Heidegger, *Plato's* Sophist, p. 31.
66. See also Masters, "Human Nature, Nature, and Political Thought," pp. 77–82.

46   CHAPTER ONE

activity alone cannot produce the movement and change or stability that characterize human nature. Activity alone does not account for the nature of natural beings because the nature of a natural being is not simply a description of what it tends to do. Activity, we have noted, also sets a standard, an internal and demanding one. To see how requires attending not simply to activity but also to what gives rise to it: the conditions of its possibility.

Aristotle calls that which makes activity possible dunamis, which is translated variously as capacity, power, capability, or potentiality.[67] Dunamis is, he explains, the power that activity has to regulate itself. He analyzes this relation between capability, *dunamis,* and activity, *energeia,* in his discussion of the Megarians in *Metaphysics* IX.3.[68] The Megarians, he recounts, say that "a man who is not building cannot build, but only the man who is building, and at the moment when he is building" (*Meta.* 1046b30–32). This means that it is only when a dunamis (or capability) is actually at work that the ability to do something is present. When it is not at work, the dunamis, as a capacity, is only potential and, therefore, absent. For the Megarians, as for some contemporary post-Nietzscheans, this means that activities emerge ex nihilo.

Aristotle thinks that this account of activity is absurd. When dunamis is treated as only present when it is in action, he argues, there can be no change or movement at all (*Meta.* 1047a15). Change or movement must happen from one thing to another. It may be true that to be capable means to have a dunamis and that not having the dunamis means not being capable, but, Aristotle insists, dunamis has its own *energeia,* or activity. The activity or actuality of dunamis lies in its being possessed even when it is not at work. The builder can have the capability to build even when he is not actually building. Not building, then, does not necessarily signal the absence of dunamis, although it can, as when, for example, the builder loses the capacity to build because of bad luck (he loses his hands, say) or he forgets how to build owing to the passage of time. Under these conditions of accident or nonuse, there can be no building activity at all. Where there is activity, it emerges not from something only potential, that is, absent, but from dunamis understood as the withdrawal into itself of the capability such that it is primed for release, that is, primed

---

67. Against the contemporary tendency to equate them, *dunamis,* power, is not the same as *bia,* force.

68. My analysis draws on Heidegger, *Aristotle's* Metaphysics, chap. 3. Because I am interested in what Aristotle's analysis teaches about his understanding of activity, I leave to one side whether Aristotle's description of the Megarian position is accurate.

for activity.[69] Dunamis, as "the source, *arche,* of change in some other thing or in the same thing *qua* other" (*Meta.* 1046a11, 1019a19–21), is the "power" of activity: it is what makes activity possible. As we saw above, without the capacity for logos there could be no activity of its use; without good habits there can be no virtuous activity.

If dunamis powers activity, this does not make activity itself any less important. Dunamis may be that from which change occurs, but it is not something inert, waiting to move to action. Rather, it effects change by way of its actualization, by doing its work, by practice. It is by performing the activities for which it is holding itself in readiness that a dunamis becomes capable in the first place. It is, in other words, by building that a builder becomes capable of building (*Meta.* 1046b34–36). The activity of building actualizes the builder's capability to build. One is a builder in the way one is a courageous or deliberative or virtuous person, for example, which is to say, only so long as the disposition to build or to act courageously or prohairetically shows itself from time to time in activity. Along similar lines, Aristotle remarks that "distance does not break off friendship absolutely, only the activity of it. But if the absence is lasting, it seems actually to make men forget their friendship" (*NE* 1157b6–13).

Human nature, then, is not determined all and only by activity, in Aristotle's understanding, for activities come from capabilities. There are, so to speak, doers behind deeds. The nature of the doer is stable. But this is not to say that nature is once and for all determined. Rather, the doer's nature is continually informed by the activities he has performed and continues to perform. This means that if the deed is the product of activity, it is not activity's sole product. For even as activities emerge from a stable character, activities are, themselves, formative of character. The more courageously I act, the more courageous I become. There can be no activity without capability, but there can also be no capability without activity. Each depends on the other. It is this interdependence between energeia and dunamis that makes possible the changes over time and movement that define the nature of human beings and also their stability. This interdependence also defines soul, the part of natural beings that contains their principle and source of motion. If the ordering or constitution of character, soul, and human nature itself is given by the interdependence between energeia and dunamis and is changeable, it is nonetheless possible, at any given moment, to distinguish among those who are and those who are not actualizing their potential. This distinction, as we have seen, rests on the practice of prohairetic activity.

---

69. Ibid., pp. 156–65.

48   CHAPTER ONE

Some commentators have taken Aristotle's definition of nature in *Metaphysics* V.4 to be equivocal. They say he defines nature in two senses, and they criticize him for sometimes favoring one and sometimes the other.[70] As "the principle of motion in natural beings, which is somehow inherent in them, either potentially, *dunamei*, or actually, *entelecheia*" (*Meta.* 1015a18–19), Aristotle's definition of nature in the *Metaphysics* involves duality, to be sure. In one sense, he says, nature is the primary stuff—matter—and, in another sense, it is form. In one sense, it is the immanent thing from which a growing thing first begins to grow, *dunamis;* in another sense, it is the genesis of growing things, their activity, *energeia*. He takes form, or *energeia*, to be primary and guiding (*Physics* 193b17),[71] and he also understands form to take its guiding orientation from matter, much in the way the shape of a statue may appear to its sculptor from the clay. But this is not to equivocate. For in the *Metaphysics,* as in the *Physics,* the *Nicomachean Ethics,* and also the *Politics,* where Aristotle both establishes the necessity of hierarchy or teleology (among species and human beings in *Politics* I and among regimes in the rest of the *Politics*) and also alerts us to its dangers, the sense of nature that he takes to be primary and guiding is nature neither as an origin nor as an end separable from growth. It is both, and neither, and is captured in the process of growth itself. A natural being becomes and reveals its nature as it grows, changes, and moves through time.

This way of understanding nature fits well with Aristotle's treatment of nature as a telos and of tele more generally: "For what each thing is when fully developed, we call its nature, whether we are speaking of a man, a horse, or a family. Besides, the final cause and end of a thing is the best, and to be self-sufficing is the end and the best" (*Pol.* 1252b31–1253a1; see also *Movement of Animals* 698b10–15; *Physics* 194a24–31). This suggests that it is the end, or *telos,* that guides movement and without which there could be no movement, only randomness. In the case of what

---

70. Annas ("Aristotle on Human Nature," p. 735 n. 12; *Morality of Happiness,* p. 146) understands Aristotle to be "adding to" his account in the *Physics* of nature as the internal source of change "the point that a thing's nature is both the matter from which the change begins and also the substance or form which is the *telos* of the completed change." Calling the matter from which the change begins "mere nature" and the form or telos of the completed change the "strong sense of nature," Annas disaggregates what, for Aristotle, co-constitutes natural beings: matter and form, or *dunamis* and *energeia* (*DA* 412a10). Irwin, *Aristotle:* Nicomachean Ethics, pp. 416–17, makes the same mistake. Arnhart, *Darwinian Natural Right,* pp. 36–39, by contrast, treats nature as "both original potential and developed potential."

71. J. Lear, *Aristotle,* chap. 2; Nussbaum and Putnam, "Changing Aristotle's Mind."

is by nature, form may be the telos of natural beings, but form itself is not static. Defined in terms of entelecheia and energeia, the form of natural beings, as their telos, is no less (and no more) kinetic than activity itself.[72] This is because to be an end is to exist in the present, as a possibility. And for something to be a possibility for a human being depends, as we have seen, not on accident or chance or force or necessity, all of which would be external to the being, but on the being's own past and present, on her habits and capabilities and on their actualization by way of prohairetic activity. The end or the completion of a natural being's coming into being is not separable from the growth process. A telos does not stand over and against the process of coming into being, directing it from without, but is, rather, paradoxical: its tense is futural while its focus is not on the future but on what is possible in the here and now as it emerges from the past.[73] Nature, understood as an end and a beginning all at once, is an ongoing process. As the domain of activity, it is also, and crucially for Aristotle, the domain of ethics and politics (*NE* 1103b26–30).

The Work of Man

The work is the maker in act.
ARISTOTLE, *Nicomachean Ethics*

From the interdependence between energeia and dunamis, the movement and change over time that characterize human nature, the soul, and virtue are possible. And from their interdependence the stability and unity over time that characterize natural beings are possible as well. What sort of unity is this? Against what Bernard Williams refers to as modernity's "dualistic distinction between soul and body," Aristotle treats the body as "ensouled" (*DA* 403a).[74] According to Jonathan Lear, Aristotle insists, against Plato, that in a virtuous person, "the 'nonrational' and rational parts of the psyche . . . function together as a harmonious and seamless whole."[75] The unity of the virtuous soul may be characterized by harmony, but,

---

72. This is in contrast to Villa, *Arendt and Heidegger,* pp. 42–52, according to whom Aristotle's teleology robs action of its initiatory power and gives action a predetermined "authoritarian" future or end. Because a natural being comes into its own not by actualizing a potential that was always already there but by forming and re-forming that potential by means of activity, that being's telos, although embedded in a past and oriented by a set of capabilities, is itself kinetic and so predetermines nothing.

73. I have more to say about this peculiar quality of Aristotelian tele in chapter 5.

74. Williams, *Shame and Necessity,* p. 23. See also J. Lear, *Open Minded,* p. 168, claiming for Aristotle an "embodied conception of human reason."

75. J. Lear, *Open Minded,* p. 169; see also Annas, "Self-Love in Aristotle," pp. 3–4.

50   CHAPTER ONE

being constituted by energeia and dunamis and, thus, a source of motion, it is not a seamless whole or a simple unity. Like human nature, it is, rather, a unity in difference, a differentiated whole. Discussing the requirements for virtue, Aristotle says that "nature, habit, and reason must be in harmony with one another; for men do many things against habit and nature, because of reason, if reason persuades them that they ought" (*Pol.* 1332b6–8). Referring to this passage, Julia Annas remarks that, for Aristotle, the "'harmony' of nature, habit and reason is compatible with reason going against the other two." Calling this "a remarkable concept of harmonization," she questions it by enclosing "harmony" in quotation marks.[76] But this *is* Aristotle's concept of harmony. "Seamless harmony" would, for Aristotle, be a contradiction in terms. Requiring not the absence of all difference, and not a oneness of soul, the harmony that characterizes the unity of the soul requires difference (and so the possibility of disharmony or conflict) to enable both the movement and the stability that define it.[77]

The work, *ergon,* of each human being is to unify his soul not by mastery—the despotic rule that eradicates difference—but by practicing the virtue of moderation, which, by preserving the balance of unity and difference proper to the soul, holds a peculiar place in Aristotle's account of the virtues.[78] For Aristotle, acting virtuously by hitting the mean depends on the past (who I have been) and on the future (who I hope to become), and it is wedded to the particular set of circumstances I find myself in now. I must answer for what I do and I am responsible for what I do, which is to say, I must account for my actions, however imprecisely.[79] By enfolding past and future into his account of activity, Aristotle is able to capture the "now" of ethics and politics without arresting it. In the moment of activity, the soul retains its internal differences.

Activities in the world produce capabilities. Capabilities, produced by activities, in turn power activities. By activities, as we have seen, Aristotle understands what I make of myself, alongside the guided making of the social and political institutions of the polity that, as a citizen, I have contributed to making. Guided making and self-making cooperate (though not in the sense that their ends always coin-

76. Annas, "Aristotle on Human Nature," p. 734.

77. Movement and dependence show the soul to be an "integration of distinct elements rather than a uniform unity." See Broadie, *Ethics with Aristotle,* p. 65.

78. Moderation, Aristotle says, preserves practical wisdom (*NE* 1140b11–12). I discuss the virtue of moderation further in chapters 2 and 3.

79. As Hans-Georg Gadamer notes, Aristotle "interpreted the Socratic equation of virtue and knowledge in such a way as to include the giving of accounts as part of the moral essence of ethics." See "Aristotle and the Ethics of Imperatives," p. 59.

cide). It is for these reasons—to preserve human agency while simultaneously recognizing the degree to which it is effected—that Aristotle has, as we have seen, a demanding account of responsibility. And this is also why he has a complex account of equity: "Equity bids us . . . to consider not so much the action of the accused but the choice, and not so much this or that part of the account but the whole story; to consider not what sort of a person an agent is now but what sort of person he has been or is usually" (*Rhet.* 1374b13–16).

The work of unity in difference in the soul—virtuous or prohairetic activity—is open to any human soul that, by virtue of being constituted by energeia and dunamis, works. As Aristotle puts it: "No *ergon* of man has so much permanence as virtuous activities, *energeiai*" (*NE* 1100b13). This work is learned by "a certain kind of study and care" (*NE* 1099b18). He is not advocating theoretical or scientific study but choosing good mentors, specifically mentors with practical wisdom. Choosing good mentors, of course, already calls for good judgment, itself a matter of the very habits that emulating the mentor is meant to cultivate. Learning how to be virtuous (learning how to act well and being well habituated), it turns out, already depends on being well habituated. Here we come up against a circularity that is characteristic of Aristotle's philosophical method. For some, this circularity gives Aristotle's politics its conservative and exclusionary bent: acting well must be grasped from the inside out. Who acts well? Those habituated to act well. Who are these? Those who exercise good judgment and choose as their mentors people with practical wisdom. Who exercises good judgment and chooses well? Those with good habits. Although it is true that, in Aristotle's understanding of virtue, those who are not properly habituated will not be able to act virtuously, insofar as good habits can be learned by anyone so disposed, in the absence of otherwise constraining social and political institutions, there is no reason to draw from this circularity an elitist conclusion. Indeed, Aristotle insists that neither birth nor wealth determines one's capacity for excellence (*Pol.* 1281a4–8, 1323a38–b6). Some external goods are required, to be sure, and not everyone will be disposed to learn good habits. But there is no necessary connection between being so disposed and the accident of birth or great wealth.[80]

In my reading, the political and, indeed, peculiarly democratic possibilities of

---

80. We have seen this already in Aristotle's treatment of birth as a matter of accident in the cases of citizen and slave identity. Further evidence of Aristotle's disaggregation of birth and wealth from virtue may be found in his rejection of traditional markers of status as qualifications for rule and his insistence, in their place, on virtue (*Pol.* III.12).

52   CHAPTER ONE

Aristotle's approach to virtue lie in its very circularity. Democracy is itself a circular mode of governance. Citizens, who are also rulers, make the laws to which they are subject. In other words, they follow their own law. In this way, democracy is a mode of governance that has its source and authority in itself. It is the self-governing regime. It is the same with the practice of virtue: when I act well, I do so because my own habits so dispose me to act. Intellectual and moral virtue both involve modes of activity—prohairetic activity—whose origin and authority lie in themselves. The self-sovereignty associated with these practices is the same as the self-sovereignty characteristic of democracy.

A unity in difference exemplifies Aristotle's understanding of the harmonious whole that is the soul and of the harmonious whole that is the polity as well, which he characterizes as not a unison but a plurality; a rhythm, not a single beat (*Pol.* 1263b35).[81] The work of each citizen (individual prohairetic activity) and the work of citizens together (collective prohairetic activity) is to unify the polity in a way that preserves its essential plurality. If the primary focus of this chapter has been on the "internal" work of human being, the ways in which each person is and is not responsible for his or her nature, and the nature of that nature itself, the rest of this book looks to the work of citizens in the creation of the social and political institutions and practices that preserve the polity as a unity in difference by shaping the identity and guiding the making of citizens (and so also any exclusions from citizenship).

Once more revealing that questions of nature are also questions of and for politics and ethics, Aristotle, in his discussions of nature in *Politics* I, anticipates his treatments of the key political institutions that will be the subject matter of the rest of his treatise. By way of the discussion of the nature of property (its proper and improper use), he inquires as to the best property arrangement for a well-constituted polity, the question to which he returns in *Politics* II. I explore this topic in chapter 2. Staging the question of natural slavery as a question of justice, he lays the groundwork for his treatments in *Politics* III of citizenship, which I have discussed in this chapter, and of justice, to which I turn in chapter 3. Aligning law, *nomos,* with force, and opposing both to nature, *phusis,* in his discussion of conventional slavery, Aristotle challenges the very legitimacy of what he also takes to be at the heart of a well-constituted polity in *Politics* III, namely, the rule of law. This is a question I take up in chapter 4. My aim is to investigate Aristotle's treat-

---

81. I discuss the harmony of the well-constituted polity in chapter 5.

ments of the practices of property, justice, and law against the backdrop of the lesson of *Politics* I: that beings by nature are also made and that the social and political institutions produced by citizens will affect the proportionate contribution of necessity and agency to a person's activity by nurturing and constraining effective agency. I end, in chapter 5, with an exploration of the constitution that best guides these institutions and practices even as it is produced by them.

CHAPTER TWO

The Use of Property

There is general agreement among contemporary readers that Aristotle advocates a system of private property for a well-constituted polity.[1] He is read in this way largely on the basis of his famous rejection of the endorsement of common ownership by Plato's Socrates.[2] There is also agreement that Aristotle's understanding of property can, without distortion, be assimilated to our own.[3] If the choice is between reading Aristotle as a defender of private property or as a proponent of common property, placing him in the first camp is warranted. But Aristotle's understanding of property cannot be so easily categorized. With no word in Greek for property as such, Aristotle describes his preferred mode of ownership as holding things as one's own for common use, *idiai kteseis, koinai tei chresei* (*Pol.* 1263a25, 40).[4] He thus seems to negotiate a middle way between common property

---

1. For commentators who read Aristotle as defending a system of private property, see F. Miller, *Nature, Justice, and Rights*, chap. 9; Mayhew, *Aristotle's Criticism of Plato's Republic*, p. 96; Swanson, *Public and the Private*, chaps. 1, 4; Dobbs, "Aristotle's Anticommunism." By contrast, Nussbaum, "Aristotelian Social Democracy," argues for a socialist account of Aristotelian property. Mayhew, *Aristotle's Criticism of Plato's Republic*, pp. 107–9, offers a convincing criticism of Nussbaum. For theorists who cite Aristotle as a defender of private property, see Schlatter, *Private Property*, p. 16; Waldron, *Right to Private Property*, p. 6; Becker, *Property Rights*, p. 62; Munzer, *Theory of Property*, pp. 128–29.

2. Aristotle does not mention that Plato's Socrates endorses common ownership only among the guardians in *Republic* V.

3. See F. Miller, *Nature, Justice, and Rights*, pp. 311–13, where he assimilates Aristotle's concept of property to "the modern Anglo-American concept of property rights" (p. 312). See also Rasmussen and Den Uyl, *Liberty and Nature*, chaps. 2–3. I agree with those who argue that there are no "rights" in Aristotle, although this issue is beyond the scope of this book: see L. Strauss, *Natural Right and History*, pp. 182–83; MacIntyre, *After Virtue*, pp. 66–67; Kraut, "Are There Natural Rights in Aristotle?"; Schofield, "Sharing in the Constitution."

4. See Jones, *Law and Legal Theory of the Greeks*, chap. 11; Harrison, *Law of Athens*, 1:201; MacDowell, *Law in Classical Athens*, p. 133.

Aristotle uses any number of words to signify what we call property, including, *ta oikeia* (the things of the household), *ta ideia* (what is one's own), *timema* (the honor paid to those

and private property, to produce an account of property that shares features of modern and contemporary conceptions of private ownership but also departs from them in important ways.

Contemporary legal and political theories tend to treat property as an individual right to the possession, use, and disposition of material things. Central to individual liberty, independence, and security, property, in these conceptions, sets up zones of sovereignty within which private owners may effectively do as they will with what is theirs. Aristotle, too, takes property to be bound with autonomy and exclusion, maintaining that a good and self-sufficient life requires a store of external goods, including material possessions, and that the possessor of goods decides how to use them. Like many contemporary advocates of private property, Aristotle opposes forced redistribution on the ground that it leads to civil strife, *stasis* (*Pol.* 1281a15–22). That he introduces and elaborates his account of property as one of the practices of managing one's own home (*Pol.* I.8–11) and opposes common ownership and other forms of legislative redistribution demonstrates his commitment to the private aspect of property.[5]

Unlike most defenders of private property, however, Aristotle advocates holding things as one's own *for common use*.[6] He endorses this mode of owning in the home, among friends and neighbors, and under his preferred constitutions, with respect to what we take to meet our daily needs (*Pol.* 1257a7–14), land and crops (*Pol.* 1263a37), wealth (*NE* IV.1–2), and political offices (*Pol.* 1279a29–33, 1309b7). This suggests that there is a public dimension to Aristotelian property as well. This

---

who possess), *ktemata* (holdings), *trophe* (material necessities), *chremata* (things in use, including *ploutos,* wealth), *pragmata* (things in action), *ousia* (estate, substance), and *choregia* (equipment of life). He uses *ktemata* and *chremata* separately and together most often in the first two books of the *Politics* to refer to what is held for use in the home. He usually uses *timema* in reference to constitutional property qualifications and *ousia* when referring to the whole of a person's estate (their possessions combined with their things in use, as well as other intangible properties). He uses *choregia* to refer to the external goods necessary to the good life of a human being and of a polity and also in its more usual sense, as one of the most important public service institutions at Athens. I will use *property* to capture all these significations, marking their differences from one another and from contemporary usage where necessary.

5. Thus, some writers conclude that property is exclusively part of the household: see Mathie, "Property in the Political Science of Aristotle"; Dobbs, "Aristotle's Anticommunism," p. 41.

6. Others who share this way of thinking about property include Rose, *Property and Persuasion,* and, I have argued, Supreme Court justice Harry Blackmun, James Madison, and Thomas Jefferson. See Frank, "Integrating Public Good and Private Right."

56   CHAPTER TWO

aspect is on display throughout his ethical and political writings: from his recommendation that wealth be used not for private gain and accumulation but to benefit the common good (*Pol.* I.8–10; *NE* IV.1–2) to the central role he accords property in enabling the polity to be well constituted (*Pol.* II.2, 3, 5), and from his claim that a well-ordered polity should have common meals open to all citizens (*Pol.* 1330a3–5) to his recommendation that in a good polity land should be divided into two parts—one public, the other private—and that each citizen should have lots in each part for reasons of justice and fairness and to inspire concord among citizens in case of border wars (*Pol.* 1330a11–20). As the practice of holding as one's own and using with others reserves of individual and collective goods, property, in Aristotle's understanding, is both private and public at the same time.[7]

Aristotelian property is dual in another sense as well. Contemporary scholars typically treat property as fundamentally instrumental. For economic efficiency theorists, it is a means to the end of wealth maximization.[8] For personality theorists, as for most Aristotle commentators, it is a means to the end of virtue.[9] If property is a means to the end of wealth and virtue, then it would seem that more property would make for a more self-sufficient, virtuous, and happy life. But this is not Aristotle's view. An excessive amount of property, he insists, will harm its possessor (*Pol.* 1323b6–10). Wealth, *ploutos*, he says, "consists in an abundance of coin and land; the possession of agricultural land and the possession of moveables, cattle and slaves, distinguished in number, magnitude and beauty. And these are all owned, *oikeia*, secure, free, and useful" (*Rhet.* 1361a13–16; *Pol.* 1256b30–32).[10] Property, in this way, is a means to the end of wealth, to be sure (*Pol.* 1256a4). But it is also something more: "All in all, wealth consists in using things rather than having acquired them. It is really the activity, *energeia*, of using things that constitutes wealth" (*Rhet.* 1361a24–25). Wealth, the sum of property, is not only what one

7. *Contra* Barker, *Political Thought of Plato and Aristotle,* chap. 9; F. Miller, *Nature, Justice, and Rights,* chap. 9; Swanson, *Public and the Private,* chaps. 1, 4; and Arendt, *Human Condition,* chap. 2, who argue that Aristotle defends individual property to safeguard a sphere of privacy. For discussion of the relation between private and public in fourth-century Athens, see Cohen, *Law, Sexuality, and Society,* chap. 4. For the embeddedness in the household of the ancient Athenian economy, see Booth, *Households,* chap. 2.

8. See, e.g., Demsetz, "Toward a Theory of Property Rights"; Becker, *Property Rights,* chap. 2; Posner, *Economic Analysis of Law.*

9. See, e.g., Waldron, *Right to Private Property;* Radin, "Property and Personhood"; Stillman, "Hegel's Analysis of Property."

10. Note that the word *oikeia* was inserted in this passage in the *Rhetoric* by the Renaissance scholar Marc-Antoine Muretus. Aristotle's repeated use of this word when he discusses property in his other ethical and political writings justifies its insertion here.

acquires for use, one's possessions or holdings; it is also, and crucially, itself an activity of use.[11]

Similarly, property may be a means to the achievement of a virtuous and happy life, but it is also itself a practice of virtue. Aristotle insists that the things we hold as our own may be used well or badly. When used well, property, somewhat paradoxically, limits its own accumulation (*Pol.* 1256b32–37). As we will see, property, to Aristotle, has a noninstrumental or constitutive role in shaping both individual character and the character of a polity. If contemporary paradigms tend to treat property as a safe haven from political life, in what follows I argue that the practice of Aristotelian property, as an activity of use bound to virtue, is instead integral to a political life. To justify this claim, the first section of this chapter examines Aristotle's account of use, the second explores the virtues of Aristotelian property, and the third, binding use and virtue, turns to the relation between Aristotelian property and politics.

The Activity of Use

In *Politics* I, Aristotle introduces property as one of the practices of managing one's own home, *oikonomike*.[12] A home must be furnished with the appropriate equipment if its functions are to be discharged. The job of the householder is to supply the goods that are "necessary for life, capable of being stored, and useful for the community of the household and polity" (*Pol.* 1256b29–30). What Aristotle calls the things of the home, *ta oikeia*, and we call property, is the sum of the equipment that is acquired for use and preserved (*Pol.* 1277b24–25). He elaborates a complicated and sometimes confusing set of relations among the activities of acquiring, using, and preserving: the end of the activity of taking, *ktetike*, is using, *chresis*, for the things taken are for use; the end of the activity of using things is

---

11. Meikle, *Aristotle's Economic Thought*, pp. 48–50, recognizes this dual role in regard to wealth. Traces of this way of understanding property may be found in Aquinas, John Locke, and the present-day property theorists Joseph Singer and Joseph Sax.

12. The relation of the householder to his property is not the only relation in the home that is of concern to Aristotle. He also considers the relationships between master and slave, husband and wife, and father and children. I discuss Aristotle on slavery in chapter 1. For a nuanced and illuminating discussion of Aristotle on gender, see Saxonhouse, *Women in the History of Political Thought*, chap. 4.

For other discussions of the household, see Bellemare, "Note sur *l'oikonomia politike*"; Booth, *Households;* Foxhall, "Household, Gender and Property in Classical Athens"; MacDowell, "*Oikos* in Athenian Law"; Singer, "*Oikonomia.*"

58   CHAPTER TWO

their preservation, *soteria;* and the end of the activity of preserving things is their use. Aristotle thus defines acquisition and preservation as activities of use. Things are taken and preserved specifically for what he calls "proper use" (*Pol.* 1257a10), which limits what is taken to meet daily recurrent needs. The central activity of the household with regard to property, then, is proper use.

Using properly what is held refers not only to the things taken for immediate use in the home. It also refers to what is held to be shared or given away among friends, among neighbors, and among citizens in a polity. Aristotle says: friends have all things in common, *panta koina philois* (*NE* 1159b31–32, 1168b8). Although this phrase is sometimes adduced as evidence that Aristotle takes friends' goods to be common goods, Aristotle objects to common ownership not only for well-constituted polities but for friendship as well.[13] He says that there is less friendship, not more, among those who hold everything in common (*Pol.* 1263a15–19, 1263b15–25). This is because under common ownership things are shared not because sharing is preferred but because it is required.[14] When friends choose a system of common ownership, they indicate that they will not count on one another to share, that they do not trust one another, and so are not truly friends.[15] Instead, referring to the appropriate property arrangement among friends, Aristotle says that friends' goods are, for the purpose of use, common goods, *pros to chresthai . . . koina ta philon* (*Pol.* 1263a29–30). This means that friends' goods are held as their own, although held in this way for use together.

Holding things as one's own for proper use is also the mode of owning suitable among neighbors, citizens, and rulers. Aristotle maintains that such things as land and crops are used properly when they are held as one's own and given over to neighbors to use when they need provisions on a journey (*Pol.* 1263a37) and that wealth, especially if held on a large scale, is used properly when it is held as one's own and used to benefit the polity as a whole by, for example, "equipping a chorus splendidly or fitting out a ship of war, or giving a banquet to the public" (*NE* 1122b19–24). Holding as one's own for proper use is, finally, the mode of owning appropriate to those who rule the well-constituted polity, insofar as political offices and the like are used properly when they are held by rulers to the common good of all the citizens of a polity, in the manner of stewardship (*Pol.* 1279a29–33,

13. For those who take it as evidence of common property, see Yack, *Problems of a Political Animal,* chap. 4; Barker, *Politics of Aristotle,* p. 49, although Barker also recognizes it as a holding as one's own for common use, p. 305.

14. See also Dobbs, "Aristotle's Anticommunism," p. 39.

15. This was Epicurus's answer to why common ownership among members of a school

1309b7). Rather than carving out a clear distinction between *oikos* and *polis,* home and city, private and public, Aristotelian property, in its use, marks continuities between how we take and use things in the home and the practices of social and political life (*Pol.* 1260b14–20). Proper use in the home becomes, among friends, neighbors, and citizens, a using with others, which is to say, common use. If we generally treat property as a moat that excludes other people from interfering with what is ours and protects a private sphere in which we can do with it what we will, Aristotelian property operates also as a bridge. Property may render us self-sufficient and independent, but Aristotle also stresses the ways in which property underscores our mutuality by engaging us in interdependent activities of use.

Note that in all these practices of property, things are used properly when they effectively disappear into their use: by being consumed to the end of living in the home or by being handed over or used to benefit others in the polity. Aristotle, however, insists that using things properly preserves them. Explaining how things may be used and preserved at the same time is the key to understanding his account of proper use. To explore this apparently paradoxical practice, I consider the word Aristotle uses to signify the equipment that belongs, as a matter of necessity, to a human life and to the life of a polity: *choregia* (*NE* 1099a34, 1178a25; *Pol.* 1288b40, 1325b41, 1326a6, 1332a1).[16] The root of *choregia* is *choros,* signifying chorus, dance (choreography), and play. Treating as categorical the difference between Aristotle's use of choregia as the necessary equipment of life and its usual significations, H. Rackham notes that in Aristotle, choregia "has almost or quite ceased to be felt as a metaphor."[17] Although Rackham does not explain his statement, the differences in usage would seem to lie in the instrumentality and necessity that characterize the material equipment of life, on one hand, and the intrinsic value and playfulness attributable to choregia in its usual senses, on the other. The material equipment of life is used to the end of the person or constitution it sustains. In the case of choregia in its usual senses, by contrast, it's the play that is

---

is inappropriate as well: "Epicurus did not think it right that their property should be held in common, as required by the maxim of Pythagoras about the goods of friends; such a practice in his opinion implied mistrust, and without trust there is no friendship." Diogenes Laertius, *Lives of Eminent Philosophers,* 10.11 (vol. 2).

16. As we will see, what Aristotle says about ousia and ktemata in his discussions of the virtue of liberality, about ploutos in his discussion of the virtue of magnificence, and about the ktemata held for chresis in *Politics* I suggests that my analysis of proper use by means of choregia would hold for these significations of property as well.

17. *Nicomachean Ethics,* pp. 42–43, note a.

60   CHAPTER TWO

the thing and, although a play may have participants and spectators, it does not have users. In the light cast by these differences, I argue that Aristotle's use of *choregia* to signify the material equipment of life is instructive precisely in its connection to the term's usual connotations. Exploring what both usages have in common points the way toward a noninstrumental understanding of use, showing how things may be simultaneously used and preserved, and thus what Aristotle understands by proper use.

Traceable to the seventh century B.C.E., the choregia, meaning specifically "defraying the costs of a chorus," had, by Aristotle's day, become an organized institution at Athens (*AP* 54.8, 56.2–3).[18] Those appointed to finance and furnish the chorus were among the wealthiest citizens in Athens (*AP* 56.3), and the task of these citizens, *choregoi,* was to provide dramatic productions with their choruses and, in so doing, to provide the polity as a whole with a public performance. This involved supplying the chorus members with everything they needed to prepare for their performance and to perform, including a space to live in and to practice in the home of the choregos, clothing, food and other things necessary for their training, costumes, and masks.[19] The choregos thus equipped the chorus even as he equipped the performance with a chorus and the city with a performance. This suggests that there were two domains of choregic activity: the household of the choregos, where he provided the chorus members with *choregia,* their necessary equipment; and the collective space of the polity, where the choregos performed the choregia by providing the production with a chorus and giving it to the city. I explore in turn the relation of each of these choregic practices to Aristotle's use of choregia.

The relation between the choregia as the equipment that sustains the chorus and the equipment of life that Aristotle calls choregia is straightforward enough. For the chorus to play, it needed its equipment. Choregia is thus necessary to the playing of the chorus. The material equipment of life taken in the home to the end of living, choregia in Aristotle's usage, is no different. The householder and other household members, like the chorus members, depend on choregia as the material equipment of life for their survival or preservation. Without costumes and masks, the chorus could not perform. If it thus depends on choregia because equipment allows it to play, choregia also depends on the chorus because they give

---

18. For a comprehensive and fascinating account of the institution of the choregia at Athens, see Wilson, *Athenian Institution of the Khoregia,* on which the following draws.

19. Hornblower and Spawforth, *Oxford Classical Dictionary,* pp. 323–24.

it its place, allowing it to be equipment. Similarly, the equipment of life may preserve the household members, but it is also preserved by them insofar as, in their use of it, they allow it to be equipment. Understood in this way, the activity of using mediates the mutual preservation of things and people. The equipment of life may belong to the household members, but this suggests that they also belong to the equipment of life. The two, like a chorus and its necessities, belong together. Choregia is thus the necessary equipment of both the household members and the chorus. This analysis suggests that preserving a thing is using it in a way that allows it to be what it is. Aristotle calls this sort of use proper use.

Paradoxically, when choregia, as the necessary equipment of life or of a chorus, is used in a way that accords with its preservation, when it is used properly, it disappears into its use. If, for example, during a play, the chorus members called attention to themselves or to their costumes, the play would not work. It would be hampered by the intrusion of equipment whose proper mode of being is to disappear into use so that the show can go on. As Peter Wilson puts it, "the task of the *khoregos* was, in an important sense, to arrange [the labor that went into the performance as] labour that conceals itself and produces the 'grace' of the choral performance."[20] Similarly, when used properly, the equipment of life disappears into its use by being consumed if it is food, for example, or by wearing well, if it is a shoe (rather than, say, giving its wearer blisters). Aristotle insists that it is the user of the house, the *oikonomikos,* who judges the house better than does its maker, the pilot who judges rudders better than the carpenter, and the diner, not the cook, who is the better judge of a banquet (*Pol.* 1282a17–23). The one who actually dwells in the home, steers the ship, eats the food—the one who uses the things *as* things in use—is best able to know and to judge them.[21] Proper use, so understood, is a practical activity having to do with things, *ta pragmata,* with which one has to do in action, *praxis* (*Pol.* 1257a10).[22] Thus, the disappearance of equipment into its use does not make that equipment instrumental to a further end. Nor does a thing's disappearing make the use in which it disappears improper. This is because, as

20. Wilson, *Athenian Institution of the Khoregia,* p. 51.

21. I take up the question of judgment explicitly in chapter 3.

22. For a helpful discussion of use as a practical activity, see Heidegger, *Being and Time,* secs. 15, 16. Somewhat paradoxically, it is artefacts (which would not exist but for their production by man) whose proper use calls for this kind of attending to a thing-in-use by not-attending to it. Natural things involve a different mode of relation between user and thing. The proper use of land for agriculture, for example, requires explicit attention and concern to monitor how wet or dry the soil is, watch for pests, and so on. Letting the land disappear into its use would render it useless.

62   CHAPTER TWO

Aristotle explains, this sort of property, equipment, is a tool not of production but of living or action. It therefore produces nothing other than the action included in its actual use (*Pol.* 1254a1–5). To use such things properly, *oikeios,* is to let them be what they are, that is, to allow them their own, *oikeion.* Allowing something its own preserves it. Holding for proper use the necessary equipment of life and play, *choregia,* is a holding that preserves, by its disappearance into use, what is in use.

As we have seen, however, choregia, in its usual sense, signifies not only the equipment necessary to sustain the chorus members and not only the tools of their performance but also the activity of the choregos in supplying this equipment. Choregia as the equipment of the chorus and choregia as the equipping by the choregos of the chorus are related, of course, in that both are necessary for the show to go on, but if choregia, as equipment, contributes to the play by disappearing into its use, the activity of the choregos in supplying it appears not to do the same. If choregia in the former sense is a tool of action, in the latter sense it is a tool of production. In Wilson's analysis the activity of equipping a production with a chorus was, indeed, a public performance by the choregos motivated by the desire for an occasion to ostentatiously display his wealth so as to enhance his own prestige, and, more broadly, to consolidate the interests of his class. Choregia, so understood, acted as a "symbolic stage" where the wealthiest citizens of Athens competed in a context of "agonistic self-assertion" to outdo one another in order to gain social and political goods.[23] Exemplifying this practice of choregia, Wilson claims, is Aristotle's celebrated magnificent man. If Wilson is right about Aristotle, however, then my analysis of choregia and its significance for understanding Aristotelian property fails. If, as I claim, Aristotelian property is best understood via its disappearance into use and noninstrumentally, then it can only be disanalogous with the choregia as a public spectacle staged by the choregos and instrumental to the end of securing social and political power.

In my reading, Aristotle's account of magnificence offers an alternative, indeed, a corrective to the choregic practice of wealth Wilson describes. Aristotle's account orients attention away from the holder of wealth and toward the works the wealth (*chremata,* or things in use, *NE* 1122a20–25) produces, thus pointing toward a practice of proper use of choregic wealth no different from the proper use of choregia as the material equipment of a chorus or householder. Aristotle calls the magnificent man, *megaloprepes,* an artist in expenditure (*NE* 1122a34–35). He is an

---

23. Wilson, *Athenian Institution of the Khoregia,* pp. 123, 142.

artist because his virtue lies in producing great works with good taste, and he is an artist in expenditure because the virtue of magnificence, unlike, say, the virtue of liberality, concerns not all actions dealing with wealth but with spending great sums (*NE* 1122a35). Aristotle insists that the motive of the magnificent man in spending his wealth is no different from the motive driving the practice of other virtues. In all cases, it is the nobility of the activity itself (*NE* 1122b7). Echoing the definitions of virtue and wealth he offers elsewhere (*NE* 1098b31–1099a4; *Rhet.* 1361a24–25), he states that the virtue of magnificence lies not in possessing wealth but in using it, for "a disposition is defined by the activities in which it is displayed and in the objects to which it is related" (*NE* 1122b1–21). The virtue of magnificence lies, in other words, in the activity of spending itself and in the achievements or works, *erga,* that the spending produces.

Wilson notes that in discussing the magnificent man and his counterparts in excess and deficiency, Aristotle "frequently employs examples from the sphere of *litourgiai* [liturgies, that is, mandatory services to the community], and more often than not, these are *khoregic.*"[24] To Wilson, this demonstrates Aristotle's endorsement of the practice of wealth to the end of securing status, prestige, and power. But in Aristotle's discussion of this virtue it is not the man himself but his activities and works that are described as "magnificent," "brilliant," and "great" (*NE* 1122b15–19). Motivated by the nobility of his activity, Aristotle's magnificent choregos spends his vast wealth to promote the greatness of his work; he defrays the cost of the chorus to display not himself but his work, in this case, the play. When used properly the "great sums," along with the choregos himself, disappear into their work. When, by contrast, he takes center stage, no less than when the equipment or the chorus fails to disappear into its use, the play does not work.[25] To be choregos simply calls for being choregos, that is, doing the activity of being choregos, namely, giving choregia: to the chorus members, to the production, and to the city. In this way of thinking, it is not only the case that the choregia belongs to the choregos, although this is true. The choregos also belongs to the choregia.

24. Ibid., pp. 141–42.

25. Wilson, ibid., p. 134, notes that it is only "in the rarest instances" that the choregos takes an observable role as a leader. His example is Alcibiades, who often appeared on stage, vying for the attention of the audience and indulging in violence against his rivals (pp. 148–55). It is not that the choregos appeared nowhere: he appeared in the *pompe,* the opening parade of the festival at which his chorus was to perform, he helped choose the judges of the choregic competition, and, if victorious, he appeared at the crowning ceremony (pp. 95–103).

64   CHAPTER TWO

Indeed, he depends on his activities and work for his magnificence no less than the work depends on him for its greatness. He is choregos only insofar as he gives choregia in all these ways and so produces the work.

Read together, Aristotle's choregia as the material necessities of life and choregia in its usual significations, as bound with play, disclose the practice of proper use. Proper use may be practical, as when choregia disappears into its activities of use. It may also be poetic, as when choregia disappears into its work. Reaching toward necessity on one hand (choregia as the sustenance of life) and toward art on the other (choregia as the activity of producing a work), practical and poetic proper use are both, in the language of chapter 1, prohairetic activities—activities informed by moral and intellectual virtue—in the domain of the natural. It is for this reason that Aristotle sometimes uses the language of nature to define modes of use (*Pol.* 1257a29, 1258b2, 1258b8). Against the backdrop of my reading of Aristotle's understanding of nature in chapter 1 and the account of proper use just provided, use according to nature is use that allows the thing in use to be what it is, namely, proper use. This understanding of proper use makes recourse to an essentializing "naturalist" teleology unnecessary.[26] In proper practical use, the thing in use and the user form a unity that preserves both. The thing in use depends on the user to preserve it as a thing in use, and the user depends on the thing in use for his self-preservation. Similarly, in proper poetic use, the work and its producer form a unity that preserves producer and work. There can be no dramatic production without a chorus equipped by a choregos, and he is not a choregos if he fails to provide, and provide for, a chorus. These unities, which depend on the disappearing into its use or work of the things in use, also, paradoxically, preserve user and thing, producer and work, in their difference.

If, when used properly, property disappears into its poetic work or practical use and thus preserves works and things, makers and users, the practice of property may also open the way to destruction, exploitation, and oppression. Consider Midas, concerned not with holding for use but rather with acquisition and accumulation (*Pol.* 1257b15–17), who died because he could not use his great wealth to meet his daily necessities. Or consider the violence that Aristotle claims accompanies money-making and usury, different modes of accumulation for an end other than use, which involve people taking things from one another (*Pol.* 1258b3–10;

26. See also Salkever, "Aristotle's Social Science," pp. 26–27.

NE 1096a6–11). Or consider the ignoble choregos, interested primarily in self-display, who generates violence and rivalries that model and produce political stasis, or rulers who hold their offices not for the common good but to private ends or to the ends of some particular interest group. Holding things for use opens the possibility of improper use or abuse, namely, use for the purpose of some end other than use or the work.

The source of malpractice lies in the breaking up of the unity between the one who uses and the thing in use or the maker and his work. When the unity brought about by proper practical use breaks up, the thing in use ceases to be a thing in use.[27] Emerging from its disappearance, it becomes something else. This breaking up first occurs when something useful stops being useful. Think, for example, of a pen or a fork or a shoe. When a pen runs out of ink or when a fork fails to pick up food, it stops being a useful thing and we stop using it as a thing in use. When a shoe fails to work properly as a shoe, when it allows water to seep in or causes blisters, it acquires an independence from its use that causes it to become the focus of our attention and concern. When a pen or a fork or a shoe fails as a thing in use, the user stops subordinating the thing to its use and treats it instead as an object of inquiry: Why has this stopped working? Similarly, when the unity brought about by proper poetic use breaks up, the work ceases to work. When the choregos takes center stage, we ask: What happened to the play? Use ceases to be practical when the failure of a thing in use causes a person to stop using it as a thing in use. It ceases to be poetic when the creator of a work eclipses his achievement. When the unity between user and thing in use or maker and work is thus broken, the good of use is no longer given by the activity of using or by the work produced by use. Using becomes instead an activity the good of which is measured and guided in some other way. This may happen with the rise of money.

Each home initially meets its own needs by taking things to the end of living. Over time, needs become more complex. As households become unable to meet their needs, barter evolves. Barter involves a giving over and taking of different things useful to the end of living, for example, wine for corn (*Pol.* 1257a25–30). As use that renders a thing in use for something else, barter involves not immediate or proper use but what Aristotle calls "not proper" use (*Pol.* 1257a11), or use that is not according to nature but not contrary to nature, either (*Pol.* 1257a29, 1258b2). The

---

27. The following draws on Martin Heidegger's discussion of equipment in "Origin of the Work of Art," p. 35.

66   CHAPTER TWO

use characteristic of barter is not proper rather than improper because the destination of the things bartered is immediate use.[28] Nonetheless, because giving over and taking things that are not the same requires a common measure of different things, not proper use can give rise to improper use, or use contrary to nature (*Pol.* 1258b8). In order to meet the requirement of commensurability among things that are different, money is introduced: "Money thus comes to be a middle, *meson,* for it measures all things" (*NE* 1133a20–22; *Pol.* 1257a32–40).[29] By making possible use that is not bound to the thing in use, money frees its holders and users from the necessity that otherwise limits acquisition and use.

In particular, money makes possible exchange for gain, retail commerce, *kapelike.* In exchange for gain, and in other practices of what Aristotle calls "wealth-getting," things cease to be things in use and become instead instruments to the end of making money. Referring to the "niggardly . . . smith who fashions the Delphian knife for many uses . . . [when] every instrument is best made when intended for one and not for many uses" (*Pol.* 1252b1–5), Aristotle criticizes the practice of making a knife to be used also as a file and a hammer. It is made to so many ends, Aristotle implies, so that it can be exchanged for many things. As Scott Meikle puts it, "What is wrong with the Delphian knife is not that it is used in exchange, but that it is made to be exchanged and is bad at its job for that reason. . . . Its use value has been compromised and diminished by design out of considerations of exchange value."[30] This is not to say that every tool must have only one use, but it is to say that each tool has its "ownmost," *oikeios,* or proper use. It is this use that can be compromised by the rise of money.

The danger posed by money is not only that it can effect an alienation from proper (or not proper) use, as in the case of the Delphian knife, but also that the art of money—the activity of wealth-getting—can replace the practice of all other arts. Money can acquire this comprehensive authority because, insofar as the products of any art may be used or exchanged, the activity of their use may become solely a means to the end of wealth-getting. Medicine may, for example, be practiced with a view to health, an end internal to the practice of medicine, or it

28. I discuss the importance of the category of not proper use in relation to the practice of reciprocal justice in chapter 3.

29. In truth, says Aristotle, things that are different cannot be made commensurable without denying their difference (*NE* 1133b15–20). Money, *nomisma,* is the measure of all things only by convention, *nomos.* The true measure, that which money can measure only relatively and by convention is use, *chreia,* that is, the activity of using things in use. I discuss this in detail in chapter 3.

30. Meikle, *Aristotle's Economic Thought,* p. 56.

may be driven by the profit motive, which, as in the case of the Delphian knife, will compromise its proper use. Philosophy may be taught and practiced for the love of wisdom or for the love of money, as, Aristotle maintains, the Sophists do (*Sophistical Refutations* 171b25–30). With the rise of money, wealth-getting threatens, in the words of William Mathie, to "take the place of [politics] as the art that orders all other arts because the end it seeks may be falsely regarded as the greatest good of human action."[31] When this happens, all aspects of life, including the practice of virtue, can become separated from their proper use and become mere means to the end of wealth.

By introducing the abstraction of value from use (in order to enable the assessment of price), money can alienate things from their proper use. When the unity of the relation of proper use is thus broken, the good of things in use is not determined in the activity of using. When a thing in practical use fails to disappear into its use, it is also alienated from its use and becomes instead, as we saw, of interest in its own right. In that case, it becomes not a means to some further end but an end in itself. The same is true when a maker fails to disappear into his poetic work and becomes of interest in his own right, to wit, the self-displaying choregos. All of these outcomes of the breaking up of the unity of proper use stem from the same source: an alienation from its use of the thing in use and a withdrawal on the part of the user from the activity of using. Under these conditions, property ceases to be a prohairetic activity of practical or poetic use and becomes instead theoretical.

There is much to be said for the fact that money frees human beings from the necessity that otherwise limits acquisition and use. Aristotle's description of ways of life "whose work or operation arises by itself" (*Pol.* 1256a40–41) is illuminating in this regard. Dependent on the gifts of nature, not on other people, nomadic herdsmen, farmers, fishermen, and hunters, says Aristotle, need not engage in retail exchange (*Pol.* 1256a30–b10). Their modes of living are defined by and limited to the taking of things to meet daily needs. Aristotle may call the nomadic life the most leisured life (*Pol.* 1256a31–32), but, as Mathie rightly puts it, "it is perhaps also least human."[32] By contrast, by virtue of its capacity to alienate from use by abstracting value, money, like the practice of theorizing more generally, has the power to free from necessity. A question, says Aristotle, is "best investigated" when it takes in abstraction what does not exist separately (*Meta.* 1078a21–23). This sug-

31. Mathie, "Property in the Political Science of Aristotle," p. 23. See also Booth, "Politics and the Household."

32. Mathie, "Property in the Political Science of Aristotle," p. 21. See also Lewis, "Acquisition and Anxiety."

68   CHAPTER TWO

gests a liberatory dimension to money and a kinship between money and thinking theoretically. Recognizing this, Aristotle treats money in a way that is not unequivocally derogatory. He recounts an anecdote about the philosopher Thales, who was "reproached for his poverty, which was supposed to show that philosophy was of no use." Thales, using his wisdom to read the stars, was able to forecast a great harvest of olives. "He gave deposits for the use of all the olive-presses in Chios and Miletus, which he hired at a low price because no one bid against him. When the harvest-time came, and many were wanted all at once and of a sudden, he let them out at any rate which he pleased, and made a quantity of money" (*Pol.* 1259a12–17). By using what Aristotle twice calls a financial scheme of "universal application," in other words, by abstraction, Thales created a monopoly and got rich (*Pol.* 1259a8, 20). Although, as he puts it, getting rich was not Thales' ambition and ought not to be the ambition of philosophers (because using wisdom for financial gain, as do the Sophists, is a mode of improper use), these sorts of stories are nonetheless useful for those who value the art of getting wealth. Aristotle concludes that "statesmen as well ought to know these things; for a state is often . . . in want of money" (*Pol.* 1259a33–34).

Aristotle implies that both money and theory, like property, have a proper use. This suggests that his typology of use is more complex than it initially appears to be, because each of his three modes of use—proper, not proper, and improper— has itself a proper and an improper aspect.[33] If proper proper use is immediate use that allows the thing in use to disappear into its use by, say, consuming it to meet one's daily needs, the wholesale and gratuitous destruction of a thing would amount to its improper proper use. If proper improper use confines the practices of wealth-getting to their appropriate domains—storing for future use, statesmanship, and so on—improper improper use allows wealth-getting to become the end of all arts and practices, medicine, virtue, and philosophy included. If proper proper use is associated with necessity and repetition, driven by the imperatives of meeting daily needs, proper improper use has the power to introduce freedom and change into human activity by liberating action from the monotonous criteria of immediate use.

This means that there is nothing inherently wrong, in Aristotle's scheme of

---

33. I deal here only with proper and improper use. I return to the category of the not proper in chapter 3, where we will see that it is the middle practice of property, what Aristotle calls not proper use, that turns use into an activity which allows for freedom and change. Use, so understood, is rooted in neither immediacy nor abstraction but in analogy, which combines both.

things, with theorizing or abstraction. Both are part of the practice of philosophy, which, like property, deals with what is one's ownmost and so "makes an inexpressibly great difference in one's pleasure" (*Pol.* 1263a42–b2 on property; *NE* X.7 on philosophy). Theory and abstraction nonetheless pose a danger to the practice of property. Insofar as money and theory must, to do their work, abstract from use, they open the possibility that use, the activity of property, will be forgotten and, along with it, the practice of property that use regulates. When property ceases to be practiced as an activity of use and is instead theorized in terms of exchange value and monetized (as it is by many present-day property theories), there is no longer any internal limit to wealth accumulation, because use is what sets that limit. When property is theorized rather than practiced, it also stops being a site of sharing in community and becomes a site of privatization, securing within a polity only the withdrawal of its members from their collectivity. Under these conditions, excessive accumulation can be limited only by external and coercive means and not, as Aristotle advocates, by education within the practice of property itself, which, he claims, is the distinctive work of the legislator (*Pol.* 1263a40). Moreover, when use is forgotten, the good of property must be referred to something outside property, such as wealth maximization. When we stay with use, by contrast, it is possible to see that the good of property lies not in an end outside property but in property itself. This, as we will see next, is the virtue of property.

The Virtue of Property

Most commentators understand Aristotelian property as an external good, instrumental to virtuous activity and so to a happy life.[34] They thus interpret property as a means to the end of virtuous activity.[35] But property, we have just seen, is not

---

34. For the distinction between external goods that are instrumental to happiness and those that are intrinsic, see Nussbaum, *Fragility of Goodness,* pp. 327–28; Sherman, *Fabric of Character,* pp. 125–26; Cooper, "Aristotle on the Goods of Fortune"; Mulgan, "Aristotle and the Value of Political Participation." Commentators agree that property is an external good, though they disagree about whether it is instrumental or intrinsic. I argue that it is both an external good and a characterological one, both constitutive of a happy life and instrumental to such a life.

35. See Cooper, "Aristotle on the Goods of Fortune," p. 177; Irwin, "Generosity and Property in Aristotle's *Politics*"; Mathie, "Property in the Political Science of Aristotle," p. 14: "Property is . . . a necessary condition of virtuous activity but its pursuit is not itself a virtuous activity nor perhaps even consistent with virtuous activity."

70   CHAPTER TWO

simply a means to a further end. As Aristotle's treatment of magnificence suggests, property is itself a site of the practice of virtue. This is no less true of the more ordinary virtues depending on lesser amounts of property, namely, moderation and liberality. Property is the site of the practice of virtue at least in part because Aristotle understands virtue as a mode of property. To see this, consider again his definition of virtue, which I discussed in chapter 1: "Of excellence, *arete,* there is the activity, *energeia,* according to it. But it makes no small difference whether we place the chief good in holding, *ktesis,* or in using, *chresis,* in habit, *hexis,* or in activity, *energeia.* For habit takes it in itself not to bring a good to completion, even when the habit lies there as a ruling principle, *arche.* But activity, *energeia,* not so; for the activity, *energeia,* will of necessity be acting and acting well, *praxis*" (*NE* 1098b31–1099a4). The language Aristotle uses is striking. He speaks of habit as a kind of holding or possession and of action as a mode of use. He speaks of virtue, in other words, in terms of property. And he does so in two ways at once. There is, on one hand, an analogy between property and virtue: just as virtue calls not for action alone but rather for action stemming from the appropriate habit, so too does owning properly call not for using alone but for use stemming from proper holding. And just as good habits emerge from acting well, so too does holding well depend on proper use. Like habit and action, then, holding and using form a reciprocal and dynamic relationship.[36] At the same time, in Aristotle's definition of virtue, the words connoting property, "holding" and "using," and the words signifying virtue, "habit" and "action," stand in for one another: "[I]t makes no small difference whether we place the chief good in holding, *ktesis,* or in using, *chresis,* in habit, *hexis,* or in activity, *energeia*" (*NE* 1098b31–33). This suggests that habit is a kind of holding and that holding is a matter of habit. It also suggests that action is a mode of use and that using is a matter of action.

Putting these points together, we can see that good habit, as a matter of holding properly, depends on using properly what is held, that is, acting well. And we can see that acting well, as a mode of proper use, depends on holding properly what one has as one's own, hence ownership.[37] As the practice of holding and using things properly, property, like any activity, already calls for good habit conjoined

---

36. *Pace* Hare, "*Eleutheriotes* in Aristotle's *Ethics,*" pp. 20–25, who claims that liberality, the virtue of property, actually signifies two different virtues—"good stewardship" (proper holding) and "generosity" (proper use)—which are in tension with one another.

37. This insight is at the heart of Aristotle's rejection, in *Politics* II, of common ownership. It explains why the argument of Irwin, "Generosity and Property in Aristotle's *Politics,*" that the virtue of liberality can be exercised in the absence of private ownership is wrong.

with acting well, that is, virtue. And, as the practice of holding and using habits properly, virtue requires property. It is by understanding property as a verb and not strictly as a noun, as an activity of use and not strictly as a fungible thing, that we see that property is bound to, is indeed a site of, virtue. And it is by understanding virtue as a verb and not strictly as a noun, as an activity and not strictly as a thing, that we see virtue as a kind of property.

Property, in this reading, is both an external good and a characterological good, or a good of the soul. Aristotle, however, appears to distinguish these categories of goods (*Pol.* VII.1; *NE* I.8). Identifying the end of a good life—*eudaimonia*—with virtuous activity of the soul, he claims, for this reason, that virtue belongs among the goods of the soul and not among external goods (*NE* 1098b18–20). Apparently limiting the goods of the soul to the virtues of intellect and character, he cites as external goods, by contrast, good children, fine birth, and beauty, as well as wealth, political power, and friends (*NE* 1099a31–b6). That property is properly categorized as an external good is evident. But Aristotle, we have seen, treats wealth not only as what is owned for use but also as the activity of use itself (*Rhet.* 1361a24–25). Property thus brings eudaimonia by way of proper use, that is, virtuous activity.[38] To distinguish categorically external from characterological goods, then, is to miss Aristotle's fundamental point that, at least in the case of the good of wealth, property is as much a practice as a tool and, more specifically, that properly practiced, property calls for virtuous activity of the soul. This is because, as the activity of holding for proper use, the necessary equipment of property is good habit conjoined with acting well, that is, virtue. It is also to miss the point that virtue is not external to property relations but rather emerges within the practice of property in the presence of a proper ordering of the soul (even as the practice of property contributes to that ordering). Aristotle's treatments of liberality and moderation underscore this dynamic and reflexive relation between virtue and property and the degree to which property is an external and a characterological good at the same time.

In *Nicomachean Ethics* IV Aristotle says that liberality is the mean in regard to the giving and taking of useful things, especially with respect to giving. Not giving enough is being mean, *aneleutheros,* that is, caring more about taking than about giving useful things. Giving in excess is illiberal in the mode of *asotia,* prodigality. Someone can give too much when he has a lot to give or when he does not have

---

38. Socrates insists on this understanding of wealth as well in the *Euthydemus* (280A–E), the dialogue that Aristotle cites when he distinguishes among kinds of goods (*NE* I.8).

72   CHAPTER TWO

much. It is not bad when the one who gives too much has a never-ending supply, because he need not worry about depleting his resources (*NE* 1120b25). When someone gives too much who does not have that much, however, two possibilities arise: a person, in order to continue to give, may take from the wrong sources. Or he may "waste his substance" and thus ruin himself (*NE* 1120a1). Wasting one's substance is not simply recklessly giving away too many things to the wrong people, for the wrong reasons, and at the wrong times, although it is that, too. One's substance, *ousia*, derived from the verb "to be," *einai*, is, at the same time, that by virtue of which somebody is who he is. Wasting one's substance is, in this sense, "losing oneself" (*NE* 1120a3–4). One has as one's substance what one holds as one's own for use. This is property in its usual signification. One also has as one's substance one's habits, and these constitute one's character, who one is. What is owned for proper use—things or habits—is what is proper to one, *ta oikeia*. As what is owned for use in both senses, property brings well-being, *eudaimonia*, by use or well-doing. Aristotle may distinguish external goods from goods of the soul, then, but, in doing so, he marks not only their difference but also the degree of their interrelation.

That property is a characterological good may be seen as well in the relation between moderation and property. In *Nicomachean Ethics* III Aristotle defines moderation as the observance of a mean regarding the pleasures of the body that man shares with lower animals, in particular, taste and touch, especially in eating, drinking, and sexual relations (*NE* 1118a25 ff.). Moderation is the mean between *akolasia*, lack of discipline, and *anaisthesia*, want of sensation. It is a mean relative to overindulging in every pleasure, as hedonists do, and to shunning all pleasure, as boorish persons do. Aristotle associates moderation with desire, specifically, desire relative to the pleasures of the body, but not those of sight, hearing, or smell because, he says, we cannot overindulge in these. Rather, it is desire for what is pleasant to the most basic of our senses, the sense of touch (*NE* 1118b1–3; *DA* 414a3–4).[39] This is why a certain gourmand wished that his throat were longer than a crane's, Aristotle reports, for his pleasure lay in the sensation of touch (*NE* 1118a34–35). As the virtue related to the pleasures of touch, moderation directs

---

39. Aristotle calls touch the most basic sense for these reasons: it mediates the other senses; it is that which allows ensouled beings to nourish and so to preserve themselves; and when the sense of touch is overstimulated, say, by a person's being hit by a car, the result can be death, whereas in the case of the other senses, excess stimulation destroys only the sense organs but not the person.

how we are toward things we desire in a most basic and unmediated way. Moderation specifically guides how we move toward these things in response to our desire for them and also in the light of our dependence on them. It is significant, in this regard, that one form of immoderation is anaisthesia; the person without desire cannot be moderate. Moderation, then, calls not for mastering desire but for being moved by the active force of desire itself.

Insofar as moderation is especially concerned with the sense of touch, it is a virtue of property. Touching requires that something be at hand to be touched. We have things at hand when we hold them, as we do in certain cases of property. Being at hand and holding signify the separateness of man and thing. At the same time, touch is distinctive among the senses insofar as, unlike hearing, seeing, or smelling, in which, Aristotle tells us, air mediates between the one who senses and what is sensed, what we touch is unmediated: nothing separates what is touched from the one who touches (*DA* 435a17–20). Given the immediacy of touching, we run the danger of forgetting that the things we touch are other than us. Property, we have seen, is the site of the belonging together of persons and things. It is the site of their mutual preservation and thus of their interdependence. It is also a site of desire insofar as we reach toward that which we need for our self-preservation. For these reasons, inherent in the practice of property is the possibility of forgetting that the things taken for immediate use are other than the one who uses them, that they have a use proper to them. As we saw, the disappearance into use of things in use produces a unity between user and thing. But, as noted, this is not an indifferent unity. A thing that disappears into its use is not nothing. Property, when used properly, is the site of the preservation of the person and of the thing as a thing in use. This means that property, properly practiced, preserves person and thing in their difference. It is the virtue of moderation that safeguards this difference, for we act moderately, in the context of the danger of forgetting difference, when we treat the things we touch, and on which we depend, in a way that respects them as differentiated, that is, when we treat them in a manner proper to *them.*

Moderation is a virtue not only of immediate use but of mediated use as well. In barter, in which things are exchanged for other things useful to the end of living, things mediate relations with other people. The things we barter and exchange with others thus disclose our dependence on one another and bind us together.[40]

---

40. Aristotle, as we will see in chapter 3, calls reciprocal justice, as the barter of goods and services, the bond of polity.

CHAPTER TWO

Seeing moderation as a virtue of property in this way allows us to understand better Aristotle's criticism of the endorsement by Plato's Socrates of common property and common spouses (among the guardians of the perfect city), which he claims make moderation, especially sexual moderation, impossible. Just as acting properly toward things we use calls for treating them in a manner proper to them, so too does acting moderately toward other people call for respecting them in their differences, by, among other things, recognizing that they are not ours to use as we will. The reason Aristotle emphasizes sex in his discussion of moderation (*Pol.* 1263b10) is that it is possible, particularly in sexual relations, to forget that those with whom we are involved are other than us.

Aristotle says that a life of moderation alone slips into a life of misery. This is because a community of exclusively moderate actors would be distinguished only by restraint. A good polity, Aristotle insists, requires moderation and liberality (*Pol.* 1265a28–40) and the practices of property that these virtues promote and on which they depend. It is to the sort of polity this might be that I turn next and return to more fully in chapter 5.[41]

The Politics of Property

Turning from the practices of the home to those of a political life, Aristotle asks in *Politics* II: in a well-constituted polity, will citizens hold everything in common, nothing in common, or some things in common and others not? His answer is that having nothing in common is impossible, for a political community, as such, is, at the very least, a site common to its citizens (*Pol.* 1260b39–41). If having nothing in common is impossible, is it better to have everything in common? Aristotle's answer, we know, is no. He may agree with Plato's Socrates that having everything in common secures unity. But to Aristotle the commonality secured by common property is the wrong sort of unity for a well-constituted polity.[42] A good polity instead requires holding things as one's own for common use.

Aristotle's question about property in *Politics* II asks about the best mode of owning for a well-constituted polity and also about the possibility of polity itself.

41. For liberality as a prerequisite to community, including political community, see Dobbs, "Aristotle's Anticommunism," p. 40.

42. For a discussion of Aristotle's appreciation of the unity appropriate to political community as a unity of the different, see chapter 5. See also Dobbs, "Aristotle's Anticommunism," pp. 32, 35.

Property, as the site of commonality, determines the degree and possibility of the sharing constitutive of a political life, which is to say, the sharing of a way of life and a form of governance (*Pol.* 1276b1–13). This means that a polity does not simply posit a particular system of property. Nor is property somehow prior to polity, needing only to be secured by law. Unlike property theorists, historical and contemporary, for whom property is either conventional and therefore manmade or pre-political and therefore "natural," to Aristotle, neither property nor polity is prior. Rather, property and polity constitute one another. Property is, in this sense, constitutional.[43]

Property's constitutionality may be seen in Aristotle's criticism of common ownership as reducing a polity to a single man (*Pol.* 1261a18–25). It may also be seen in the later chapters of *Politics* II, where Aristotle judges existing constitutions through the lens of their property arrangements, including their arrangements of offices. Aristotle is critical of Phaleas' constitution, for example, because it equalizes property and treats its policies regarding property as separable from the organization of its domestic institutions (education [*Pol.* 1266b34] and the distribution of honors [*Pol.* 1266b40, 1267a40]) and its foreign policy (*Pol.* 1267a24). He criticizes Sparta for failing to provide common meals at public cost (*Pol.* 1271a28–31) and for its vast inequalities in property distribution (*Pol.* 1270a15). Sparta's defeat, Aristotle says, was largely due to the "faulty nature of their laws respecting property" (*Pol.* 1270a32). Finding much that is praiseworthy about Carthage, Aristotle nonetheless maintains that by choosing magistrates with an eye to merit and wealth instead of on the basis of merit alone (*Pol.* 1273a30), Carthage allowed wealth to count for more than excellence, making the whole polity avaricious (*Pol.* 1273a39).

Property's constitutionality may be seen as well in Aristotle's classification of regimes. He initially classifies regimes on the basis of whether their rule is by one, few, or many, and whether the rulers promote the common interest or their own. Monarchies, aristocracies, and polities, ruled respectively by one, few, and many, are rightly framed, for they aim at the common good. Tyrannies, oligarchies, and democracies, ruled respectively by one, few, and many, are bad, for they aim at the interest of the ruler or rulers (*Pol.* 1279a26–30). Just after he taxonomizes regimes on this basis, however, Aristotle says that, in truth, wealth and poverty underlie the

---

43. F. Miller, *Nature, Justice, and Rights,* chap. 9, treats property as a "constitutional application."

classification (*Pol.* 1279b34–1280a2). Consistent with his reclassification on the basis of wealth and poverty, his ensuing commentary focuses most extensively on oligarchies and democracies: oligarchies are, after all, ruled by those who own the most, the wealthy (*Pol.* 1279b18–19); democracies are ruled by the free in general (*Pol.* 1317a40), that is, by those who in general do not possess much property but are poor (*Pol.* 1279b19–20). Wealth and poverty determine a polity's constitution because whereas other capacities may belong to the same people, it is impossible for a person to be both wealthy and poor (*Pol.* 1291b2–13). Insofar as wealth and poverty cannot be shared, they threaten the commonality necessary to polities. Indeed, polities based on wealth or poverty, Aristotle says, "are originally based on a mistake, and, as they begin badly, cannot fail to end badly" (*Pol.* 1302a5–7). The original mistake of oligarchies and democracies is the same. Taking wealth or freedom (thus poverty), respectively, to be the measure of polity, they do not recognize that a true polity must pay attention to virtue (*Pol.* 1280b8).

The practice of virtue—bound, as we have seen, with the proper practice of property—alters a polity's arrangement of property and, hence, its constitution. When things are held as one's own for common use, those with wealth act liberally by contributing to common meals, by allowing needy citizens access to their lands to use (*Pol.* 1263a35–37; *AP* 27.3), and by distributing public revenues among the poor "in such quantities as may enable them to purchase a little farm or, at any rate, make a beginning in trade or farming" (*Pol.* 1320a37–40). Indeed, those with the most wealth, as we have seen, act magnificently by financing choregic performances, fitting out ships for war, providing public banquets, and offering sacrifices to the gods on behalf of the city (*NE* 1122b19–24). In using their property well, these citizens benefit the collective and contribute to the reduction of material disparities between themselves and the many, making it possible for these two groups to approach greater equality. For their good works on behalf of the city, these citizens receive honor from the many and gain their good will and their trust (*Pol.* 1320b10). The proper practice of property thus alters the constitution of a polity from one based on inequality and strife to one of greater equality and concord. If wealth and poverty, as statuses associated with property ownership, cannot be shared, this is not true of the things that are held as one's own, for these may, and in Aristotle's political and moral economy ought to, be shared by way of proper use. The proper practice of property, as we will see more fully in chapter 5, thus works to actualize a polity as a site of sharing and concord.

The kind of sharing characteristic of the proper practice of property is best accommodated not by a regime of common ownership because this property arrangement brings about total unity. Neither is it accommodated by tyranny, in which there can be nothing in common between ruler and ruled, nor by oligarchy, in which wealth tends to mastery, or by democracy, in which poverty tends to slavery (*NE* 1161a33–34; *Pol.* 1295b14–24). The right sort of commonality is present, Aristotle maintains, in regimes that include a large middle class of property holders with sufficient property to avoid the despotisms of wealth and poverty present in oligarchies and democracies (*Pol.* 1279a17–22). This propertied class is not a simple aggregation of the very rich and the very poor but rather possesses characteristics that are a virtuous mean between the vices of wealth and poverty (*Pol.* 1292b25–29, 1295a25–31), specifically, the virtues of moderation and liberality (*Pol.* 1265a28–40, 1326b31–32).[44] Moderation and liberality, as the virtues of property, are virtues of the practitioners of property and of the good polity itself.

Holding as one's own for common use is better than either common ownership or strictly private ownership. But even the proper practice of Aristotelian property, it could be argued, will have the effect of institutionalizing disparities among those with a lot of property, those with less, and those without any at all. Even if property is reconceived as the power to hold things for use with others, this power may still be withheld. And even if things held for use are given away, property may simply reinscribe social hierarchies by producing patronage relations.[45] The problem with any form of private property is that it establishes and safeguards social inequalities that are potentially inimical to a good political life. Aristotle, as we have seen, explicitly criticizes the leveling effects of equalizing institutions, defending instead a property qualification for citizenship and celebrating differential property ownership among citizens as characteristic of well-constituted polities (*Pol.* 1266a39–b33).

Although it is true that wealth in Athens afforded citizens the opportunity for self-display, increased their public profiles, and bolstered their political power, Aristotle insists that the wealthy ought to spend their great sums on things "for which the whole polity is enthusiastic" (*NE* 1123a2–5), in other words, as we have seen, to benefit the collective.[46] He may argue against the kind of property equalization effected by Phaleas' constitution, but he advocates voluntary equalization as a complementary mechanism to the education of virtue, insisting that "property should become common by friendly use and that no citizen should be in want

44. For discussion, see Morrow, "Aristotle's Comments on Plato's *Laws*."
45. Veyne, *Bread and Circuses*, pp. 70 ff.
46. Finley, *Politics in the Ancient World*, pp. 35 ff.; von Reden, *Exchange in Ancient Greece*, p. 74.

78   CHAPTER TWO

of sustenance" (*Pol.* 1330a1–3, 1270a40). Indeed, Aristotle objects to legislatively enforced property equalization for the same reason many contemporary liberal-democratic theorists do, namely, because it is a coercive form of redistribution that treats everyone as equals without regard to their distinction.[47] This is most productively read not as a celebration of inequality but as an argument against a particular kind of equalization. Aristotle disfavors this sort of equalization not only as a way of determining the proper distribution of property in a polity but as the criterion for the just distribution of any goods in a polity, including power. In polities based on this sort of equality, namely, certain forms of democracy, there may be some element of justice, he says, but, by taking equality on the basis of freedom to mean that citizens are entirely equal, these polities and their institutions "strip away the qualifications of the persons concerned and judge badly" (*Pol.* 1280a13–14). Aristotle rejects democracies ruled by decrees for much the same reason. Decrees, determined by aggregating the votes of citizens who are individuated and equated on numerical grounds alone, do not respect qualitative or, in his words, proportional or geometric individuation. In order to be just, distributions of power, property, and other goods must recognize differences among people. As he puts it: "For persons who are equal the shares must be equal. For those who are unequal the shares must be unequal" (*Pol.* 1282b20–21). By recognizing differences and comparing those differences using a common measure, just distributions (and well-ordered polities more generally) accommodate both equality and distinction.[48] Aristotle thus rejects strict equalization of property because by leveling differences that come about by the exercise of diverse habits, talents, and faculties, it does to people what money does to things: it abstracts from the differences that reflect and produce individuality.

If we assume that a well-constituted polity is better understood as being committed to an equality hospitable to individual distinction and plurality, the connections Aristotelian property has to virtue underscore its political promise. Insofar as Aristotelian property is a matter of holding things as one's own, it individuates and distinguishes. As the site of proper and common use, it also integrates members of a polity into webs of interaction. Dependent on (even as it cultivates) the self-generated good will of those who hold and use, Aristotelian property reflects

---

47. Most liberal democrats do not argue for strict egalitarianism, and the reasons they give often resonate with those of Aristotle: see, e.g., Rawls, *Theory of Justice;* Dworkin, "What Is Equality?"; Kateb, "Democratic Individuality and the Claims of Politics."

48. See Frank, "Democracy and Distribution."

a dual commitment to freedom and responsibility. Promoting integrated human activity and also individual ethical habituation, Aristotelian property reflects a dual commitment to collective action and individuation. Politics calls for individuation, initiative, and autonomous action, as well as membership, recognition of interdependence, and acting well with others. Aristotelian property calls for holding things as one's own, or being an owner, hence individuation, as well as use together, hence sharing in community. Treating property as an activity of proper use, and, hence, as a site of virtue reveals property's ethical, political, and, indeed, democratic potential. It does so by disclosing the ways in which the practice of property, bound as it is to the habits and actions of political agents, can produce a self-governing collectivity that also preserves individual distinction. This reading of Aristotelian property reveals the degree to which the dualities of politics—private and public, independence and dependence, individual and community—depend on property. This relation is not instrumental. Rather, politics depends on property insofar as property, what we hold as our own for use together, is, as such, a practice that is constitutive of a political life. This mode of owning is adequate to the richness of the dualities of politics, because it is itself a duality. Property is mine, that is, not yours. In being mine, it differentiates me from you. At the same time, in differentiating me from you and you from me and each one from every other, it treats us as distinctly equal.[49]

Property is what is proper to one. The substance of what is proper to one consists in one's *ousia*, possessions, wealth, that which is present for immediate and everyday use, equipment that is useful for a good life.[50] To waste one's ousia, in this sense, is to become poor, *aporos*. To waste one's ousia, we saw, is also to lose oneself (*NE* 1120a1–4). What is one's own, in this latter sense, is what is most proper to one, one's being, who one is.[51] If what is proper to one is who one is, and what is proper to one is property, then, in some sense, what one has is who one is. One has as one's own one's habits, and these constitute who one is, for one is who one has been. Who one is and who one has been, are, accordingly, questions of property. If ousia is what one has as one's own in a double sense (things and character), aporia has a double sense as well. Aporia is poverty (*Pol.* 1279b9, 1279b34, 1289b32). It is also a question, puzzle, or difficulty (*NE* 1146b6). Studying property

49. Hegel's account of property, like Aristotle's, exposes property's duality: See *Phenomenology of Spirit*, pp. 259, 258.

50. For this description of ousia, see Heidegger, *Metaphysical Foundations of Logic*, p. 145.

51. See Jones, *Law and Legal Theory of the Greeks*, p. 202.

is studying wealth and poverty. It is also studying the question or puzzle of who one is to be. Studying the question of property continues, in this way, the study, begun in chapter 1, of being and not-being, identity and difference. I turn in chapter 3 to a further exploration of these questions in the context of Aristotle's treatment of justice.

CHAPTER THREE

The Virtue of Justice

Justice is judgment as to what is just.
ARISTOTLE, *Politics*

For Aristotle, as for present-day political philosophers, justice concerns the proper treatment of other people. In the *Nicomachean Ethics,* Aristotle distinguishes comprehensive justice from particular justice. Comprehensive justice is the lawful. Justice in its particular sense, which Aristotle divides into a number of specifications, including distributive, corrective, and reciprocal justice, is the fair or the equal. Readers generally take comprehensive justice to be more fundamental than the specifications and, therefore, to shape or guide them. In the words of Richard Kraut, "lawfulness is the one characteristic that all justice has in common."[1] This statement reflects Aristotle's understanding of the relation between a whole and its parts. As parts of the whole of justice, distributive, corrective, and reciprocal justice share the defining characteristic of the whole, namely, lawfulness.

Aristotle's appreciation of law calls any straightforward understanding of the relation between lawfulness and justice into question, however. As we saw in chapter 1, when slavery is mandated by law or convention, *nomos,* but not by nature, Aristotle deems slavery unjust and equates laws that institute it with violence or domination. As we will see in chapter 4, when the policies of a regime are directed not to the common good but rather to the interests of private individuals considering only their own advantage (*Pol.* 1292a5–32, 1293a31, 1293b31), doing justice requires breaking the law. Aristotle, indeed, maintains that the laws of most cities aim at domination (*Pol.* 1324b5–7) and, even when they do not, he insists that equity is required as a corrective to law because the universality characteristic of laws can produce injustice in particular cases (*NE* V.10). These examples suggest that, to him, justice is more fundamental than law, not the other way around. Lawfulness may be "the one characteristic that all justice has in common" but, to Aristotle, it is also the case that lawfulness depends on justice (*NE* 1129b12). This means that justice is as much the measure of lawfulness as lawfulness is the measure of justice.

---

1. Kraut, *Aristotle: Political Philosophy,* p. 103.

82   CHAPTER THREE

Deferring a more detailed examination of the relation between justice and law-fulness to chapter 4, this chapter explores Aristotle's understanding of justice by taking seriously his insistence on the bidirectional nature of the relation between a whole and its parts. As we saw in chapter 1, in his account of the relation between a polity and its citizens, Aristotle maintains both that citizens, as parts, take their bearing from the polity, as a whole, and also that a polity, constituted by its citizens, takes its bearing from them. Accordingly, he explores the nature of the polity by way of his investigation of citizenship. In a similar fashion, in order to illuminate justice as a whole, this chapter focuses on the specifications of justice enumerated by Aristotle. Legal and political theorists tend to focus on his accounts of distribution and correction.[2] This is understandable. In Aristotle's hands, these specifications appear to work, institutionally and substantively, in much the same way that they do in contemporary law and politics. He treats distributive justice as a legislative matter concerning who, in a polity, should get honor, wealth, power, offices, and other divisible goods and benefits. We do the same. He treats corrective justice as a matter for the magistrates, concerned with correcting voluntary and involuntary wrongs. So do we. For him, as for contemporary law and politics, distribution and correction are matters of equality.

If Aristotle's accounts of distribution and correction continue to be authoritative, the same cannot be said of his treatment of the fair exchange of goods and services. Indeed, most contemporary legal and political philosophers neglect his account of reciprocal justice entirely, and few Aristotle scholars take it very seriously.[3] Among those who do, most treat it as a theoretically weak account of market exchange, relegate it to his economic theory, or dismiss it as muddled or incoherent.[4] That is unfortunate, for Aristotle calls reciprocity the bond and "salvation" of a polity (*NE* 1132b31–34, 1133a1–2; *Pol.* 1261a30–32). He does so not because a political life is the same as a life of economic exchange. Aristotle does not

2. See, e.g., Rawls, *Theory of Justice,* pp. 10–11; Waldron, "Wisdom of the Multitude"; Nussbaum, "Aristotelian Social Democracy"; Nussbaum, "Nature, Function, and Capability"; Weinrib, "Aristotle's Forms of Justice."

3. For a definitive response to those who claim that reciprocity is not properly understood as a form of justice, see Danzig, "Political Character of Aristotelian Reciprocity," pp. 401–3. Whereas Danzig claims that reciprocity is a form of corrective justice, I argue the reverse, namely, that correction, along with the other specifications of justice, are forms of reciprocal justice.

4. See, e.g., Finley, "Aristotle and Economic Analysis"; Joachim, *Aristotle: The Nicomachean Ethics,* p. 150. For two recent exceptions, see the very different accounts of Meikle, *Aristotle's Economic Thought,* and Danzig, "Political Character of Aristotelian Reciprocity."

see the market as what holds a polity together (*Pol.* 1280a32 ff., 1280b30 ff.). This suggests that his account of reciprocal justice is not a theoretically thin account of a market economy. Rather, as we will see, it is a rich and nuanced treatment of an ethical and political mode of exchange, what historians have called reciprocative or gift exchange, that operates at many levels of citizen relations.[5] Exemplified in the commercial exchange of material goods and services, it is at work as well in facilitating the citizen practice of rotational rule and, as we will see in chapter 5, in cementing friendship and social harmony among the classes of a well-constituted polity (*NE* 1155b34, 1162b22–65b37).

Like all practices of justice, comprehensive and particular, reciprocal justice involves two standpoints: the author or doer of justice and the subject or sufferer of justice who receives, or fails to be given, his due. Unlike distributive and corrective justice, however, which are administered by a polity's officials, reciprocity is practiced by members of a polity with one another. Reciprocity thus accommodates a key feature of justice understood as the proper treatment of others that is missing from distribution and correction. In reciprocal justice alone the practitioner and the subject are both doers and sufferers *at the same time.* When I exchange the house I have built for the shoes you have made, I administer (my) justice and receive (your) justice. When you exchange the shoes you have made for the house I have built, you administer your justice and receive mine. There is, thus, a mode of equality among the practitioners of reciprocal justice that is absent from the practices of distributive or corrective justice, which political officials administer but do not, as officials, receive. Without this sort of equality, there can be no exchange, Aristotle says, and members of a polity "feel they are in a position of slaves" in relation to one another (*NE* 1133a1–3).[6]

Reciprocal equality is of an odd sort, however, for, as the varying contexts of reciprocity make plain—house builders exchange with shoemakers, citizens exchange with noncitizens, the many exchange with the better off—it does not ef-

---

5. Millett, "Sale, Credit and Exchange"; Wilson, *Athenian Institution of the Khoregia.*

6. As we will see in the course of this chapter, to call the equality characteristic of reciprocal justice reciprocal equality is not to ignore Aristotle's refusal to reduce reciprocal justice to the mere reciprocity he attributes to the Pythagorean conception (*NE* 1132b28–30), nor is it to ignore that under a system of rotational rule, distribution and correction exemplify precisely the equality exemplified by reciprocal justice, albeit extended over time: as a citizen today I am subject to the justice of the ruler who will tomorrow, as citizen, be subject to the justice I authorize as ruler. I return especially to this last point in the final section of this chapter.

84   CHAPTER THREE

face the differences or inequalities among its practitioners. Reciprocity somehow accommodates both equality *and* difference. This capacity is evident if we look not only at the parties practicing reciprocity but also at the goods they exchange. The housebuilder and the shoemaker exchange houses for shoes, but this does not mean that houses are identical to shoes. To maintain social harmony, the many may demand material goods while the better off demand honor, but this is not to efface the differences between material goods and honor. Reciprocity, in each case, establishes an equivalence that does not elide the differences among the things or people being equated.

The recognition of difference in sameness that is characteristic of reciprocal justice is, we will see, the work of practical wisdom, *phronesis,* specifically, good judgment.[7] This suggests that reciprocity is the bond of polity because the practices of reciprocity teach, even as they depend on, phronesis, an intellectual virtue preserved, Aristotle insists, by moral virtue. The practices of reciprocity exemplify, in other words, what in chapter 1 I called prohairetic activity. Against the modern sensibility that sets justice and morality apart, reciprocal justice underscores the centrality of virtue to justice, something suggested already by the fact that Aristotle discusses justice as part of his general investigation of virtue. Focusing on reciprocal justice, we will see, helps explain why Aristotle calls comprehensive justice the exercise of virtue as a whole (*NE* 1130b18) and why he describes the specifications of justice as concerning a part of virtue, namely, that which enables people to refrain from overreaching, *pleonexia,* or taking more than their fair share, especially in dealings of money, honor, or safety (*NE* 1130b3).

If acting justly is a matter of acting well, this means that both comprehensive and particular justice require good judgment on the part of their practitioners and that doing justice requires attending to virtue. This is true, of course, of other practices of citizenship as well, as we have seen in the case of property and, as we will see in chapter 4, in the case of law. Owing to the peculiar way in which it alone embodies the simultaneity of standpoints crucial not only to an adequate understanding of justice but to a harmonious political life, however, reciprocal justice has a particularly intimate relation with practical wisdom, *phronesis.* Like other political practices, it teaches and depends on phronesis. Unlike them, it also models the practice of phronetic judgment itself. The work of reciprocal justice, so un-

---

7. If living in accordance with moral virtue is living in accordance with one's own nature, *oikeiosis,* living this way in regard to other human beings is justice, which depends in crucial ways on good judgment. See Engberg-Pedersen, "Discovering the Good," pp. 175–77.

derstood, thus parallels the basic work of the soul in activity as described in chapter 1, that is, the soul doing and suffering its own virtue and, thus, retaining its identity in difference by means of prohairetic activity. Read through the lens of reciprocity and its virtues, justice, to Aristotle, concerns not only the proper treatment of others but also the doing and having of one's own.

Reciprocity

Reciprocal justice regulates exchanges of services, of previously distributed goods, and of other things of use between two people. Coming in *Nicomachean Ethics* V.5, after the discussions of distributive and corrective justice in V.3 and 4, respectively, reciprocal justice appears to combine the principles of these two modes of justice and to operate against their backdrop. Briefly, distributive justice is concerned with allocating a polity's divisible goods and involves a relation to persons as well as to things (*Pol.* 1280a14, 17). Treating as commensurable the ratios between persons and things, Aristotle maintains that a distribution is just when the ratio between the persons and the ratio between the things is geometrically or proportionately equal (*NE* 1130b30–1131a33). Corrective justice, concerned with rectifying voluntary and involuntary wrongs, demands equality only between the parties to the transaction. Treating as commensurable the loss sustained by one party to a transaction and the gain received by the other, Aristotle represents corrective justice in terms of arithmetic or numerical equality (*NE* 1132a1–2). Reciprocal justice requires commensurability as well. Indeed, it appears to treat as commensurable the parties to an exchange and the things being exchanged: "as builder is to shoemaker, so many shoes to a house" (*NE* 1133a23–25), or "as farmer is to shoemaker, the amount of the shoemaker's product is to the farmer's product for which it exchanges" (*NE* 1133a32–33). For reciprocal as for distributive justice, equality is geometric or proportional. As such, reciprocal justice may be similar to distributive justice and, insofar as it regulates voluntary transactions, it may appear to be a mode of corrective justice. Aristotle maintains, however, that reciprocity "does not coincide" with either of them (*NE* 1132b23–25). Two key features distinguish Aristotle's discussion of reciprocal justice from his treatment of the other specifications. First, he highlights and questions the commensurability characteristic of reciprocal justice. Second, he shifts the standpoint from that of an authority administering justice—a judge in the case of corrective justice, a legislator in the case of distributive—to that of the parties to the exchange. I explore these differences in the sections that follow.

COMMENSURABILITY

At the outset of his discussion of reciprocal justice, Aristotle canvasses several possible explanations for what might allow for commensurability among different things. Most commentators take his answer to be money. Aristotle says that all things exchanged "must be able to be compared in some way. . . . It is to meet this requirement that man has introduced money . . . for it is a measure of all things . . . how many shoes are equal to a house or to a given quantity of food" (*NE* 1133a19–22, 1133b16). Scott Meikle rightly points out, however, that "simply establishing a measure cannot itself create a commensurability. . . . Indeed, measure presupposes commensurability."[8]

Aristotle concludes, instead, that "really and in truth it is impossible for things so very different to become commensurate" (*NE* 1133b19–20). This is fully consistent with his understanding of things (*Physics* II.3) but surprising given its context, namely, his discussion of exchange, which would seem to require commensurability. Because each sort of thing has its own material, form, function, and end—its own four causes—and these are specifically different from one kind of thing to another, he does not, in the end, provide a theoretical account of commensurability at all. For some scholars, this constitutes a failure.[9] In my view, Aristotle's rejection of commensurability in his treatment of reciprocal justice suggests a practice of justice that makes it possible to compare different things or persons using a common term, thus recognizing and establishing their equality, while appreciating them in their differences.

How, without a theoretical account of commensurability, is exchange possible at all, let alone fair or equal exchange? Aristotle answers by looking to use, or *chreia*.[10] Use, he says, is the "one thing" by which all things are measured; it "holds everything together" (*NE* 1133a25–26, 1133a27–28). It is, thus, a common term. But use, as we saw in chapter 2, also safeguards differences among things. A shoe is for wearing (*Pol.* 1257a10), as, we can infer, a house is not. This suggests that use allows for exchange without rendering commensurable things that are incommensurable because, insofar as use takes its bearing from the things in use, it remains par-

---

8. Meikle, *Aristotle's Economic Thought*, p. 22.

9. Ibid., pp. 14–17, 25, 36. *Contra* Danzig, "Political Character of Aristotelian Reciprocity," pp. 400, 412–13, who rightly argues that Aristotle's aims are "far less theoretical."

10. Usually mistakenly translated as "demand," *chreia* is also sometimes translated as "need," which is better but does not capture the fact that, for Aristotle, as we saw in chapter 2, chreia is a prohairetic activity.

ticular to the things themselves. Aristotle's understanding of use is distinctive.[11] It is not a matter of satisfying wants when that is understood in a way characteristic of some utilitarians, who treat subjective pleasure or satisfaction as the measure of an exchange—the common term—and accordingly claim that an exchange is fair or equal when a shoemaker, say, receives as much satisfaction or pleasure from X houses as does a builder from Y pairs of shoes. Understanding use that way equalizes the things being exchanged in terms of pleasure.

Aristotle's approach to use is different. Whereas mutual desire motivates exchange in his view, too—I want your house just as you want my shoes—and this desire implies the anticipated pleasure of having the thing that one gets in exchange, pleasure, so understood, is not the same as the pleasure that grounds the commensurability of exchanged things in utilitarianism. The utilitarian view considers pleasure itself to be measurable. The commensurability of pleasure derived from the attainment of each exchanged thing, we just saw, determines the justice of the exchange. To Aristotle, however, pleasure is not measurable. Rather, the pleasure that desire anticipates is the pleasure one derives in use and, as we saw in chapter 2, it is inseparable from use as determined by the things in use themselves. How do things in use determine their use? How do we know, for example, that a shoe is for wearing? In the primary mode of use discerned by Aristotle—proper use (*Pol.* 1257a14)—the answer is "we do not *know*." Proper use is immediate, unreflective, and quotidian. When used properly, things disappear into their use. In our daily conversations, for example, we choose our words immediately and, for the most part, unreflectively. When we attend closely to our words, the conversation, now a matter of concern, becomes stilted. At the extreme, when we stop talking and attend closely to a single word, perhaps playing the childhood game of repeating it again and again—"bird, bird, bird, bird, bird"—the word ceases entirely to be a thing in use. This mode of using a word is so out of place in an everyday exchange (though not for a young child learning the word for the first time) that the oft-repeated word becomes nonsensical. How, we wonder, might we ever just use it again? Or consider the case of riding a bicycle. The ride is smooth so long as we unreflectively and immediately use the bicycle for riding. When we begin self-consciously to steer clear of each approaching rock or pothole, or think too

11. I agree with Meikle's analysis of chreia insofar as he rejects its translation as "demand" and recognizes that chreia cannot be what makes products commensurable. But insistent as he is on finding a solution to the commensurability problem, he does not see the key role of chreia in simultaneously marking the incommensurability of things and allowing for their exchange: see Meikle, *Aristotle's Economic Thought,* chap. 2.

88   CHAPTER THREE

hard about which gear to engage, we stop treating the bicycle as a thing in use and turn it into an object of scrutiny. Such reflections make for a bumpy ride. With respect to use that is proper to a thing, the answer to "what is it for" is given by its immediate and unreflective use.

The case of exchange is different. Aristotle calls the sort of use involved in the barter of shoes for a house "not proper use" (*Pol.* 1257a12–14). Unlike proper use, in which a thing disappears into its use, in barter the thing is an object of scrutiny as a thing to be exchanged. But not proper use is not "improper use" (*Pol.* 1257a9). The use involved in barter is not improper because the destination of the thing being exchanged is proper or immediate use even if that sort of use, at the moment of exchange, is secondary. When a shoemaker and a builder exchange shoes and houses, the house is for the shoemaker to inhabit and the shoes are for the builder to wear, both in the mode of proper use.[12] Proper use is immediate. The use characteristic of barter, by contrast, is mediated by the determination of what the things to be exchanged are for. This determination is not essentially different from the determination of the purpose of a thing of immediate use. In both cases, the determination of the purpose, based on the four causes (material, form, end, and function), is more or less inchoate. But in the case of the mediated use of barter, the determination of use sometimes has to be made explicit.[13] This might occur, for example, when the shoemaker and the housebuilder are unable to come to an immediate agreement about how many shoes to exchange for how many houses. When that happens, an explicit discussion about the material, form, function, and destination of the shoes and houses will arise.[14]

Whether inchoate or explicit, the determination of the use of the things to be exchanged is made by the parties to the exchange on the basis of the specific properties of the goods. Insofar as this is the case, the equality characteristic of reciprocal justice is one that accommodates, indeed, that depends on, differences. Even the explicit determination of use, a product of reflection between the parties to an

---

12. They are in the proper mode of use, that is, unless the exchangers are in the shoe or the real estate business, when the profit motive may alienate from use and alter the practice of exchange. I return to this point in the context of the rise of money just below.

13. This transition from inchoate to explicit, from private to public, is effected in acts of positive reciprocity here under discussion. It is also effected in acts of negative reciprocity discussed by Allen, *World of Prometheus*, p. 64.

14. There is a fundamental difference between this account of the "value" of the things to be exchanged based in the four causes and the more usual accounts of value based on, for example, labor, professional standing of the makers, or supply and demand.

exchange, stays with these particulars. The uses "giving shelter" and "protecting one's feet" are, after all, as incommensurable as the items "houses" and "shoes."

For exchange, however, comparison must be possible. How does use allow things to be compared, as Aristotle claims, "sufficiently" for the purposes of a particular exchange (*NE* 1133b19–21)? Use is a common term and "holds everything together" insofar as the articulation of specific differences also fosters an appreciation of how incommensurable things may be treated *as if* they were the same. This appreciation shows itself as the agreement between the parties to the exchange.[15] That agreement—how many shoes the builder should get for how many houses—reflects the parties' judgment about how to equalize shoes and houses on the basis of these items' specific differences. It reflects the parties' judgment about what is fair and, in this way, it justifies the exchange. The agreement the parties reach is contingent. Lodged in a consensus between specific people about specific uses of specific items, it justifies only the exchange of this house for those shoes. Recognizing that, in truth, different things cannot be made commensurate, the equality characteristic of reciprocal justice, determined by use and understood in terms of the specific properties of the things in use, is thus sufficient only for the purposes of (this) exchange. This means that doing reciprocal justice is a matter of being attuned to the particularities of, and differences among, things, and of producing a marriage of the like with the unlike that asserts the identity between these things without denying their differences.

When barter becomes retail trade—when a thing is exchanged for money and money is then used to buy a different thing—the agreement between the parties to the exchange can be expressed by money, which Aristotle calls the "exchangeable representation of use" (*NE* 1133a26–29). Money, *nomisma,* is a token or sign that agreement—a convention, *nomos*—has been reached. Price thus reflects the agreement of the practitioners of reciprocity and reflects writ small the trust among the members of the polity as a whole that helps maintain its community. Price, so understood, may be an abstraction from use, but it need not be determined independent of use, nor need its presence make reciprocative exchange based on use any less primary.[16] Money may, however, change the terms of exchange. Not proper

15. "The decisive thing was that parties to a transaction should be satisfied with the terms, which would be negotiated without much attention to legal niceties." The permissive character of Athenian legislation is evidenced by a law providing that "mutual agreements should be binding on both parties." For references and discussion, see Millett, "Sale, Credit and Exchange," p. 178.

16. Millett, "Sale, Credit and Exchange," p. 182.

90   CHAPTER THREE

use can become, as we have seen, improper use. As itself an instrument of comparison, money becomes, in Aristotle's word, the "intermediate" between items of exchange, measuring how many shoes are equal to a house or to a given amount of food (*NE* 1133a20–21), indeed, measuring all things. When money mediates exchange, it can attenuate the reflection and discussion about specific uses that, as we saw, mediate the barter of a house for some shoes. When reflection and discussion are attenuated, the contingency of the agreement can be forgotten, and money can take on a life of its own, alienated from the specific uses of things and alienating people from things.

The rise of money, indeed, encourages people to focus on exchange value rather than on use. Alienating things from their uses, money can cease to be the token of an agreement reached on independent grounds by two parties to an exchange and become instead a force that shapes and structures those agreements. By orienting them toward wealth-getting, money can also distort people's faculties and character (*Pol.* 1258a11–14). On this basis, Meikle, for example, argues that, for Aristotle, money produces "social arrangements that come into being independently of the activities of citizens themselves and yet have a large role in shaping those activities since citizens have no choice but to accommodate to them."[17] According to such a reading, after money is introduced, calculations of wealth maximization, rather than the parties' considerations of specific and proper use, will determine exchange. Aristotle is, to be sure, wary of and worried about money. He does not, however, blame money for structuring social arrangements in wealth-maximizing ways. The problem lies, rather, in people's distorted faculties and character, specifically, in their unmoderated desires, *pleonexia*. Attributing these distortions and the shape of social structures to the rise of money leaves unexplained how, once money is introduced, it is nonetheless possible, in Aristotle's scheme of things, to lead a life not dictated by wealth-getting.

The introduction of money and social arrangements directed at wealth-getting (usury, for example) can, to be sure, lead to violence and compulsion (*Pol.* 1258b3–10; *NE* 1096a6–8), but the effects of money and the deformations it encourages can also be countered. In Aristotle's words, "money has its name *nomisma* because it exists not by nature but by law *nomos* and it is in our power to change it and make it useless" (*NE* 1133a30–32). Citizens may counter money's effects, in both their col-

---

17. Meikle, *Aristotle's Economic Thought,* pp. 74, 68–81. See also Booth, "Politics and the Household," p. 223. On how money effects this separation, see Simmel, *Philosophy of Money,* p. 307.

lective and individual capacities, specifically by prohairetic activity, namely, that activity by which they make themselves citizens and by which they produce the social and political institutions that guide them. "First among necessary offices" in a regime, Aristotle maintains, is the office charged with the care of the market. The responsibility of the holder of this office is to inspect contracts (*Pol.* 1321b13–14; *AP* 51) and to nullify fraudulent transactions, that is, those arranged with a view to money-making to the detriment of one of the parties to the exchange. By virtue of its oversight, this office, itself a product of collective citizen action, encourages fair exchanges of goods and services among citizens. This office is supervisory, not preemptive, and that means that the holder of the office has no mandate to substitute his determination of fairness for the agreement reached by the parties.[18] Judgments regarding fair exchange thus remain largely with the citizens.

The alienating and corrupting effects of money may be countered not only by a regime's institutions but by the individual practices of citizens as well, specifically, by a commitment on the part of the parties to an exchange to attend to the specific and proper uses of the things to be exchanged. This, as we saw in chapters 1 and 2, depends, for Aristotle, on intellectual and moral virtue. To claim a role for virtue in the determination of fair exchange is not, however, to side with those who argue that the standing or worth of those who produce the things to be exchanged determines fair exchange.[19] According to that reading, the higher the standing of the producer, the more justifiably costly the product. This status-based understanding of worth, like the deterministic understanding of money, obscures the fact that, for Aristotle, virtue is a prohairetic activity or practice. The worth of the producer matters when worth, as Judith Swanson rightly puts it, is glossed in terms of the producer's "talents or expertise and, insofar as these presuppose integrity or other moral qualities, his moral virtue. Put differently, because the caliber of a good or service reflects the excellence (or lack thereof) of the producer—who chooses what to produce (a cure, a lecture, a table) and is responsible for its quality (a fraudulent cure, an organized lecture, a sturdy table)—the producer's excellence merits reward."[20] So understood, the producer's worth is given not by the producer's standing but, as we saw in chapter 2 regarding the magnificent man, by the

18. For discussion, see Mayhew, *Aristotle's Criticism of Plato's* Republic, p. 110.

19. Danzig, "Political Character of Aristotelian Reciprocity," pp. 418–24, adopts this position. For other references, see Meikle, *Aristotle's Economic Thought,* pp. 133–35; Swanson, *Public and the Private,* pp. 83–86.

20. Swanson, *Public and the Private,* p. 84.

92   CHAPTER THREE

excellence of his product as it reflects back on the activity of producing it and, in this way, on the agent of that activity. Fair exchange is, therefore, assessed both in terms of the things to be exchanged and in terms of the virtue of those who produce them.[21]

Reciprocal justice thus depends on the intellectual and moral virtues of its practitioners in a number of ways: their excellence as producers of good things (or not), their excellence as users of these things and as judges of that use, and their capacity to arrive at an agreement that reflects the proper uses of these things. If fair exchange depends on virtue in all these ways, Aristotle also insists that virtue is learned by the practice of fair exchange: it is "by taking part in transactions with others that we become just or unjust" (*NE* 1103b14–16, 1178a12). I turn next to an explanation of how this is the case.

PARTIALITY

Exchangers characteristically bring to their exchanges a concern for their own good. It is only because the shoemaker desires the builder's house and the builder wants the shoemaker's shoes that they decide to exchange in the first place. At the same time, reciprocal justice, like all practices of justice, concerns the proper treatment of others. It is important that the shoemaker give the builder the right kind and number of shoes in the right way at the right time. Bringing together two modes of concern that are usually set in opposition, reciprocal justice marries a concern for one's own good with the proper treatment of others not by canceling them out to produce impartiality but rather by producing the kind of partiality characteristic of *phronesis,* practical wisdom.

Citing popular opinion, Aristotle says, "the man who knows and concerns himself with his own interests is thought to have phronesis, while political officials [in their concern for the good of others] are thought to be busybodies" (*NE* 1142a1–3). Aristotle seems to be of two minds about this opinion. Although he agrees with its

21. *Contra* Meikle, *Aristotle's Economic Thought,* chap. 2, who collapses persons into things, insisting on a quantitative assessment; and Danzig, "Political Character of Aristotelian Reciprocity," pp. 401, 417–22, who understands worth "as defined by the values of the city, values that are in turn reflected in the prices of the marketplace." For Danzig, the value of a producer is determined by how lucrative his profession is.

My reading casts a new light on the possibilities for artisans—the ur-producers of the polity—one that is fully consistent with the account of identity offered in chapter 1 in that the cultivation of phronesis by production is similar to the practice of phronesis that Aristotle associates with citizen-rulers.

central thrust, namely, that phronesis is "identified especially with that form of it which is concerned with a man himself" (*NE* 1141b33), he also suggests that "perhaps one's own good cannot exist without household management nor without a form of government" (*NE* 1142a8–10). He thereby gestures toward an enlarged sense of the good of the self that involves, as well, the good of others. The good of others known by the one with practical wisdom is, however, of a peculiar kind. As I demonstrate next, such a person, the phronimos, is able to treat others properly only by recognizing the limits of his capacity to know their good, that is, by knowing his own partiality.

This dimension of phronesis may be clarified by considering its relation to the virtue of moderation. Like all the virtues, moderation is possible only under the guidance of phronesis (*NE* 1144b20). It is also impossible to be phronimos without virtue (*NE* 1144b30). Moderation holds a special place in Aristotle's account of the virtues: it preserves phronesis (*NE* 1140b11–12).[22] Moderation thus preserves that by which it and all the other virtues are guided. As we saw in chapter 2, the practice of moderation safeguards the otherness of others. Plato's dialogue *Charmides* suggests that it does so insofar as it is a kind of self-knowledge. There, Socrates says that moderation is knowledge that one knows what one knows and that one does not know what one does not know (167B–C). Socrates' interlocutor draws from this the conclusion that to be moderate is to know what one knows and does not know, that is, to know all. Socrates rejects this definition. He says that it is impossible for a person to know what he knows and does not know (167A). But if that is the case, how can moderation be a kind of self-knowledge? Knowledge of what one knows and does not know, says Socrates, is not the same as knowledge of self (170A). The knowledge of self is knowledge *that* one knows and does not know (170D). This is what Socrates, in the *Apology,* calls human wisdom (20D–23C). Moderation, in other words, is that knowledge of oneself by virtue of which one knows that one cannot know what one knows and does not know and thus that one is not and cannot be all-knowing. This suggests that moderation is a sort of self-knowledge possessed by those who keep within bounds, who know that their mortality distinguishes them from gods (*NE* 1177b34, 1178a1–3, b8–23), who, as

---

22. Plato says the same (*Cratylus* 411E) and, like Aristotle, he bases this claim, in part, on their etymological relation. See, for discussion, North, *Sophrosyne,* p. 204 n. 27. Alasdair MacIntyre disputes this etymology as "ingenious but false," accepting nevertheless the "double character" of the relation of moderation to practical wisdom: see "*Sophrosune,*" p. 5.

94   CHAPTER THREE

Aristotle puts it, "mind their own" (*Rhet.* 1381a24–26) and, in so doing, leave others to mind their own as well.[23]

Understanding the limits of his capacity to know what is good for someone else, the phronimos nonetheless (or perhaps, therefore) acts well toward others. It is in recognition of this limitation and its possibilities that Aristotle maintains that in acts of reciprocity, it is the one receiving the benefit who determines whether it is fitting (*NE* 1163a17–22). It is also why he claims that it is always the user of a thing who judges it best (*Pol.* 1282a17–23). It is this chastened understanding of the possibilities for knowing fully the good of another, combined with a concern for one's own good, that is at the heart of Aristotle's account of phronesis (*NE* 1140b7–9).

The relation between reciprocal justice and phronesis is complicated and multilayered. The former depends on the latter, for without phronesis a person would be unable to discern what is to his own good and to act well toward others. Reciprocity depends on phronesis as well insofar as discerning the use of things, namely, that which makes possible both the production of good things and their exchange, is a matter of phronesis. Reciprocity also teaches phronesis because it requires that human beings attend to the particular goods of exchange sufficiently to make them well, to determine their specific uses, to share their perceptions of these particulars, and so to adjudicate their fair exchange. If, as Aristotle says, phronesis is knowledge of particulars grasped by experience (*NE* 1142a14), reciprocity provides an exemplary occasion for experiencing particulars, whether things or people. In addition to this relation of mutuality wherein reciprocity depends on even as it teaches phronesis, the two are connected in another way. Both practices require treating things and people equally while recognizing their distinctiveness. This similarity comes out most clearly in Aristotle's understanding of the practice of good judgment, which he treats as "convergent" with phronesis (*NE* 1143a25).[24] In this way, as I show next, reciprocal justice does not only depend on phronesis. It also models the practice of phronetic judgment.

23. *Contra* Rosen, "Note on Aristotle's *De Anima*," p. 129, who argues that by failing to articulate a conception of the psyche as unified in knowing, Aristotle fails to achieve an adequate conception of the self-knowing or sensing psyche, thus rendering self-knowledge impossible.

24. As Ronald Beiner points out in *Political Judgment*, p. 155: "Our world of experience (including political experience) is a world of identity and difference. To identity and difference correspond the dual faculties of identification and discrimination. Judgment encompasses these two correlative capacities."

Good Judgment

An understanding of phronetic judgment as a dual process of equalization and distinction in the world of experience differs from accounts that treat judging as a deductive process, modeled on a syllogism, in which particulars are subsumed under a general rule.[25] According to those accounts, when there is no general rule driving the activity of judging, the resulting judgment is unjustified and hence unjust. When judgment is understood as a deduction from a universal premise, however, that which good judgment must appreciate, namely, difference, is rendered commensurable or indifferent.

Aristotle's invention of the syllogism as a model of judgment might suggest that he too understands judgment as the subsumption of particulars under a general rule. Indeed, he is sometimes treated as the authority for the syllogistic account of judging.[26] But in Aristotle's hands, the syllogism, when applied to practical matters, is not driven by the general rule or major premise. As he explains in the *Nicomachean Ethics,* "if a man knew that light meats are digestible and wholesome but did not know which sorts of meat were light, he would not produce health" (*NE* 1141b18–21). The minor premise, the one that identifies particulars—"that is light meat"—is instead key (*DA* 434a17–20; *NE* 1143b1–5; *Movement of Animals* 700b25–701a1, 703a5). If perception does the primary work of judgment, Aristotle's account of judgment is, nonetheless, cognitive, involving some universalization and abstraction. As we have seen, phronetic judgment encompasses two correlative capacities. It appreciates particulars in their differences and it compares those differences under a common term. But it finds the common term without rendering the particulars general. Phronetic judgment can do this because, as I read him, Aristotle understands it as a practice of thinking analogically.

Consider the definition of analogy Aristotle offers in the *Poetics:* "Analogy is possible whenever there are four terms so related so that the second is to the first, as the fourth to the third" (1457b16–17). He provides this example: "A cup is in relation to Dionysus what a shield is to Ares." Analogies call for the perception of particulars in their own right, and hence in their differences. Aristotle's example calls for knowing Dionysus and his cup and knowing Ares and his shield. Analo-

---

25. Legal formalists tend to claim that a judgment may be deduced analytically simply by applying a universal rule to particular facts. Critical scholars and antifoundationalists, by contrast, determine the justice of judgment by measuring it against general standards given by, for example, political ideology, sympathy, or alterity.

26. See, e.g., Scalia, "Rule of Law as a Law of Rules."

96   CHAPTER THREE

gies call for the perception of particulars in relation to other particulars. We must know the relation of Dionysus *to* his cup, namely, that Dionysus is a lover of wine, and the relation of Ares *to* his shield, namely, that Ares is the god of war. Finally, analogies call for perceiving the relation between Dionysus and his cup, on one hand, and Ares and his shield, on the other. Analogies bring all of these different relations together in a fourfold unity: Dionysus is to his cup *as* Ares is to his shield. As their representation suggests, they identify what is different: A/B = C/D or A:B::C:D. This process of identification represents the generalization necessary for the practice of judgment. But analogies identify what is different not by subsuming particulars but by highlighting particularity. Indeed, in order to work, analogies must be articulable into their different moments.[27] In this way analogies achieve generality and preserve particularity at the same time.

Because to perceive is to grasp by way of experience, analogies depend on a certain familiarity with the individual terms and their relations. But analogies also put familiar terms together in new ways, and this with double effect. They disclose previously unrecognized similarities: Dionysus is to his cup *the way* Ares is to his shield. They also render the familiar strange. We may, Aristotle says in the *Poetics,* "put the fourth in place of the second, and the second in place of the fourth," describing the cup as "the shield of Dionysus" and the shield as "the cup of Ares" (1457b20–22). This is the generative power of analogy.[28] In their capacity to identify and discriminate, analogies mirror the practice of phronetic judgment. This is no accident. For Aristotle argues that to judge is to think analogically (*DA* 431a20–b1; see also 426b8–427a15).

The relation of likeness or equality that analogies posit cannot be justified logically or proven or demonstrated.[29] There are no a priori rules or criteria for judging analogousness or for phronetic judging. This is not to say that analogousness rests on a fact in the world that one simply perceives (or does not), or on something common in human nature, or in a shared culture, or that analogies are something one "gets" in an instant and whose authority is thereby somehow firmly

27. Note that successful analogies produce a *homonoia,* or concord, that is both unifying and differentiating. As we will see in chapter 5, this is precisely the attribute Aristotle takes to be necessary to a good political association.

28. See Davis, *Poetry of Philosophy,* p. 118. *Contra* Allen, *World of Prometheus,* p. 286, who claims that "two unlike things *turn out* to have something in common" (my emphasis). In my view, they do not "turn out" to have something in common but rather their commonality is produced or generated by the analogy, if successful.

29. See, e.g., Drucker, "Just Analogies?"; Bambrough, "Aristotle on Justice"; Zashin and Chapman, "Uses of Metaphor and Analogy."

established. It is also not to say that analogies are something one gets on one's own and not in the course of conversation. Analogousness is none of these things because analogies cannot be gotten prior to their use. This use depends as much on how analogies are received as on the expertise of their maker. That this is so is evidenced by Aristotle's insistence that metaphors (the building blocks of analogy) cannot be taught and by the fact that, in discussing analogy, Aristotle provides no rules or criteria but only examples. This means that like the use that allows for the reciprocal exchange of goods and services, the felicitous use of analogies arises in and depends on a context of discursive exchange. Felicitous analogy, or phronetic judgment, the mode of thinking by which citizens determine the right thing to do, is not Aristotle's solution to the problem of justice but rather a discursive practice by means of which citizens confront problems of justice daily.

If this is right and Aristotle's treatment of justice offers no a priori solutions, how might we explain his recourse to mathematical measures in his discussions of reciprocity, distribution, and correction? Aristotle figures reciprocal justice as a proportional equality of the form $A/B = C/D$ or $A/C = B/D$ (*NE* 1133a7–10), where A is the shoemaker and B the builder, and C represents shoes and D, houses; he figures distributive justice as a proportional equality of the form $A/B = C_1/C_2$ (*NE* 1131b4–9), where A and B are citizens of a polity and C_1 and C_2 are shares of goods being distributed;[30] and he represents corrective justice in terms of arithmetic equality (*NE* 1132a1–2). Scholars treat these formulae as Aristotle's "abstract and objective" and universally applicable measures of justice.[31] Justice is a matter of equality or fairness, and so we use mathematical equations to model the process of abstraction required to establish equality among things or people that are different. As I read them, however, Aristotle's formulations are not meant to imply mathematical rigor or deductive logic in determining justice. Rather, the proportional equality characteristic of reciprocal and distributive justice, taking the form A:B::C:D (though somewhat differently for each), represents an analogy. The same is true of corrective justice, which can be understood in terms of propor-

30. Because the goods of reciprocal justice are different (citizens exchange shoes for houses) but the parties to a particular distribution are allotted shares of the same thing, I represent the goods of reciprocity as C and D and the goods of distribution as C_1 and C_2.

31. See, e.g., Allen, *World of Prometheus*, p. 290. Although most commentators take Aristotle's recourse to mathematics at face value and applaud or criticize him for his rigor, a few, including Winthrop, "Aristotle and Theories of Justice," p. 1204, and Corcoran, "Aristotle's Poetic Justice," have noted the oddity of Aristotle's use of mathematics given his insistence throughout the *Nicomachean Ethics* that the material he will be treating in that book, justice presumably included, is imprecise and inexact and must be respected as such.

98 CHAPTER THREE

tional equality as well, when A:B = 1. As such, Aristotle's formulae for justice model the mode of thinking appropriate to a practice of judging that is not theoretical but practical and not deductive but generative. Doing justice so understood is not a process of abstraction from particularity and not an erasure of difference but rather a practice that, as a matter of phronetic judgment, accommodates equality and difference.

Doing justice involves producing felicitous analogies, which is to say, practicing the virtue of good judgment. This may seem to be a tautological claim, or at least a trivial one that could have been made without this chapter's detours and arguments. It could not. For, in the course of this chapter, we have seen that phronetic judgment involves a proper attunement to the particularities of, and differences among, things and persons, and that it involves thinking analogically about these particulars to produce a marriage of the like with the unlike that asserts their equality without denying their differences. The differences between persons and between things, measured in terms of some particular quality that shows them to be *un*equal, are necessary for a proper understanding of their equality. And doing justice calls for simultaneously recognizing differences among persons and among things and comparing these differences using a common measure that does not erase their differences. Justice, so understood, is a matter of equality, to be sure, but an equality that accommodates distinction.

Cultivated most immediately in the everyday practices of reciprocal justice in a polity, phronetic judgment is, in the first instance, not a gift of rulers but a virtue of the practitioners of fair exchange, citizens and noncitizens alike.[32] Aristotle seems, however, to associate the practice of phronetic judgment only with rulers. Comparing the ruler to the flute player and the subject to the flute maker, Aristotle says that the only excellence the subject needs is true opinion, whereas phronesis is the excellence peculiar to rulers (*Pol.* 1277b26–30). This may be so when there is a division of labor between using and making. Aristotle maintains, as we have seen, that it is the user of a thing and not its maker who judges it best—the diner, not the chef, the resident, not the architect (*Pol.* 1282a17–23). He insists that "it is difficult, if not impossible, for those who do not perform to be good judges of the performance of others" (*Pol.* 1340b24–26). When labor is divided between making and using, making, in Aristotle's view, must be subordinated to using, the maker to the user, and the ruled to the ruler. Using office—the activity of ruling—thus offers a

---

32. Kraut, *Aristotle: Political Philosophy*, p. 151, notes that the practices of fair exchange extend not only to citizens but to noncitizens as well.

special opportunity to rulers for exercising phronetic judgment, specifically in the form of political wisdom, *politike*.[33]

But labor is not always so divided. All members of a polity, and not exclusively the rulers, practice reciprocity. Practitioners of reciprocity are both makers and users. The shoemaker makes shoes and uses houses; the builder makes houses and uses shoes. In making houses or shoes, in exchanging them, and in using them, exchangers practice phronetic judgment. Aristotle's treatment of analogical thinking in the *Poetics* similarly suggests, in line with the argument of chapter 1, that all users of language (all first-level possessors of logos and of the intellectual and moral virtue that informs it) are at least potential practitioners of phronetic judgment. Perhaps it is because he sees the everyday practices of reciprocity as necessary for the cultivation of phronetic judgment that Aristotle says that to be a good ruler one needs first to learn how to be a good subject (*Pol.* 1277b14, 1333a1–2). And, perhaps for this reason, too, only a political life of ruling and being ruled in turn, the political corollary of reciprocal justice—in which practitioners of phronetic judgment are the makers and users of their own justice and their own laws—offers all members of a polity the possibility for fully developing and using phronetic judgment.

Aristotle's expectations of reciprocal justice are high. He claims that reciprocity, or what he calls "proportionate requital," is the bond and "salvation" of a polity (*NE* 1132b33; *Pol.* 1261a30–31). In the words of D. G. Ritchie, reciprocity "provides a form of *philia* or association for an activity more basic than any other to the life of the polity."[34] As we have seen, reciprocal exchanges provide people with goods and services to meet their daily and immediate needs. Reciprocity is basic to the life of a polity, in this sense, because it ensures a subsistence. The association formed by reciprocal exchanges of this sort is akin to what we might call a market. This form of association is, however, not adequate to a polity. As Aristotle points out, the polity is an association to the end not merely of life but of a good life (*Pol.* 1280a32 ff., 1280b30 ff.). As we have seen, indeed, reciprocal justice in the context of exchanges of goods and services, though often geared toward subsistence, does not result only in an association to the end of mere life. Teaching phronesis even as they depend on it, the practices of commercial exchange, a mode of prohairetic activity, cultivate virtues that, in Aristotle's understanding, orient a polity toward a good life. As we saw in chapter 2, the virtue of proper use establishes continuities between what we tend to divide into separate private and public spheres. Similarly,

---

33. I explore the relation between phronesis and politike in chapter 4.
34. Ritchie, "Aristotle's Subdivisions of 'Particular Justice.'"

100   CHAPTER THREE

the practice of phronetic judgment, on which the determination of not proper use depends, establishes continuities between the reciprocal justice governing commercial exchanges and such more obviously political and social phenomena of reciprocity as, in the words of Lawrence Becker, "rituals of gift giving, unspoken understandings between lovers, patterns of family life, expectations among friends, duties of fair play, obligations of citizenship."[35]

If, in exchanges of goods and services, these shoes are exchanged for that house now (even if delivery of one or the other good occurs later), these other acts of reciprocity generally occur over time. I receive a gift from you now and I give you one next year. Becker notes that the fundamental question to be asked about these practices of reciprocity is: "How can a benefit, unasked for by the recipients, obligate them to make a return?"[36] Aristotle's answer to this question may be found in the following passage, which appears early in his discussion of reciprocal justice but which most commentators treat as not germane to his account: "We set up a shrine of the Graces in a public place to remind men to return a kindness; for that is a special characteristic of grace, since it is a duty not only to repay a service done one, but another time to take the initiative in doing a service oneself" (*NE* 1133a2–5).[37] Return is crucial to the practice of reciprocity. It is also only half of Aristotle's description of that practice. The shrine reminds people to do service. This means that initiation is important as well.[38] Return or repayment cements the bonds of a polity.[39] Initiation, that is, giving freely, generates those bonds in the first place (*Pol.* 1253a40; *NE* 1162b34). Reciprocity holds a polity together, then, by generating and regenerating relations among its practitioners, citizens and noncitizens alike.

Reciprocity is the salvation of polities in another sense as well. In the giving characteristic of both initiation and unasked-for return, a person acts and exists for himself. This is Aristotle's definition of a free person, one who "exists for himself and not for another" (*Meta.* 982b26–27). Reciprocity thus presupposes and

---

35. Becker, *Reciprocity,* p. 73. For rich accounts of the phenomena relating to reciprocity at Athens, see Millett, "Sale, Credit and Exchange"; Wilson, *Athenian Institution of the Khoregia.*

36. Becker, *Reciprocity,* p. 73.

37. For general discussion of the Graces, see MacLachlan, *Age of Grace.*

38. In making this claim, I differ from Danzig, "Political Character of Aristotelian Reciprocity," p. 410, who claims that repayment only is of the essence of reciprocity.

39. The extensive anthropological literature concerning the Kula ring and the Potlatch attests to this.

teaches freedom, that is, it presupposes and teaches equality and distinction among its practitioners and, thus, opens the way to their friendship. Aristotle calls friendship and reciprocity the bond of a polity (*NE* 1132b31–34, 1155a23–24) and, as we will see in chapter 5, the friendship appropriate to a political life is one that, like reciprocal justice, depends on even as it promotes freedom, equality, and distinction among its practitioners. Aristotle seems to say, however, that friendship makes justice unnecessary: "When men are friends they have no need of justice, while when they are just, they lack friendship" (*NE* 1155a27–29). When he says that friends have no need of justice it is not because friends' selflessness somehow makes justice unnecessary. Rather, the justice appropriate to friendship, reciprocity, is not externally imposed. As the product of the friends' own virtue, justice, so understood, and friendship are coextensive (*NE* 1160a7–9, 1162b29–31).[40]

The political corollary of reciprocal justice is rotational rule: citizens as makers and users of justice rule and are ruled in turn (*Pol.* 1261a31–36). Citizens take up offices as a duty of citizenship, a repayment to the polity, and they must, as part of that return, use them well. Citizens also step down from office to give the reins of power to others. In regimes thus governed by reciprocity, citizens rule and are ruled as free men (*Pol.* 1277b8–9). Because they exist for themselves, they must be ruled in their own good, and they must rule in their own good as well. Practicing phronetic judgment, learned in their daily reciprocal exchanges, these citizens bring to the institutions of justice an enlarged understanding of their own good that is, as such, leavened by a concern for the proper treatment of others.

Justice and Virtue

How exactly does phronetic judgment take account not only of the good of the judge but of the proper treatment of others as well? Phronesis is an intellectual virtue that carries the moral virtues in its wake: in Aristotle's words, "it is not possible to be good without phronesis or to have phronesis without moral virtue" (*NE* 1144b33–34).[41] This is because we need to discern the particulars of a situation in order to do the right thing in the right way at the right time, and, as Aristotle's dis-

---

40. Aristotle does distinguish the equality appropriate to justice (proportional equality) from that appropriate to friendship (equality in quantity). I explore this point in chapter 5.

41. *Contra* those who, noting Aristotle's positioning of his treatment of justice in *Nico-*

102   CHAPTER THREE

cussion of weakness of the will, *akrasia,* in *Nicomachean Ethics* VII makes plain, character affects perceptions. Any choice or judgment I make is embedded in who I am. As we saw in chapter 1, *prohairesis,* choice, is close to our "prejudice" or prejudgment. Without prejudgments, nothing would ever be familiar and, because discernment comes with experience, we could not properly discern particulars.

This bidirectional relation between phronesis, the virtue of good judgment essential to the practice of justice, and the virtues of character demonstrates that these virtues and justice are not opposed. Like justice, the virtues of character are relational. They guide and inform our treatment of particulars in the world, be they things or people. And, like the virtues of character, justice must regard the good of the self. This means that, to do justice, the practitioners of justice, a polity's noncitizens, citizens, and officials, must exercise virtue in the form of good judgment. It also means that, to do justice, distribution and correction, like reciprocity, require virtue. Consider in this light the passage in *Nicomachean Ethics* V, in which Aristotle introduces justice. Justice is virtue, he says, although not simply, *haplos,* but with regard to the other (*NE* 1129b26; see also 1130a12–13, 1130b1–2). Aristotle's Kantian readers take him to be counterposing justice to the other virtues: whereas justice pertains to the good of other people, the other, simple virtues regard only the good of the self.[42] To those who prioritize right over good, what matters for the virtues are habits or intentions—what goes on "inside" a person—whereas what matters for justice are actions, which take their place among persons in the world. Insofar as justice regards other people but virtue, in its concern for proper habits, does not, these writers argue that justice, but not virtue, is fundamentally political and somehow improves on or is "higher than" virtue.[43] The Kantian distinction is thus read into Aristotle's text, making him a proponent of the view that justice sets the parameters not only for individual moral worth but also for the goodness or moral worth of the polity itself.

It is true that, to Aristotle, justice is essentially political. Justice is the key question for political philosophy (*Pol.* 1282b24). Every political community has a jus-

---

machean *Ethics* V, argue that justice forms a transition from the moral virtues to the intellectual ones; see, e.g., Winthrop, "Aristotle and Theories of Justice," p. 1202.

42. See the accounts cited by O'Connor, "Aetiology of Justice," p. 145 n. 32; Kraut, *Aristotle: Political Philosophy,* p. 101. This is one of the sites of contemporary moral philosophy's debate about whether Aristotle's moral philosophy is egoistic or altruistic: see Kraut, *Aristotle on the Human Good,* chap. 2.

43. See, e.g., Barker, *Political Thought of Plato and Aristotle,* p. 322. For justice as "super virtue" see Kraut, *Aristotle: Political Philosophy,* p. 125. *Contra* Heyman, "Aristotle on Political Justice."

tice that is appropriate to it (*NE* 1159b27; *Pol.* 1309a36–39). Good lawgivers aim to promote justice (*NE* 1160a13). It is nonetheless a mistake to conclude that, for Aristotle, justice, not virtue, is the measure of a polity or that justice is fundamentally different from the other virtues.[44] As we have seen, justice is virtue not only with regard to others. Dependent on the partiality characteristic of good judgment and on moral virtue, justice is virtue also with regard to oneself. Justice is virtue, Aristotle claims, *but not haplos.* Contrary to accounts that read this statement as elevating justice over virtue, Aristotle seems to be suggesting that virtue is the larger whole of which justice is a part. Rather than justice somehow improving on or being higher than virtue, it is justice that is virtue qualified. This means that justice is an adequate measure of the goodness of a polity insofar as it is itself good (*Pol.* 1283a38–40). We have seen what this means in the context of reciprocal justice, in which virtue is tied to the activities of making and using and to the practice of good judgment. As I show next, the activities of reciprocal justice and its virtues are no less necessary to the proper practices of distribution and correction.

DISTRIBUTION AND CORRECTION

Examining distribution, correction, and reciprocity at work in oligarchies and democracies in *Politics* III.9, Aristotle maintains that these practices in those regimes are plagued by a fundamental error. In oligarchies, whose constituting principle is inequality based on wealth, distributions are just when goods are allocated to citizens in proportion to their wealth (*Pol.* 1280a27). In democracies, whose constituting principle is that all are equally free, distributions are just when goods are allocated to citizens in equal shares (*Pol.* 1280a25). Insofar as they distribute goods on the basis of equality, these regimes practice justice. Aristotle insists, however, that oligarchies and democracies are not entirely just because each misconstrues equality (*Pol.* 1280a10–13), oligarchies by taking inequality to be wholly determined by wealth, democracies by taking equality to be wholly determined by freedom (*Pol.* 1301b35–1302a8). The oligarchic and democratic practices of correction and reciprocity are no more (or less) just than their practices of distribution. These regimes may have "agreements about imports, and engagements that they will do no wrong to one another, and written articles of alliance" (*Pol.*

44. Tessitore, *Reading Aristotle's* Ethics, pp. 35–47, and Winthrop, "Aristotle and Theories of Justice," argue that Aristotle's treatment of justice needs to be supplemented by ethics, Tessitore in the form of virtue, Winthrop in the form of friendship. I see ethics, and specifically virtue, not as a supplement but as part of the political practices themselves.

104   CHAPTER THREE

1280a39–40), but these contracts, Aristotle maintains, merely ensure that the parties do no injustice to each other. Leaving the affiliation among citizens and between polities "of the same character after as before their union" (*Pol.* 1280b29), these regimes merely enjoy the name polity without truly being one (*Pol.* 1280b8).

The practices of justice in these regimes are flawed for two reasons. First, oligarchs and democrats are bad judges in their own cases; and, second, they imagine themselves to be speaking of the whole of justice but practice a limited justice (*Pol.* 1280a21–23) or a "part of justice only" (*Pol.* 1281a10). These practices of justice are flawed, in other words, owing to a dual partiality. Unlike the partiality characteristic of the phronimos, the partiality of oligarchs and democrats leads them to practice justice only to their own advantage. Although their practices of justice may determine what is due, they understand equality as simple commensuration. Taking what is different to be the same (*Pol.* 1283a3–10, 1280a9–11), they "strip away the qualifications of the persons concerned and so judge badly" (*Pol.* 1280a13–14). Perhaps as a corrective to the dual partiality that mars the practices of justice in these regimes, when Aristotle discusses distribution and correction theoretically in the *Nicomachean Ethics* he assumes an impartial standpoint. He describes distributive justice from the standpoint of the legislator and corrective justice from that of the judge, whom Aristotle calls "a sort of living justice" (*NE* 1132a20–23). Delba Winthrop explains that Aristotle frames these discussions in this way to teach citizens that justice requires learning "to calm the anger which is at the core of righteous indignation at injustice and to overcome the natural, unreflective concern for one's own good."[45] In Winthrop's view, Aristotle's discussions of the specifications of justice assume an impartial standpoint to teach citizens what Winthrop calls the "habit of justice," specifically that justice calls for impartiality.[46] In the light of the dangers posed by the partiality practiced in oligarchies and democracies, this makes sense. As we saw, at least part of the reason for the poor practices of justice in those regimes is that people "are passing judgment on themselves and most people are bad judges in their own case" (*Pol.* 1280a13–15).

Aristotle is not sanguine, however, about the possibilities for impartiality, especially when it comes to the offices of the magistracies: "In forensic oratory . . . it is other people's affairs that are to be decided, so that the judges, intent on their own satisfaction and listening with partiality, surrender themselves to the disputants instead of judging between them" (*Rhet.* 1354b32–1355a1). Indeed, he maintains

45. Winthrop, "Aristotle and Theories of Justice," pp. 1203–4.
46. Ibid., p. 1203.

that judges "will often have allowed themselves to be so much influenced by feelings of friendship or hatred or self-interest that they lose any clear vision of the truth and have their judgment obscured by considerations of personal pleasure or pain. In general, then, the judge should, we say, be allowed to decide as few things as possible" (*Rhet.* 1354b9–14). When judges allow their passions to cloud their judgment, they substitute their own good for the good of the disputants before them and so pass judgment on themselves. When that happens, justice becomes what is to the advantage of the judge. The standpoint of corrective justice may be impartially represented by the office of the judge, but impartiality of office is no safeguard against an officeholder's partial exercise of judgment.

One might argue that the fault in such cases lies not with the office but in the particular judge and that true impartiality would cure the deficit of judgment. But this is not so. Legislators, producing universal laws that are uniformly applied to everyone in the polity, can fail to do justice owing not to the faulty implementation of these laws but to the very fact that they are framed to apply to everyone impartially. Because they are so framed, without regard to difference, laws need correction in the form of equity, *epieikeia* (*NE* 1137b26–29). Like the leaden rule used by Lesbian builders whose material allows it to shape itself to what it measures, equity enables those applying the laws properly to attend to as many of the particular circumstances, characteristics, and habits of the actor as possible and so to provide a more exacting treatment than does legal justice (*NE* 1137b29–31; *Rhet.* 1374b13–16). Impartiality, as reflected in the laws, may aim at the common good (*NE* 1129b14–19), but by treating what is in the common good as what is good for each citizen, impartiality mistakes the whole for the part or one part for another and is therefore not itself a good basis for judgment.[47] Whether the defect of judgment is not enough impartiality or too much, the source of the defect is the same, namely, that it is not the good of the particular citizen but the good of one, or many, or all others that is brought to bear in the determination of what is just for that citizen.

To say all of this is not to claim that judges and the law are incapable of doing justice, nor is it to claim that there is something inherently unjust about distribu-

---

47. This is the case whether the good of many others refers to average cases (as it does in the case of law) or to the many who are the ruling democrats. In the first instance, the failure to do justice stems from the laws' generality. In the second, it stems from the laws' bias in favor of the majority. Aristotle signals this problem also in his critique, in *Politics* II.3, of the celebration of communal women, children, and property by Plato's Socrates. Under those conditions, too, Aristotle says, "all" and "each" get confused.

tive and corrective justice. The point is, rather, that there is nothing in the office of the judge *qua* office or in the institution of law *qua* institution that can produce the partiality characteristic of good judgment. This partiality depends not on a denial of self-interest on the part of the practitioners of justice but on the good judgment of these practitioners about their self-interest and also about the interests of those who are subject to their justice. Partiality, so understood, is cultivated in the first instance, as we have seen, in the practice of reciprocal justice. This suggests that it is the practitioners of reciprocal justice who teach the "habit of justice" to officials and not the other way around.

Aristotle makes a similar point when he contrasts forensic oratory to political oratory. He calls the latter "a nobler business, and fitter for a citizen" because "in political oratory there is less inducement to talk about non-essentials" and, treating general issues, it "is less given to unscrupulous practices than forensic oratory." This is because "in a political debate the man who is forming a judgment is making a decision about his own vital interests" (*Rhet.* 1354b23–30). Partiality, properly practiced, is integral to good judgment. Such partiality is different from the kind that allows the judge to substitute his good for that of the disputant before him or the kind that makes officials poor practitioners of distributive and corrective justice. It is also different from the partiality that makes people bad judges in their own cases. Aristotle's remarks in the *Rhetoric* underscore that the right kind of partiality is bound with a concern for one's own good, the sort of concern that citizens typically bring to the assembly and to their other associations with fellow citizens and noncitizens, most especially, as we have seen, in the practices of reciprocal justice. This sort of partiality, combining a concern for one's own good and for that of another, produces, even as it depends on, the judgment characteristic of the phronimos. The justice this sort of judgment produces does not simply aggregate the good of each to produce a good for all, and it is distinct from the good of the whole. Instead it seeks and finds a commonality that is good for individuals and the community at the same time (*Pol.* 1264b17–21).[48]

Against the backdrop of this understanding of the partiality proper to good judgment, as elucidated in the practice of reciprocity, consider once more Aristotle's accounts of distribution and correction. As in reciprocal justice, where just exchange requires knowing the use of the things to be exchanged, so too does just distribution require knowing the use of the thing to be distributed. In both cases

---

48. I discuss the content of this idea of a common good and how it may be achieved in chapter 5.

the answer to the use question emerges not from an appeal to a fixed standard, not from the office of an impartial legislator, but from deliberation and judgment among citizens.

Distributive justice, says Aristotle, is exercised in the distribution of honor, wealth, and other things of use, *chremata,* which may be allotted to members of a polity in equal or unequal shares (*NE* 1130b30−33). For persons who are equal, the shares must be equal. For those who are unequal, the shares must be unequal (*NE* 1131a20−24; see also *Pol.* 1280a11−13, 1282b20−21). Distributive justice involves at least four terms: two persons to whom goods are distributed and two shares of what is being distributed. The just is the equal in that it demands that the ratio between the shares be equal to the ratio between the persons. A distribution is just, Aristotle maintains, when the difference in the amount allocated to each person is in proportion to some relevant difference between them, and the ratio between the persons and the ratio between the shares is equal. Aristotle calls the relevant difference desert or merit: "For all agree that justice in distribution needs to be based on some idea of desert, although all do not mean the same idea of desert" (*NE* 1131a24−29).

What counts as relevant difference? What counts as merit or desert? Aristotle offers the following analogy to explain desert in the case of the distribution of political offices: "It is not proper to give an advantage in respect of flutes to those of better birth, for they will not play any better, but it is superior performers who ought to be given the superior instruments" (*Pol.* 1282b31−35). Taking this analogy as Aristotle's general formulation of desert, some of his interpreters conclude that offices ought to go to those who are best able to perform the tasks associated with office-holding. Emphasizing performance, they maintain that the criterion of just desert is determined by the contribution the person receiving political office will make to the common good of the polity as a whole.[49] Stressing that actually performing depends on *being able* to perform or on *having the capacity* to perform, others argue that goods in general and political offices in particular are to be distributed to everyone except those who cannot use them at all.[50] Each interpretation captures important Aristotelian insights about justice and about political participation. However, mirroring the oligarchic and democratic principles of

---

49. See, e.g., Waldron, "Wisdom of the Multitude," p. 572; Heyman, "Aristotle on Political Justice," p. 854; Allen, *World of Prometheus,* pp. 286−87.

50. See Nussbaum, "Aristotelian Social Democracy"; Nussbaum, "Nature, Function, and Capability."

108   CHAPTER THREE

justice, contribution and capacity, respectively, offer, on their own, only partial accounts of desert.[51]

For Aristotle, by contrast, capacity and contribution must be taken together: "The persons who should be in office are those most capable of holding office" (*Pol.* 1273b5–6), and holding office calls for using it "with a view to the life of excellence" (*Pol.* 1284a1–3). Capacity and contribution together constitute what Aristotle calls virtue. "In any office of stewardship . . . more virtue than ordinary is required in the holder of such an office" (*Pol.* 1309b7). As we saw in chapter 1, he defines virtue as a matter of using what one has, for, however good his dispositions may be, man does not demonstrate excellence if he does not act well, and only by acting well can he come to have a good disposition in the first place (*NE* 1103b23). The activity of proper use is contribution. At the same time, action by itself does not amount to virtue, for it is not possible to act well without having the appropriate habits (*NE* 1103b24). If a person does something but does not do it from the appropriate habit or disposition, he may be acting in conformity with some principle or other, but the action is not freely his own. A stable disposition to act well is thus necessary for acting well to be preferred; acting well and preferring good acts both depend on good habit, or the capacity to act well. Taking virtue as the criterion for distributive justice requires that determinations of just distribution be made not on the basis only of capacity, because there can be no capacities that are unaffected by action. And such determinations cannot be made on the basis only of the contributions of actors, because actions emerge from habits. Determinations are to be made instead on the basis of contribution and capacity, action and habit. Habits and actions both count because how we come to act the way we do is bound to who we have become by virtue of our habits. And our habits are formed from our actions.

What kind of criterion of distribution does this account of virtue offer? None really, at least not in the usual sense of criterion,[52] that is to say, none if we understand a criterion as an abstract and generalizable common measure. So understood, desert would commensurate in the way that other common terms do, thus reducing Aristotle's account of the proper practice of distributive justice to distribution in oligarchies and democracies. Virtue, however, is not and cannot be a

---

51. For a fuller discussion of these interpretations, see Frank, "Democracy and Distribution."

52. Here I agree with Bernard Yack, who recognizes Aristotle's refusal of "determinate standards of merit" as guides "in choosing standards of distributive justice": see *Problems of a Political Animal,* p. 166.

common term. It is also not an external standard. It is, rather, what in chapter 1 I called an internal standard that serves as a reflection of citizen activity and must be referred to each citizen himself. Who should get political offices? Those who will use political offices well. Who will use them well? Those disposed to hold them well. What determines who gets political offices? The actions of those who hold and use political offices, namely, the practitioners or makers of distributive justice. Who holds political offices? Those who rule and are ruled in turn. Like reciprocal justice, distributive justice, so understood, is produced by the actions and habits of citizens. It is guided not by an external or higher authority but by citizens participating in the political process. Authority is thus immanent in the practices of politics, via virtue. The distributive determinations made by these citizens in turn shape the citizens themselves and therefore the polity.

This is not to say that distributive determinations, any more than do the determinations of fair exchange, proceed without criteria. The criteria of capacity and contribution—like those of making and using—arise from the partial perspectives of actors positioned within the chain of habit and action. Determination of who should get a particular political office will depend on who will use it well. This is not to collapse capacity into performance but to insist on both at the same time. These factors depend in crucial ways on the practice of phronetic judgment because proper use, as a matter of acting well, depends on properly discriminating what needs to be done. All of these "criteria" of desert—habit, action, and, centrally, phronetic judgment—arise in a political context.[53] It is perhaps for this reason that Aristotle says that practical wisdom, *phronesis,* and political wisdom, *politike,* have the same disposition, even if their essences are not the same (*NE* 1141b24).

Virtue, understood as the combination of contribution and capacity, actions and habits, using and making, is the measure of desert in corrective justice no less than in distributive justice. Demanding equality between two terms only, namely, the parties to the transaction, corrective justice supplies a corrective principle in transactions in which "it makes no difference whether a good man has defrauded a bad man or a bad one a good one, nor whether it is a good or a bad man that has committed adultery; the law looks only at the nature of the damage, treating the parties as equal, and merely asking whether one has done and the other suf-

---

53. In this sense, in Josiah Ober's words, "democratic practice is proleptic to political theorizing" in Aristotle too: see *Athenian Revolution,* p. 11, for this phrase, although Ober would not apply it to Aristotle.

fered injustice, whether one inflicted and the other has sustained damage" (*NE* 1132a2–7).

Corrective justice determines the mean between the loss sustained by one and the gain received by the other. The equal, in this sense, is a mean between greater and lesser, that is, numerical equality (*Pol.* 1301b30). The practitioners of oligarchic and democratic justice, and most contemporary Aristotle commentators as well, take the equality of the parties, abstractly understood, to guide a particular correction between two parties. But Aristotle does not use abstract equality as his standard for correction. This would be to take a part of justice for the whole. Rather, corrective justice returns the two parties to where they were before one party's "doing" and the other party's "suffering," as Aristotle puts it, rendered them unequal. An activity or "contribution" on the part of one party, in other words, interfered with the other party's activity or capacity to act. To correct inequality requires attending to the parties' *differences* with respect to capacity and contribution, action and habit, in a word, with respect to their virtue. If, in acts of reciprocity, or voluntary acts of exchange, one party's doing or initiative opens the possibility for community, in involuntary acts of exchange one party's doing strikes at the other party's capacity to initiate and thereby threatens the possibility for community. By setting itself the task of undoing that damage, corrective justice recognizes the reciprocative power to initiate (and impede) action and underscores the degree to which prohairetic activity is at the heart of the initiative or doing conducive to community.

If, in these ways, the virtues central to reciprocal justice are at play in distribution and correction as well, Aristotle seems to maintain, in discussing legal justice, not that virtue guides law but that law guides virtue: "The law bids us to do both the acts of a brave man . . . and those of a temperate man . . . and those of a goodtempered man, and similarly with regard to the other virtues and forms of wickedness, commanding some acts and forbidding others" (*NE* 1129b19–24). Indeed, he says, the just man exercises complete virtue when he follows the law (*NE* 1130b23–25). If Aristotle appears to treat law as more fundamental than or prior to virtue in these ways, he also insists that only a "rightly framed law" guides virtuous activity, a "hastily conceived one less well" (*NE* 1129b25). As we will see in chapter 4, rightly framing laws, like distribution, correction, and reciprocity, is a prohairetic activity guided by phronetic judgment. Laws may prescribe certain acts. But these acts, says Aristotle, are only accidentally just, for acting justly or unjustly consists only accidentally in performing particular acts (*NE* 1137a11). The justice of an act is determined not only by the act but also by the disposition from which the action was done. One who acts justly on purpose is a just man (*NE* 1136a4). It is, after all, how an action is performed that determines its justice (*NE* 1137a5–9). Acting justly calls for having the disposition or habit to do what is just, preferring to do what is just, and actually doing it (*NE* 1129a8–10). Acting justly and preferring just acts, in this way, depend on good habit (*NE* 1137a23–24). When laws attend to acts alone, they do not attend to habit and so take an accidental feature to be essential. Properly practiced, which is to say, supplemented by equity, laws are able to attend to "what sort of person the actor has been or is usually" (*Rhet.* 1374b16). They attend, in other words, to a person's habits and actions together, that is, to his virtue. In this way, as we will see in the next chapter, law, no less than justice, is guided by virtue. Justice in all its myriad forms must be guided by virtue. When it is, citizens, in their habits, actions, and judgments—by virtue, in other words, of their virtue—determine their own, and hence their polity's, justice.

CHAPTER FOUR

The Rule of Law

The laws of politics are similar to works, *erga*.
ARISTOTLE, *Nicomachean Ethics*

Aristotle classifies and evaluates regimes in a number of ways, most famously, according to the group in whose interest rulers rule (*Pol.* 1279a25–1279b10). As we saw in chapter 2, he also classifies and evaluates regimes on the basis of their distribution of wealth and poverty (*Pol.* 1279b16–20). Equally important, though less remarked on, is his classification of regimes based on the presence or absence of law and on the presence or absence of just laws.[1] Regimes such as tyrannies, family oligarchies, and democracies ruled by demagogues are, he says, regimes in name only because they are governed not by laws but by decrees, that is, ordinances addressed to particular people under particular circumstances rather than uniformly applied to the whole population (*Pol.* 1292a5–32, 1293a31).[2] He calls deviant regimes that are governed by laws enacted not in the common good but in the interests of the rulers only (*Pol.* 1279a29–33, 1279b6–10, 1282b12–14). On these grounds, Aristotle may rightly be called a proponent of the rule of law.

Many commentators read Aristotle's endorsement of the rule of law to mean that he insists on a sharp distinction between reason and desire, treats the rule of law as reason's victory over desire, and takes the job of the rule of law to be disciplining and ordering the overreaching, *pleonexia*, of desire.[3] According to that reading, the source of law's disciplinary power must lie outside those whose unruly desires it regulates. For those who see Aristotle's rule of law as protecting the political order from the overreaching of the many, this is reason to reject it as

---

1. Whether the laws are written or unwritten would seem not to make a difference (*NE* 1180a35).
2. The difference between decrees, *psephima*, and laws, *nomoi*, insisted on by Aristotle (*NE* 1137b28–29; *Pol.* 1292a36–37), did not become salient until 403–402 B.C.E. See, for discussion, Ostwald, *Nomos and the Beginnings of Athenian Democracy*, p. 2; MacDowell, *Law in Classical Athens*, p. 45.
3. See, e.g., Wolin, "Norm and Form"; Wolin, "Transgression, Equality, and Voice."

antidemocratic.[4] For those who see it as protecting the political order from governmental overreaching, this is what makes the Aristotelian account attractive, a first step en route to a constitutional polity.[5]

In my view, Aristotle's account of the rule of law does not fit easily with such interpretations. Aristotle may call law "reason unaffected by desire" (*Pol.* 1287a33) and refer to law as a compulsive and regulatory mechanism meant to guide behavior (*NE* 1180a22–24), but he also defines law as a rule proceeding from phronesis, which, we saw in chapter 3, combines reason and desire and as powerless to compel and capable only of educating (*Pol.* 1263b41).[6] He locates the authority of law not outside those whose desires it is meant to regulate but, variously, in the person of such superior virtue that he is a law unto himself (*Pol.* 1284a14, 1284b28–34, 1288a25–26), in the few (*Pol.* 1286b5–8), and in the collective wisdom of the many (*Pol.* 1281b1–10, 1282a14–17). Moreover, to Aristotle, laws, *nomoi,* include not only the decisions of magistrates and written legislation enacted by those holding political offices but also religious norms, customs, and equity.[7]

Aristotle's many and, at times, conflicting accounts of law suggest, I think, that the rule of law and the rule of men must be understood together. Rejecting the opposition between reason and desire or lawfulness and power that drives most treatments of the rule of law, this chapter challenges the view of Aristotle's rule of law as "essentially different" from the rule of men.[8] Aristotle worries about the

---

4. Two different sorts of critical analysis operate here: Ober, *Mass and Elite,* takes Aristotle to be privileging laws rather than men; Cohen, *Law, Violence, and Community,* chap. 3, takes Aristotle to be privileging an elite group of men, the magistrates, rather than the many.

5. Shklar, *Political Thought and Political Thinkers,* chap. 2; L. Strauss, *Natural Right and History;* E. Miller, "Prudence and the Rule of Law." For further endorsements of this position, see Hayek, *Road to Serfdom,* and Dworkin, *Law's Empire,* who, for different reasons, take the rule of law as guarding against the exercise of state power. Note that "constitution" in these latter accounts signifies a restraining framework for politics that offers designated procedures for changing laws. As we will see, this is not exactly how "constitution" was understood in fourth- and fifth-century Athens.

6. I agree with Gerald Mara, correspondence with author, April 11, 2000, and Yack, *Problems of a Political Animal,* pp. 182–83, that "reason unaffected by desire" expresses not Aristotle's own understanding of law but his representation of the "legalistic" views of others.

7. MacDowell, *Law in Classical Athens,* p. 44.

8. Ober, *Mass and Elite,* p. 303–4, notes that there existed in fifth-century democratic Athens a tension between the rule of law and the rule of men, but it never bothered the Athenians, who "saw that unrestrained popular will was dangerous, . . . [and also] that excessive constitutional checks and balances along with a fully articulated law code threatened the interests of the masses." Ober claims, erroneously in my view, that Aristotle sees the rule of law and the rule of men as "essentially different" from one another.

114   CHAPTER FOUR

overreaching of citizens and of rulers, to be sure.[9] He worries about the overreaching of the polity as well. In his words, "there may be a want of self-discipline in polities as well as in persons" (*Pol.* 1310a19–20). He also, to be sure, sees the rule of law as moderating excesses in the exercise of sovereign power on the part of rulers, citizens, and the polity as a whole. In his view, however, law, too, must be moderated, for the laws of most cities aim at domination (*Pol.* 1324b7). Accordingly, Aristotle insists that good citizens must, in the name of justice, disobey laws when they are unjust, tantamount to mere force, and that equity, as practiced by the virtuous person, is a necessary corrective to the injustice laws can effect owing to their generality and thus their inability to accommodate the changeability and particularity of human affairs.[10] He thus sees the rule of men as moderating excesses in the sovereignty of law.

Aristotle, in other words, holds both that the rule of law moderates the rule of men and that the rule of men moderates the rule of law. He is able to do so by treating law as an everyday practice of political power, issuing from practical wisdom, that is, the combination of reason and desire.[11] Attenuating in this way the opposition between the rule of law and the rule of men does not erase the tension between the two.[12] It highlights the point, as formulated by Leo Strauss, that "no law, and hence no constitution, can be the fundamental political fact because all laws depend on human beings."[13] This recognition opens the way to an examination of the question of authority at the heart of any discussion of the rule of law. Seeing the rule of law as a question of political authority, in turn, opens the possibility that it is also a matter of political authorship and responsibility—responsibility

9. See *Nicomachean Ethics* V for Aristotle's discussion of justice, framed in response to the problem of overreaching, *pleonexia*.

10. Aristotle is concerned with two problems, that of generality (*NE* V.10), as discussed in chapter 3, and that of the laws' potentially static nature, which, combined with their generality, prevents them from being able to adapt to the changing circumstances that characterize the world of human affairs (see *Pol.* 1269a10–14).

11. See J. Lear, *Aristotle,* chap. 5, who explains that, in Aristotle's view, desire is not to be controlled by reason when determining what is to be done. It is right desire in conjunction with true reason that moves to action.

By reading Aristotle's account of the rule of law as a way of life, I fit my analysis with those of Yack, *Problems of a Political Animal,* chap. 6, and Shklar, *Political Thought and Political Thinkers,* p. 22. I draw on the idea of a practice found in MacIntyre, *After Virtue,* p. 187, and Wittgenstein, *Philosophical Investigations,* secs. 143–242.

12. This tension is elegantly explored in the context of Plato's *Statesman* in Lane, *Method and Politics in Plato's* Statesman, pp. 150–53.

13. L. Strauss, *Natural Right and History,* p. 136.

to, and of, both a constitution and a people.[14] The rule of law, so understood, may be a coercive and disciplinary force, but it is also a marker of the congruence between a polity's constitution and its citizenry and a hallmark of justice or fairness. If chapters 1 and 3 attended primarily to the coercive aspects of law and its necessary subordination to the virtue of justice, this chapter continues that line of inquiry while also exploring the equally important embeddedness of law in the acquiescence and customary practices of citizens. My aim is to produce an account of law, as the rule of men, that need not always stand opposed to equity and that can guide and inform the practices of justice even as it emerges from them.

The Laws of Citizens

> There are two parts of good government; one is the actual obedience of citizens to the laws, the other part is the goodness of the laws which they obey.
>
> ARISTOTLE, *Politics*

Aristotle maintains that citizens must have good laws and also that citizens must be habituated to abide by those laws (*Pol.* 1310a14–17). Hence, for many Aristotle commentators, as for contemporary legal theorists more generally, the rule of law represents a general disposition to follow rules.[15] This interpretation is understandable. Without such a disposition, the force of law and the stability of the constitution, as the way of life of the people in a regime (*Pol.* 1295a41–b1), would always be in question. It is certainly true that, to Aristotle, the rule of law represents and requires a habit of obedience on the part of citizens. It is for this reason that he maintains that laws should be changed only rarely. As may be seen in his treatment of the controversial figure of Theramenes in his *Constitution of Athens* (*AP*), however, the rule of law also depends on sometimes withholding that obedience.[16]

14. See Pitkin, "Idea of a Constitution."

15. As Yack puts it: "[T]he rule of law represents for Aristotle a moral disposition . . . to follow and apply general rules" (*Problems of a Political Animal,* 201). Yack attributes this disposition to citizens (196) and to rulers (200). He writes that these citizens and rulers are disposed to "follow" general rules (197, 200, 203, 206, 208), that they are disposed to "follow and apply" general rules (201), and that they are disposed to "follow and govern by means of" general rules (196). These inconsistencies are apparent only: in fact, they disclose the breadth of Aristotle's understanding of the rule of law: it is a moral disposition to follow, apply, and govern in accordance with general rules on the part of both citizens and rulers. See also Austin, *Province of Jurisprudence Determined;* Bentham, *Introduction to the Principles of Morals;* Kelsen, *General Theory of Law and State;* Hart, *Concept of Law.*

16. There is some controversy about the authorship of this text. For convincing evidence that the author is Aristotle, see Mara, "Culture of Democracy," pp. 310–11; Keaney, *Composi-*

116   CHAPTER FOUR

Aristotle describes Theramenes as playing an important role in Athens's constitutional development during a period of political turmoil (*AP* 28.5) in the later years of the Peloponnesian War.[17] During this period, between 411 and 402 B.C.E., Athens underwent a series of rapid regime changes, from democracy to oligarchy to democracy to oligarchy and finally back to democracy again.[18] Aristotle recounts that Theramenes supported Athens as both oligarchy and democracy. Consistent with his treatment of good citizenship—which he associates with obedience to the laws of a regime—Aristotle praises Theramenes for his loyalty to each regime. Theramenes also, however, had a hand in changing Athens twice from democracy to oligarchy and in moderating the first oligarchy (the Four Hundred), although he was executed for his attempts to moderate the second (the Thirty). Commending him not only for abiding by the law, Aristotle maintains that he "worked for the good of any established government so long as it did not transgress the laws, and in this way showed that he was able to participate in governing under any kind of political setup, which is what a good citizen should do." Stressing that Theramenes would "rather incur enmity and hatred than yield to lawlessness" (*AP* 28.5), Aristotle saves his highest commendation for Theramenes' refusal to follow, and active discouragement of, Athens's unlawful policies.

This suggests that Theramenes is a model citizen to Aristotle not simply because Theramenes possessed a disposition to follow general rules. If this were the case, Aristotle would not have commended his refusal to follow Athenian policies. Aristotle praises him because he supported only lawful or just policies. Aristotle's commentary on Theramenes underscores two related points. The first is that a disposition to follow rules may be actualized or withheld. The second is that what guides that actualization or withholding is citizen judgment. In Aristotle's view, then, the rule of law depends not only on a habit of obedience but also on active disobedience when citizen judgment determines that the polity's policies are unjust. It is not any and all citizen judgment that is determinative of lawfulness, however. Knowing how and when to disobey the laws of one's regime depends on good

---

tion of Aristotle's Athenaion Politeia; Day and Chambers, *Aristotle's History of Athenian Democracy,* chap. 1.

17. There is a heated debate in the literature about Theramenes and about Aristotle's treatment of him. For discussion, see Frank and Monoson, "Aristotle's Theramenes at Athens."

18. During this same period the laws of Solon were redacted and codified in order to determine which of them would remain in force after 402: MacDowell, *Law in Classical Athens,* pp. 46, 47, 53.

judgment, which Aristotle sees as key in discerning good laws (*NE* 1181a15–25). Aristotle attends to Theramenes' withholding or actualization of his disposition to follow rules because, in Aristotle's view, he was "outstanding in intelligence and judgment" (*AP* 32.2). It is for his phronetic judgment, in other words, that Aristotle distinguishes him as a model citizen.

Aristotle's commendation of Theramenes sets Aristotle's treatment of law apart from the dominant paradigms of the rule of law in contemporary legal and political philosophy: positivism and natural law theory. For advocates of legal positivism, the authority of laws and their legitimacy lie in their having been validly enacted by those in power.[19] For advocates of natural law theory, in contrast, the authority of laws and their legitimacy lie in their conformity with some transcendent standard beyond the practices of politics.[20] Aristotle's approval of Theramenes' refusal to support Athens's lawless regimes shows that, for Aristotle, unlike for legal positivists, justice is the measure of a regime's laws, not the other way around. This is not to say that Aristotle endorses a natural law paradigm, however, for the source of justice is not a transcendent and apolitical moral code. Instead, as we just saw, it is the good judgment of citizens that decides which laws to follow and thereby produces and preserves the rule of law.

Judgment is a political practice. In Aristotle's political philosophy, it has an ethical dimension as well, for good judgment is guided by practical wisdom and preserved by moral virtue, specifically the virtue of moderation (*NE* 1140b14). We have seen already in previous chapters that Aristotle's ethical philosophy links good judgment as a mode of practical wisdom and moral virtue. Most accounts of the rule of law, however, insulate law from the requirement of good judgment and from practical wisdom and moral virtue as well. Consisting of general principles, equally applied, laws, these accounts argue, must be prospective and knowable and not in contradiction with other provisions.[21] The rule of law, thus conceived preeminently in terms of due process and equal treatment, is meant precisely to preempt individual judgment and to be blind to differences in virtue.

On these grounds, indeed, some scholars distinguish the practice of judging from the practice of law. Recognizing the close affiliation between Aristotle's

19. See, e.g., Austin, *Province of Jurisprudence Determined;* Bentham, *Introduction to the Principles of Morals;* Kelsen, *General Theory of Law and State;* Hart, *Concept of Law.*

20. Aquinas, *Summa Theologica,* Questions 90–97; Finnis, *Natural Law and Natural Rights.*

21. For discussion of the Greek appreciation of this account of law, see Cohen, *Law, Violence, and Community,* pp. 56–57. For a contemporary analogue, see Fuller, *Morality of Law.*

analyses of judging and law—he offers no separation-of-powers doctrine as between legislation and adjudication and indeed defines citizenship as sharing in ruling *and* judging (*Pol.* 1275a23)—Bernard Yack, for example, nonetheless distinguishes the two based on the play of practical wisdom in each.[22] Practical wisdom, he says, is alive in adjudication but "dead" in law: it may be a source of law, but in "law . . . reason is dead, an already determined judgment applied to future unknown circumstances."[23] This captures well enough an intuitive distinction between legislation and adjudication, between laws that are "on the books" and thereby reified ("dead") and decisions in the courts that require the presence of a judge, whom, as we saw, Aristotle calls "living justice" (*NE* 1132a23). To call reason in legislation dead, however, presupposes that the laws on the books somehow apply themselves to particular circumstances. When legislation is understood instead as in need of evaluation and interpretation for its application by lawgivers no less than by judges, it, like adjudication, requires a lively practical wisdom and good judgment.

Scholars do not only insulate law from good judgment and practical wisdom. They insulate it from moral virtue as well. Yack, for example, characterizes Aristotle's classification of regimes in terms of lawfulness as a "move from virtue to lawfulness."[24] This is not surprising given his desire to reconcile Aristotle's rule of law with popular sovereignty for, like others who share this commitment, he takes popular sovereignty and virtue to be antithetical.[25] To safeguard popular sovereignty from the impact of differential virtue via the equal treatment promised by law, Yack elevates law over judgment. With the same end—the protection of popular sovereignty—in view, it was the practice of fifth-century Athens's radical democrats to treat not law but judgment as the supreme authority.[26] If they emphasized the role of judgment in determining law, their understanding of judgment differed from that of Aristotle. For radical democrats, judgment was determined by aggregating the votes of citizens in the assembly. "Laws," accordingly, mostly took the form of decrees passed by the assembly for specific actions, which, as noted, Aristotle does not consider to be laws at all. Judgment, understood as ma-

22. Yack, *Problems of a Political Animal*, p. 189.

23. Ibid., pp. 180, 184, 205.

24. Ibid., p. 196.

25. This assumption is also at the root of Ober's and Cohen's assessments of Aristotle's rule of law as antidemocratic.

26. For discussion, see Ober, *Mass and Elite*, p. 301; Allen, *World of Prometheus*, pp. 175–83. The Stranger in Plato's *Statesman* subordinates law to judgment as well but to judgment not of the people but of the political expert. I return to this point below.

joritarian vote aggregation, is not the proper measure of law for Aristotle. As we have seen, the proper measure is, rather, good judgment, informed by practical wisdom and moral virtue.

Insisting, in these ways, on the dependence of laws on men, Aristotle reconciles popular sovereignty with the rule of law by means of the dependence of both on virtue. Before exploring how he is able to effect this reconciliation, consider first two typical interpretations of his rule of law that defend the more common view that virtue has no place in a democratic account of the rule of law. Focusing on the institutions of adjudication that he claims Aristotle sets up to guard the rule of law, David Cohen argues that Aristotle sharply limits the power of popular deliberative bodies by entrusting magistrates with broad disciplinary authority to maintain civic virtue.[27] By insisting that the authority of law belongs not to the people but to a body of magistrates and giving these magistrates the power to interfere in the lives of the people by scrutinizing their morality, Aristotle produces, Cohen claims, a "censorial" model of the rule of law that justifies precisely the overreaching most moderns take the rule of law to guard against.[28] "Seen from the standpoint of his treatment of the rule of law," writes Cohen, "Aristotle appears as far more hostile to democratic principles than is often thought to be the case."[29] Focusing not on institutions but on the superior capacity of the few for practical wisdom and virtue, Eugene Miller, like Cohen, reads Aristotle's rule of law to be irreconcilable with popular sovereignty. According to Miller's reading, Aristotle rightly celebrates monarchy and aristocracy above all other regimes because, by giving the "freest possible reign" to practical wisdom guided by moral virtue, these regimes vest the rule of law in the virtuous one or few.[30]

If Yack, Cohen, and Miller are correct, then reading Aristotle's rule of law as hospitable to popular sovereignty requires pushing to one side the cornerstones of his ethical philosophy. But are they? The force of Cohen's interpretation depends on the institutional arrangements that give rise to and maintain the offices of the magistrates and on the standard the magistrates use to determine what law de-

27. Cohen, *Law, Violence, and Community,* p. 35.

28. Aristotle's understanding of human nature is, according to Cohen, largely responsible for his account of the rule of law. Without law and guardians of law to impose order and to control that element of human nature which tends toward "savagery" the appetitive aspect of that nature will reduce human beings to "anarchy": *Law, Violence, and Community,* p. 37. For a different account of Aristotle's understanding of human nature, see chapter 1.

29. Cohen, *Law, Violence, and Community,* p. 43.

30. E. Miller, "Prudence and the Rule of Law," pp. 193–206.

mands in any particular case. These go together. Aristotle defines citizenship as the sharing in ruling and adjudicating. Being a magistrate, then, is a practice of citizenship. If the office of the magistrate is occupied by citizens who rule and are ruled in turn, then those holding office today will tomorrow be citizens regulated by those next in office. Magistrates are, by virtue of this system of rotation, accountable to the citizenry, not, as Cohen suggests, set apart from them.[31] The sort of accountability generated by rotational rule comes up repeatedly in Aristotle's political philosophy, for being a good magistrate involves taking into account what it would mean to be subject to the judgment of another (*Pol.* 1279a11–13), thus exhibiting what Hannah Arendt called an "enlarged mentality."[32] Magistrates are accountable to the citizenry in another way as well. Their job is, in Cohen's words, to "institutionaliz[e] the community's common judgments about good and bad, just and unjust."[33] The morality a magistrate enforces, in other words, is that of the community. Laws may be required, as Cohen says, "to make the natural community into a well-ordered one as well," but they are as much a product of the common sense of the community as they are a disciplinary power over and against it.[34]

If the criticism of Aristotelian rule of law as antidemocratic on institutional grounds is open to challenge, what is to be made of the claim that once the virtue of practical wisdom is added to the mix, Aristotelian rule of law cannot but be

31. See Ober, *Mass and Elite,* pp. 86–91, who, like Cohen, reads Aristotle's account of the rule of law as a disciplinary response to fifth-century Athenian democracy. He nonetheless argues that there is, in general, nothing about such positions as magistracies that makes them a priori antidemocratic because magistrates would likely align themselves in their applications of the law with the people to maintain their constituency. A similar intuition is at play when Lani Guinier, *Tyranny of the Majority,* chap. 1, speaks of the democratic constraints that operate when systems of rotation are in place.

32. Arendt, *Lectures on Kant's Political Philosophy,* p. 43: "To think with an enlarged mentality means that one trains one's imagination to go visiting." For Arendt, drawing on Kant, this involves an impartiality that I called into question in chapter 3. Nonetheless, for Arendt and for Kant, as for Aristotle, the proper practice of judgment calls for putting oneself in the place of another and also recognizing the limitations on one's capacities to do so.

To the degree to which the magistrates are constrained by their audience not simply because the people elect them from time to time but also insofar as in each particular judgment they are accountable to their deliberative audience, the institution of the magistrates turns out to be more democratic than is usually recognized. For an exploration of this theme, see Allen, "Democratic Theory of Judgment."

33. Cohen, *Law, Violence, and Community,* pp. 37–38.

34. "When we find that the usual Athenian word for a law was *thesmos* in the seventh and sixth centuries but *nomos* in the fifth and fourth, that is significant. It marks the change to a democratic attitude, and implies that the validity of a law depends rather on its acceptance by the community than on the power of a ruler." MacDowell, *Law in Classical Athens,* p. 44.

undemocratic? Returning briefly to Aristotle's treatments of practical wisdom and virtue, discussed at greater length in chapters 1 and 3, I offer next a reading of Aristotle's rule of law that, with Yack, takes it to be an everyday practice belonging to citizen-rulers, with Miller, takes it to be a practice involving practical wisdom and moral virtue, and, with Cohen, takes it to be integrally bound up with the practices and institutions of judging. Unlike all three, however, I insist that these elements are interconnected. It is by judging what is the right thing to do, using phronetic judgment informed by virtue, that citizens make and unmake the rule of law that guides their polity.

As we saw in chapter 3, practical wisdom, *phronesis,* in its partiality, brings together the features that most accounts of Aristotle's rule of law set apart: reason and desire. Determined not by appetite alone, nor by the thought of an end for which means must then be found, for "we deliberate not about ends, but about what contributes to those ends" (*NE* 1112b11, trans. modified), practical wisdom is, rather, true habit in action in accordance with right desire in relation to what is good for human beings (*NE* 1139a25, 1140b21).[35] It concerns what makes a life good, for the particular person as for people in general (*NE* 1140a26–28), and calls specifically for "right discrimination of the equitable," that is, for good judgment (*NE* 1143a24). Practical wisdom is an intellectual virtue, Aristotle says, but it is distinct from the other intellectual virtues. Reason plays a role in guiding good judgment, but practical wisdom is not the same as science, *episteme,* in which reason knows a set of universal and invariable rules (*NE* VI.3). Reason and desire combine to originate action in art as well as in practical wisdom, but practical wisdom is not the same as art, which involves production in accordance with a fixed design (*NE* VI.4). Whereas the ends of action in art and the objects of knowledge in science are determined by something other than the practices of art and science themselves, the same is not true for practical wisdom, for which good action is its own end (*NE* 1140b6), and the rule guiding the person with practical wisdom is given to the agent by the agent himself. What is to be done is determined in this way from the "inside out."[36]

What gives practical wisdom's good judgment its bearing? Properly discerning the particulars of a situation, Aristotle says, depends on moral character. The

35. The modified translation belongs to Nussbaum, *Fragility of Goodness,* p. 297, who, along with Sherman, *Fabric of Character,* pp. 70–71, persuasively distinguishes Aristotle's formulation of practical wisdom from narrowly consequentialist or instrumental ones.

36. I take this formulation from McDowell, "Virtue and Reason," p. 331. See also Sherman, *Fabric of Character,* p. 2, for the nonimpartiality of phronesis.

choice I make about what is to be done—my judgment—is, in this sense, an embedded choice, one determined by my habits, which reflect who I have been and therefore who I am. "It is evident," says Aristotle, "that it is impossible to be practically wise without being good" (*NE* 1144a36). As we have seen, some commentators conclude, on the basis of Aristotle's account of practical wisdom and virtue, that the political order he endorses must be exclusionary and antidemocratic. There is plenty of evidence in Aristotle's writings to support this conclusion: he excludes from citizenship women and slaves on the basis of their inferior practical wisdom. He excludes artisans and laborers on the ground that what they do interferes with the cultivation of the virtues necessary for citizenship.

There is, however, nothing intrinsic to Aristotle's understanding of practical wisdom to support these exclusions. He does say that because we think that capacities for good judgment are affected by age, this "implies that nature is the cause" of some being more practically wise than others. As he explains later in the same passage, this means that it is "because experience has given them the eye that they see aright" (*NE* 1143b6–15). Nature, informed by experience or, as I argued in chapter 1, by one's past and present actions and habits and not something fixed or necessary, is the key to the practice of practical wisdom: "Each man judges well the things he knows, and of these he is a good judge" (*NE* 1094b30).

If practical wisdom does not, in principle, support the political exclusions with which it is often associated, neither does moral virtue, to which Aristotle insists practical wisdom is wedded. Recall that, to Aristotle, virtue is constituted by dynamically and reflexively related habits and actions. Acting well depends on good habits, and these are formed by acting well. There is also a reciprocal and dynamic relationship between practical wisdom and virtue: practical wisdom depends on virtue insofar as properly discriminating what is to be done depends on being properly habituated, and virtue depends on practical wisdom insofar as acting well depends on properly discriminating what is to be done, which is to say, on good judgment. As we have seen repeatedly, Aristotelian virtue provides no external standard or criterion against which to measure people. It is also not an inherent or fixed trait that people have or lack. Virtue, specifically as it informs prohairetic activity, sets a standard, to be sure, but it is an internal standard, one that, like Aristotle's understanding of "good," whose embodiment, he claims, varies from case to case, is best expressed in imprecise terms and is best understood analogically (*NE* I.6). As a product of habit-producing actions and action-altering habits, virtue, so understood, is a mode of being by way of prohairetic activity that can be "very generally shared" (*NE* 1099b18; *AP* 36.2). There will always be those who choose to act badly (*NE* III.5), but each of us also has the potential to act well.

Acting in accordance with practical wisdom is not acting for some predetermined end, and it is not following a predetermined rule. The rule, we have seen, is, rather, internal to the action. It is the same with the practice of virtue: when I act well, I do so because my own habits so dispose me to act. Virtue and practical wisdom are both modes of activity whose origin and authority lie in themselves. The self-sovereignty associated with these practices, I argued in chapter 1, is the self-sovereignty characteristic of a chastened understanding of democracy, one whose members have made themselves virtuous citizens. As I argue next, the self-sovereignty associated with these practices of virtue is also that which is characteristic of a chastened conception of the rule of law, one that, owing to the enlarged role for the participation of those who follow their own rule, is, at the same time, the rule of men.

To see how Aristotle's appreciation of virtue recasts the relation between the rule of law and the rule of men, consider the habits and actions that constitute virtue. Each generates the other. Each also limits the other. And they are always in flux. Although they depend on one another, habits and actions do not do the same work in the soul. Habits are in a sense "always already" (but only in a sense because, as we have seen, habits are altered by actions and, therefore, they too are changeable). They offer stability over time and generate rule-governed, because habitual, behavior. Practical wisdom depends on habit. Law, according to Aristotle, does too. It "has no power to command obedience except that of habit, which can only be given by time" (*Pol.* 1269a20). This is why, Aristotle explains, laws should be changed rarely.[37] The link between law and habit means that "a readiness to change from old to new laws enfeebles the power of the law" (*Pol.* 1269a22–23). If law depends on the force of habit, it depends also on activity: "It is impossible that all things should be precisely set down in writing; for enactments must be universal, but actions are concerned with particulars" (*Pol.* 1269a10). Law may depend on a moral disposition but it is not fully governed by that disposition. It depends as well on the "not-yet" of habits, namely, as Aristotle's treatment of Theramenes makes plain, actions. Actions either reinforce the habits that gave rise to them or

---

37. It is also why readers tend to conflate the rule of law with a habit of obedience only. Aristotle's position that laws should be changed rarely is consistent with the earlier Athenian commitment to the *graphe paranomon*. See Boegehold, "Resistance to Change"; Hansen, *Sovereignty of the People's Court*.

124 CHAPTER FOUR

resist these habits, altering them in the process. "Hence we infer," says Aristotle, "that sometimes and in certain circumstances laws should be changed" (*Pol.* 1269a14).

The Stranger in Plato's *Statesman* puts the problem of law forcefully: "Law could never accurately embrace what is best and most just for all at the same time, and so prescribe what is best. For the dissimilarities between human beings and their actions, and the fact that practically nothing in human affairs ever remains stable, prevent any sort of expertise whatsoever from making any simple decision in any sphere that covers all cases and will last for all time" (294b).[38] The Stranger uses this limitation of law to argue for subordinating law to the judgment of the political expert or statesman. In contrast, Aristotle locates the authority of law in the good judgment of practically wise citizens. Treating law as an everyday practice of good citizenship, Aristotle in this way puts forward a more dynamic conception of law.

To treat law as an everyday practice of good citizenship is not to elide Aristotle's distinction between *politike,* political wisdom, which belongs to rulers, and *phronesis,* practical wisdom, which belongs to citizens. Politike and phronesis, Aristotle maintains, have the same disposition, but they have a different being (*NE* 1141b24). They have the same disposition because the skills and virtues a person needs to promote his own well-being are the same as those a good ruler needs to promote the well-being of a polity. They have a different being insofar as politike, and the activities of legislation, or *nomothetike,* that Aristotle associates with it, are concerned with the good of a people and a polity as a whole (*NE* 1094a29–b12), whereas phronesis primarily concerns a person's own good, although, as we saw in chapter 3, that often involves attending to the proper treatment of particular others, as in the practice of reciprocal justice and the institutions of adjudication more generally that Aristotle treats as prohairetic activities. Politike, in other words, is phronesis applied to the affairs of the city. Because it is not usually the case that citizens, as part of their everyday practices of citizenship, deliberate about the good of their polity as a whole, politike, unlike phronesis, is an everyday practice of citizenship only when and insofar as citizens are also statesmen, as when they vote on a city-wide policy or make decisions with respect to the fundamental terms of their cooperation. Aristotelian politike is, nonetheless, distinct from the sort of expertise that Plato's Stranger has in mind, for it emerges not from

---

38. This is translated by C. J. Rowe in *Plato: Complete Works,* and discussed in Lane, *Method and Politics in Plato's* Statesman, pp. 150 ff.

a privileged source but from the practices of good citizenship. Consider Theramenes again. Aristotle calls him a model citizen and also an exemplary statesman (*AP* 28.5). He is thus a follower of the law and also a "maker and adjudicator of the law," using his phronesis to practice politike in order to discourage Athens's lawlessness and thereby to correct Athens's unlawfulness from within the practice of law itself.[39]

The dynamic and reflexive relation between the habits and actions that constitute virtue maps the relation between following the law and either making or unmaking it. Just as habits govern actions but do not and cannot fully determine them, so too do laws govern actions even as laws need sometimes to be changed by, and in order to accommodate, those actions.[40] This suggests that laws do not and cannot depend on habit alone. They must depend on activity as well. The result, as we saw in the case of Theramenes, is that citizens are subjects of law in two senses: they are subject to the laws and they are the laws' authors. They are governed by law even as they may modify it by activity. Following the laws (or not) matters: when laws are not followed, the activity of withholding the disposition to follow laws can unmake the laws; when the laws are followed, the disposition to follow, now actualized, remakes the laws. Rule-following is also rule-making.[41] Theramenes was executed, Aristotle reports, shortly after the Thirty began to worry that "he might become a leader of the people, *prostates,* and overthrow their regime" (*AP* 36.1).[42] Aristotle's commentary on Theramenes ends here, and the lessons he appears to want to impart to his readers are twofold: first, Theramenes was executed because the Thirty were concerned that others would follow in his footsteps and refuse to support the unjust laws of their regime, thereby unmaking it; second, as Theramenes was crushed so was the lawfulness that guided his political efforts.

Understanding the rule of law as also and at the same time the rule of men helps to underscore the differences between Aristotle's appreciation of law and the paradigms that dominate contemporary thinking. Aristotle's rule of law has neither the predictability of positivism nor the moralism of natural law accounts. Under-

39. I take this phrase from Kraut, *Aristotle: Political Philosophy,* p. 107.

40. Aristotle makes the same point in *Nicomachean Ethics* V when he insists that equity, a matter of human judgment, is necessary to correct for law's inability to accommodate the particularities of human activity owing to law's generality (*NE* 1137b13–25).

41. For similar accounts of the rule of law, see Radin, "Reconsidering the Rule of Law," pp. 807–17; Michelman, "Law's Republic." See also Cover, "Nomos and Narrative."

42. For discussion of *prostates,* see Rhodes, *Commentary on the Aristotelian* Athenaion Politeia, pp. 447, 97.

126 CHAPTER FOUR

standing the rule of law as a practice of phronesis and politike explains why Aristotle's rule of law is reducible to neither paradigm. Not to the first because to understand the rule of law as given by positive laws produced by those in power would be to understand it as a product of art rather than as an activity of phronesis and politike.[43] And not to the second because to understand the rule of law as a set of universal and invariable axioms—given by natural law or natural justice or any order that lies beyond the human and variable one—would be to treat it as the subject matter of science rather than as an activity of phronesis and politike.[44] If Aristotle's rule of law does not offer the predictability of positivism, it nonetheless guides and compels behavior. If it is a product of the habits, actions, and good judgment of citizens, it is not all and only a product of these. As I show next, the source of justice and the rule of law is also the polity's *politeia*, or constitution.

The Laws of Polities

Men should not think it slavery to live according to the
rule of the constitution; for it is their salvation.
ARISTOTLE, *Politics*

"Laws are, and ought to be, framed with a view to the constitution," Aristotle states (*Pol.* 1289a13–17, 1282b10–11).[45] This is true of regimes whose laws are oriented to the common good and of those whose laws favor the interests of the rulers. Each of these regimes, better and worse (although not the extreme oligarchies and democracies or tyrannies that Aristotle treats as constitutions in name only), has a particular constitution that originally formed it and that continues to preserve it (*Pol.* 1337a14–16). The constitution is, in this way, the measure of a regime's laws. In *Politics* II, where Aristotle's evaluation of laws from the standpoint of constitution is most evident, he assesses regimes by subjecting them to two tests: he looks at the fit between the regime's laws and its constitution, and he compares the varying con-

43. The positive legislation of a regime is indeed the product of art, specifically the art of politics, but this legislation, as we will see below, is not the same as the rule of law or the just nomoi, which are the measure of the regime's legislation.

44. Aristotle's discussion of natural justice in *Nicomachean Ethics* V shows how far it is from accounts of natural law. For discussion, see Wormuth, "Aristotle on Law"; Yack, "Natural Right."

45. Richard Bodéüs calls this the "principle of the constitutionality of the laws" and maintains that "when called on to judge the qualities of a political regime, [Aristotle] tended to place the accent, first and foremost, on the conformity of its laws with the orientation of its constitution." See "Law and the Regime in Aristotle," p. 239.

stitutions to the best constitution.[46] In other words, he evaluates them in their own terms and against a common standard.

What might Aristotle have in mind when he invokes the "constitution" as the standard by which to measure a regime's laws? He defines the constitution as that which determines both a polity's arrangement of offices and its end, or *telos* (*Pol.* 1278b8–10). He identifies a polity's constitution with its government, *politeuma* (*Pol.* 1279a25–27), that which comprises the offices of the polity and thus its collective authority.[47] We may be inclined to read his definitions of constitution in a positivist or descriptive manner as saying that the constitution of a polity *is* its arrangement of offices. However, Aristotle's use of "constitution" as a critical standard in assessing the existing laws of varying regimes demonstrates that this would be a mistake. Consider his assessment of the laws of Sparta. He criticizes the laxity of Sparta's laws regarding women (*Pol.* 1269b19–22) and Sparta's inadequate regulation of property (*Pol.* 1270a16). He criticizes laws that encourage births without taking into account the poverty this can bring to families (*Pol.* 1270b1–7) and those that open the offices of the ephorate to all, because when poorer people hold these offices, he maintains, there is a greater susceptibility to bribery and corruption (*Pol.* 1270b7–10). He thinks little of the laws that regulate common meals in such a manner that not all citizens are guaranteed sustenance (*Pol.* 1271a30–35). Insofar as Sparta's existing laws are too democratic (the ephorate, births) or too oligarchic (inadequate regulation of property and women, common meals) they are bad, he explains, because they "defeat the intention, *prohairesis,* of the constitution" (*Pol.* 1269b14) or promote its "deterioration" (*Pol.* 1270b17).[48] Aristotle, in a word, judges Sparta's existing laws to be unconstitutional. This is not to say that Sparta's laws have not been enacted by the proper authority but, rather, that, even if properly enacted, they are bad for Sparta. A parallel may be noted between Aristotle's treatment of laws, as explored in the first section of this chapter, and his treatment of constitution: although there are positivist versions of each, neither laws nor constitutions are, for Aristotle, explicable in purely positivist terms.

Aristotle's criticism of Sparta's existing laws appears to suggest what would be constitutional laws for Sparta: they would be neither too democratic nor too oligarchic but oriented to a mixed, that is, a democratic-oligarchic, constitution.

46. Ibid., pp. 239–40.

47. F. Miller, *Nature, Justice, and Rights,* pp. 149–50.

48. Aristotle's discussion of Carthage proceeds in a similar fashion, with his harshest criticism directed at legislation that inclines the polity toward oligarchy (*Pol.* 1273a5–6, 1273a25–38).

128   CHAPTER FOUR

Maintaining that "there is a true union of oligarchy and democracy when the same state may be termed either a democracy or an oligarchy" (*Pol.* 1294b14–15), Aristotle points to the Spartan constitution as a model for this sort of union (*Pol.* 1294b20–35, 1265b34–1266a1). Laws that would thus be consistent with Sparta's constitution would also preserve it. There is a bidirectional relationship between constitution and law: constitutions guide laws, and laws preserve constitutions. That this is so is clear from Aristotle's claim, mentioned above, that where laws do not rule, there is no constitution. Tyrannies, family oligarchies, and demagogic democracies—unmixed forms of deviant constitutions—ruled not by law but by decrees, are, he insists, constitutions in name only (*Pol.* 1292a32). This means that laws are both the cause and effect of a polity.

Sparta's existing laws are bad, in Aristotle's judgment, because they do not conform to its constitution. Sparta thus fails his first test for evaluating regimes in *Politics* II. It also fails his second test. He maintains that Sparta's constitution compares badly with the best constitution because, although Sparta's includes virtue or excellence (*Pol.* 1293b16), it "has regard to one part of excellence only—the excellence of the soldier, which gives victory in war" (*Pol.* 1271b2–4).[49] Like most of the constitutions of the ancient world, including those of the Cretans, the Thracians, the Persians, the Scythians, the Celts, the Carthaginians, the Macedonians, and the Iberians (*Pol.* 1324b8–22), it overemphasizes warlike virtue. In doing so, Sparta's constitution orients the spirit, or *thumos,* of its citizens (the source of the love of freedom and the power of command necessary for a free political life [*Pol.* 1328a1–8]) toward conquest and domination and, thereby, paradoxically, toward unfreedom (*Pol.* 1333b11–1334a10).[50] This point parallels the one Aristotle makes about the dangers of the practice of mastery in the home, discussed in chapter 1. Political conquest, like domestic conquest, produces unfreedom for its subjects, for those who practice it no less than for those over whom it is exercised.

Aristotle devotes much space in the *Politics* to criticizing Sparta's constitution not only because Sparta's error is so prevalent in the ancient world but also because the quest for conquest characteristic of Sparta has become all too present in Athens, the polity of primary concern to him. This was not always the case. Pericles' speeches (advocating war against Sparta in 432–31 B.C.E., eulogizing the war dead after the first campaign in 431–30, and just before he dies in 430 of the plague

---

49. For a terrific account of Aristotle's criticisms of this virtue, see Salkever, "Women, Soldiers, Citizens," pp. 172 ff. See also Laix, "Aristotle's Conception of the Spartan Constitution."

50. For discussion, see chapter 1.

that has devastated Athens) also celebrate warlike virtue. They do so, however, not for the purpose of expanding Athens's empire and conquering and enslaving others. Pericles argues instead that the Athenians should wage war only for the purposes of self-defense and to prevent Athenian enslavement.[51] Advocating warlike virtue, but not for the sake of conquest, Pericles in many ways anticipates Aristotle, who also endorses war as a necessity, that is, to protect against enslavement, preserve good government (*Pol.* 1333b39–1334a2), and, more generally, as a means to the end of peace (*Pol.* 1333a34–36).[52] If during his lifetime Pericles was more or less successful in his attempts to moderate Athens's war effort, after his death, Athenian military strategy changed. By the time of the Melian Dialogue in 416, for example, and on through the constitutional crises experienced by Theramenes in the later years of the Peloponnesian War, Athens's strategy had become entirely geared to the empire-building and conquest Pericles had decried.[53] By 411, both abroad and at home, justice and lawfulness in Athens had become matters of might and domination, driven by the desire for conquest.

Aristotle analogizes the quest for conquest characteristic of the Spartan constitution to the quest for material gain he describes in *Politics* I. Both he represents as problems of overreaching, *pleonexia*. In his words, "although [the Spartans] truly think that the goods for which men contend are to be acquired by excellence rather than by vice, they err in supposing that these goods are to be preferred to the ex-

51. See *Landmark Thucydides,* secs. 1.141, 1.144, 2.61, 2.63 (advocating war to prevent Athens's enslavement to Sparta, in self-defense, not as a preemptive strike, calling this a matter of justice, and describing war as "a necessity"); sec. 2.39 (underscoring the differences between Athens and Sparta in military matters); secs. 2.39–41 (denouncing pleonexia).

52. Although I agree with Salkever, "Women, Soldiers, Citizens," that there is in Pericles "the polarized opposition of male, war, and polis, on the one hand and female, peace, and family on the other" (p. 168) and that this presupposes and reinscribes an opposition of polis to oikos that Aristotle rejects (pp. 166–69, 179), I do not think that Pericles epitomizes the pleonexia that can accompany warlike virtue that Aristotle is condemning. This is because, as noted in footnote 51, above, Pericles does not advocate war with the aim of mastery, conquest, and gain.

53. In 416 Athens tried to convince the Melians to surrender into slavery without bloodshed. The Melians refused, offering neutrality instead. The Athenians rejected this option, arguing that "the strong do what they can and the weak suffer as they must" (5.89). Athens invaded Melos and conquered the island, put all the men to death, and sold the women and children into slavery. For the full account see *Landmark Thucydides,* secs. 5.85–116. For the position that this "realism" pervades Thucydides' entire account of the war, see Ste. Croix, *Origins of the Peloponnesian War,* pp. 5–34; Walzer, *Just and Unjust Wars,* chap. 1. *Contra* Mendelsohn, "Theatres of War."

cellence which gains them" (*Pol.* 1271b9–12, 1333b5, 1334b2–5). Curbing constitutional pleonexia of this sort calls for the same remedy required to curb individual overreaching in relation to external goods, namely, as we saw in chapter 2, self-regulation on the part of the citizens of a polity. Self-regulation depends on the recognition that gain is not an end in itself but must, rather, be subordinated to that which is its own end: acting well, or the practice of virtue. The key to self-regulation is, specifically, the virtue of moderation, learned first in the home in the context of one's relations with family and property.[54] As Stephen Salkever notes, that Aristotle understands Sparta's defects in terms of a deficit of moderation is plain from his criticisms of Sparta's existing laws regarding women and property.[55]

To Aristotle, however, the resources for moderating overreaching are not only ethical. Aristotle judges Sparta's laws to be bad not only because they show a deficit of moderation, understood as a domestic virtue, but also because they are not in conformity with Sparta's constitution, and he judges Sparta's constitution to be bad because it is not in conformity with the best constitution. This means that absent from Sparta are not only the ethical resources for moderating pleonexia but the political resources for doing so as well, and that suggests that the resources for moderating pleonexia are to be found in politics as well as in ethics. Indeed, Aristotle insists on a second remedy for overreaching alongside self-regulation on the part of citizens, and that is regulation in the form of laws that teach citizens that "there must be war for the sake of peace, business for the sake of leisure, things useful and necessary for the sake of things honorable" (*Pol.* 1333a34–36). As demonstrated in the first section of this chapter, self-regulation and regulation by law depend on one another.

To explore more fully Aristotle's political remedy for constitutional overreaching, consider once more his description of the Spartan constitution. It combines oligarchic and democratic elements, he says, in such a way that it "may be termed either a democracy or an oligarchy" (*Pol.* 1294b15). Aristotle calls this mixture a fusion of "both extremes" (*Pol.* 1294b19). Characteristic of extreme democracies is a pleonexia for freedom that teaches citizens to understand freedom as license (*Pol.* 1317b10–15). Characteristic of extreme oligarchies is a pleonexia for gain that orients citizens to mastery and the enslavement of others (*Pol.* 1295b13 ff.). It is no

---

54. For Salkever on moderation and implications for an elevated role for women in Aristotle's ethical thought, see "Women, Soldiers, Citizens," p. 179.

55. Ibid., p. 180.

surprise that Sparta's constitution, combining both of these extremes, does not have the political resources to moderate the warlike virtue it encourages. As a union of democracy and oligarchy, it is captive to the excesses of each. This analysis suggests that warlike virtue is not itself the problem, however. The problem lies, rather, in Sparta's constitution.

Oriented by the excesses fused as Sparta's constitution, warlike virtue becomes a vice. If Aristotle begins by suggesting that Sparta's laws would be improved if they conformed better with its constitution and appears to praise its constitution for successfully mixing democracy and oligarchy, he ends on a significantly different note, claiming that in a good constitution "there should appear to be both [democratic and oligarchic] elements *and yet neither*" (*Pol.* 1294b35–36, emphasis added). Aristotle implies that insofar as it is only a fusion of oligarchy and democracy, Sparta's constitution has neither the ethical nor the political resources to moderate the pleonexia characteristic of its laws and of its citizens. Indeed, it instead encourages overreaching. As we will see in chapter 5, the same is true of similarly mixed constitutions. Aristotle's claim regarding a good constitution points to a more promising set of constitutional arrangements. To explore what these might be, I return to Aristotle's *Constitution of Athens,* specifically to the constitutions with which he associates Theramenes: the Constitution of the Five Thousand and the ancestral constitution.[56]

Aristotle's account of the development of the Constitution of the Five Thousand gives the impression that the Athenians conducted remarkably orderly and thoughtful deliberations. He describes in detail (*AP* 29.1–31.3) the procedures they followed to set up a governing body of no fewer than five thousand citizens for the "salvation" of the city (*AP* 29.2) and commends the good judgment of the leading advocates of this change in the direction of oligarchy—Theramenes, Pisander, and Antiphon (*AP* 32.2)—for their deliberate attempts to sustain norms of lawfulness in highly volatile times. These politicians guided legislation and published their plans. They submitted their proposals to scrutiny and ratification (*AP* 29.1–2, 30.1, 30.2, 32.1). Similarly, after the short-lived oligarchic rule of the Four Hundred, Theramenes, this time joined by Aristocrates, and suspicious of both the ill-considered and unaccountable exercises of power by the Four Hundred and the prospect of similar exercises of power by the triumphant democrats, successfully

---

56. The paragraphs that follow concerning the Constitution of the Five Thousand and the ancestral constitution draw on and modify material in Frank and Monoson, "Aristotle's Theramenes at Athens."

132   CHAPTER FOUR

reinvigorated the principle of the rule by the Five Thousand. Aristotle's commentary on the Constitution of the Five Thousand thus associates Theramenes with a procedural lawfulness that is captive to neither democratic nor oligarchic ideology. Aristotle explicitly mentions only two features of the Constitution of the Five Thousand in the *Constitution of Athens*. The Five Thousand were all to be capable of military service "with full equipment" (as hoplites), and "there was to be no pay for any public office" (33.1–2). Restricting (at least full) political participation to citizens who "possess heavy armor" may be characteristic of a mixed oligarchic-democratic constitution (*Pol.* 1297b2), but abolishing pay for public office is at odds with that constitution and with democratic constitutions more generally (*Pol.* 1294a40–b5, 1297a40–b1). Both procedurally and substantively, then, the Constitution of the Five Thousand displayed characteristics of oligarchy and democracy and neither.

To shed more light on this combination, I turn next to Aristotle's association of Theramenes with the ancestral constitution. Calls to return to governance by the ancestral constitution appear twice in the *Constitution of Athens* in the course of Aristotle's report on the period 411–402: in Cleitophon's rider to a proposal resolving to change Athens's democracy into the regime of the Four Hundred (29.3) and in Athens's peace treaty with Sparta, which ultimately led to the Thirty (34.3).[57] Scholars maintain that these references reflect a widespread movement at the time calling for a return to the ways of the past but that there is not much to be learned from them because all the political factions in Athens during that period defended the ancestral constitution. Radical democrats invoked it to claim traditional support for their ideas, and oligarchs invoked it so as to appear to be defending a democratic platform when, in truth, their aims were to secure power for a few. Most scholars, therefore, treat invocations of the ancestral constitution as a rhetorical tool deployed by these parties or clubs to suit their political purposes.[58]

Aristotle's account, especially in the context of the peace treaty negotiations, does not readily support such an interpretation. He reports that, unlike those who invoked the ancestral constitution in the name of democracy and those who did so with the aim of establishing oligarchy, the group of citizens led by Theramenes advocated the ancestral constitution for something other than partisan reasons. Aristotle refers to the members of this group as *gnorimoi,* notables, but distin-

---

57. For details, see Fuks, *Ancestral Constitution,* chap. 1.

58. See Finley, *Use and Abuse of History,* chap. 2; Rhodes, *Commentary on the Aristotelian Athenaion Politeia,* pp. 376–77.

guishes them from the oligarchs, whom he also calls gnorimoi, by maintaining that the gnorimoi of Theramenes' group did not belong to any political club (*AP* 34.3).[59] Aristotle's intention to disassociate this group from any partisan political platform may be gleaned from the fact that he names its members: Archinus, Anytus, Cleitophon, and Phormisius. One would expect these men to have oligarchic sympathies because just after their call for the ancestral constitution, the Thirty was established, with Theramenes as one of its members. But none was a member of the Thirty. On the contrary, Archinus, Anytus, and Phormisius were prominent democrats.[60]

Comprising democrats and oligarchs, this group may be understood as bipartisan, advocating a mix of democratic and oligarchic arrangements acceptable, by means of negotiation and compromise, to members of either party. As we have seen, however, Aristotle does not advocate bipartisanship, a mix of oligarchy and democracy, as a constitutional virtue in the *Constitution of Athens* or in the *Politics*. Nor is bipartisanship what distinguishes Theramenes or his supporters. They are more accurately described as nonpartisan. Indeed, Theramenes' distinction, and Archinus's as well, lies in not acting from set ideological predispositions. A prominent democrat, Archinus refused to follow not only oligarchic policies but democratic ones as well (*AP* 40.1–3). A prominent oligarch, Theramenes, as we have seen, refused to follow democratic and oligarchic policies.

On all four occasions on which Theramenes acted, Athens, whether oligarchy or democracy, was not being ruled by a systematic and stable set of laws and procedures. Owing to its lawlessness, Athens under these regimes was, in Aristotle's taxonomy, tantamount to a tyranny (*Pol.* 1292a5–33, 1292b5–11), effectively without a constitution at all (*Pol.* 1293b28–31).[61] In his words: "Oligarchy or democracy, al-

---

59. For discussion of *gnorimoi* in contrast to the *demos,* see Rhodes, *Commentary on the Aristotelian* Athenaion Politeia, pp. 88, 345, 427, who describes the multiplicity of uses to which Aristotle puts these terms, sometimes using them to denote a distinction between the wealthy and the poor and sometimes without class connotations.

60. About Cleitophon less is known other than that Aristotle associates him with an earlier attempt to bring back the ancestral constitution by reference to the laws of Cleisthenes on the ground that "Cleisthenes' constitution was not democratic but similar to that of Solon" (*AP* 29.3). See Rhodes, *Commentary on the Aristotelian* Athenaion Politeia, p. 431–32. Anytus was also one of Socrates' three accusers (Plato, *Apology* 18B).

61. For excellent discussions of Aristotle on lawfulness that stress the narrowness of his category of lawless constitutions and underscore that, for Aristotle, even defective legal systems are "in a way just" and that even defective laws must be obeyed, see Kraut, *Aristotle: Political Philosophy,* pp. 105–8, 111–18, 373–84.

134   CHAPTER FOUR

though a departure from the most perfect form, may yet be a good enough government, but if any one attempts to push the principles of either to an extreme, he will begin by spoiling the constitution and end by having none at all" (*Pol.* 1309b31–34). Aristotle's commendation of Theramenes does not convince P. J. Rhodes. Accepting that Theramenes may have opposed some extreme oligarchic and democratic regimes in the name of fidelity to the law, Rhodes says, "It is hard to apply a charge of illegality to the democracy overthrown in 411," thus implying that Aristotle's praise of Theramenes for his overthrow of that democracy rests on ideological grounds.[62] Aristotle's commentary in the *Constitution of Athens* suggests otherwise. Calling the post-Periclean democratic leaders demagogues and deceivers who "induced the people to follow an unsuitable course of action" (28.3) and "whose main aim was to be outrageous and please the people with no thought for anything but the present" (28.4), Aristotle describes their actions as contrary to *nomos,* law, "corrupting" and "violent" (28.3). His remarks, along with his pejorative use of the word *demagogue,* do not simply reflect ideological bias against democracy.[63] Aristotle generally uses *demagogue* to signify "the extreme democracy in which the *demos* considers itself above the laws" (*Pol.* 1292a5–33).[64] To Aristotle, then, the democracy of 411 was no more legal than the other regimes Theramenes worked to overthrow.

By disregarding the policies of Athens when Athens was an extreme oligarchy and an extreme democracy, Theramenes refused to participate in the destruction of Athens's constitution. There is more at stake here for Aristotle, however. Against those who call Theramenes a destroyer of all constitutions (*AP* 28.5), Aristotle suggests that, by refusing to yield to Athens's lawlessness, Theramenes was an exemplar of lawfulness, acting to preserve Athens's constitution. The constitution proper to Athens, in Aristotle's view, is obviously neither oligarchy nor democracy. Nor is it, like the Spartan constitution, a fusion of the two. Instead, Athens's proper constitution, like Theramenes and like the constitutions and procedures he advocated, is better understood as moderate or nonpartisan. As we will see in chapter 5, oriented toward oligarchy and democracy and neither, Athens's proper constitution aims at the well-being of all.

---

62. Rhodes, *Commentary on the Aristotelian* Athenaion Politeia, p. 361.
63. Ibid., pp. 323–24, 358.
64. Ibid., p. 323.

Constitution

A man may be a safer ruler than the written law,
but not safer than the customary law.

ARISTOTLE, *Politics*

We saw above that citizens are the source of their laws and that a polity's laws are oriented toward its constitution. This is not meant to reproduce by way of an opposition between citizen and constitution the usual opposition between the rule of men and the rule of law. It is the everyday practice of law on the part of a polity's phronetic citizens and politikoi rulers that makes (or unmakes) its laws, and lawfulness is guided by a polity's proper constitution even as laws themselves and lawfulness—understood as practices of good citizenship—preserve that constitution. The rule of law is thus simultaneously a practice of good citizenship and grounded in a good constitution. So understood, the rule of law disciplines the three kinds of pleonexia I identified at the start of this chapter: the overreaching of the many, of the few, and of the polity as a whole. The rule of law, however, does not stand over and against a citizenry, its rulers, or the polity, for the source of law's disciplinary power does not lie outside those whose desires it regulates. Instead, the rule of law is a practice of self-discipline insofar as citizens, rulers, and the polity itself exercise moderation.

As we saw in chapter 3, moderation allows rulers to act justly (*Pol.* 1277b16–17), that is, to know their limits so that they may refrain from substituting their own good for that of the citizens. Moderation allows citizens to practice reciprocity, including fair exchange, friendship, and rotational rule. Moderation allows polities to avoid becoming captive to the quest for conquest. Moderation, an ethical and political virtue, is thus responsible for stemming the tendencies to overreach on the part of rulers, citizens, and polities. Most important, perhaps, is that moderation preserves or saves practical wisdom, whose imperative nature (*NE* 1143a8) generates the laws that guide and command the citizen-ruler in much the same way that the rule of law guides and commands a political life. Rulers are guided by practical wisdom in the form of politike. As we have seen, those who are ruled are guided by practical wisdom in the form of a concern for their own well-being and if, as citizens, they require only "true opinion" in relation to their polity's laws (*Pol.* 1277b28–30), by practicing moderation, they preserve the capacities for the practice of politike that come into active use when it is their turn to

136 CHAPTER FOUR

rule.[65] As Aristotle puts it, the good citizen "should know how to govern like a free-man, and how to obey like a freeman," for these are "the excellences of a citizen" (*Pol.* 1277b14–15).

If there is a direct relation between practical wisdom and law, and practical wisdom gets its bearing from moral virtue, what might be the political analog of moral virtue? Aristotle's answer, as is suggested by his account of Theramenes, is the constitution. Just as virtue is composed of sedimented habits, with no precise and identifiable source, that are generated by actions and that themselves generate but do not fully determine activity, so too is constitution, as Aristotle's endorsement of the ancestral constitution implies, a product of long and unvarying habit, a "way of life of a people" (*Pol.* 1295a41–b1), generated by a series of actions that have, by repetition and acquiescence, acquired the force of law. If virtue "preserves" practical wisdom and so produces (even as it is guided by) good judgment and thereby lawfulness, the polity's proper constitution, by introducing predictability, pattern, and order into individual practices, safeguards and preserves lawfulness to produce (even as it is guided by) the common judgment of the community, its common sense or consensus. In a sense, then, the rule of law is simply the product of practically wise habits and actions. But these, in series, amount to something more than a simple aggregation. They amount to nothing less than a polity's constitution.

Aristotle's rule of law, guided and preserved by constitution, is not simply conservative and backward-looking. For Aristotle, the polity's proper constitution refers not to time immemorial but rather to a way of life whose origin may be in the past but whose force lies in its everyday practice. For Aristotle, furthermore, a constitution is not so rigid that it cannot change to accommodate new circumstances. Athens's ancestral constitution, for example, refers not to an irretrievable or forgotten past. Sharing the lawfulness characteristic of the Constitution of the Five Thousand, it is also for "the future" (*AP* 33.1). Unlike the rule of law of natural law theory, which, similar to that offered by Plato in the figure of the Stranger, reifies and freezes law by locating it out of time in an invariable realm that transcends that of human affairs, and unlike the positivist paradigm, which, similar to that of fifth-century radically democratic Athens, reifies law by treating it as a "dead" rule

65. Without this sort of account of the phronesis of citizens, phronesis would have to appear ex nihilo in citizens when they became rulers. In light of his critique of the Megarians, discussed in chapter 1, Aristotle would have to reject such an account of the emergence of the virtue of judgment. Instead, as we saw, virtue comes into active use from habit, which we hold for use.

for the future, written in stone, a product of aggregated majoritarian judgment but not necessarily of practical wisdom and good judgment, Aristotle's rule of law looks back to the past and forward to the future, remaining, as an everyday practice, in the domain of ethics and politics. Aristotle's rule of law, like the constitution that guides it and the practices that produce and preserve it, is changeable, albeit in the form of the incrementalism and gradualism associated with changes in habit. In this way, it safeguards the stability of a polity and is also able to recognize and accommodate the variability of human affairs.

As is plain from Aristotle's commentary on Theramenes and the constitutions with which Aristotle associates him, Aristotle's rule of law depends crucially on virtue, specifically, as we have seen, on moderation. It is the practice of virtue, along with the good judgment it depends on and preserves, that makes the rule of law, and indeed the constitution itself, a prohairetic activity of citizenship. The rule of (good) law, so understood, dependent on the rule of (good) men, does not contradict popular sovereignty but instead promotes a political and citizen-oriented practice of law that, while guided by the constitution, also founds and refounds it daily. Insisting that both the rule of law and the rule of men take their guidance from the constitution does not contradict popular sovereignty because the authority of the constitution, as the way of life of the people, lies in citizens' participating as makers and subjects of their own law. This politically rich circularity affiliates the sovereignty of law with popular sovereignty, both being practices of citizenship regulated over time by the constitution those citizens authorize.[66] Chapter 5 explores the constitutional program for Athens that Aristotle affiliates with these practices.

66. Michelman, "Law's Republic," pp. 1501–3. See also Dicey, *Introduction to the Law of the Constitution,* pp. 406–14.

CHAPTER FIVE

The Polity of Friendship

Aristotle's readers agree that the "true aristocracy" described in *Politics* VII and VIII, composed of virtuous, spirited, and like-minded citizens, is Aristotle's most preferred regime. It comprises two classes: property-owning citizens (warriors, politicians, priests) who, on the basis of age, rule and are ruled in turn, and noncitizens (slaves, laborers, foreigners, women).[1] Unlike other regimes, in which classes of citizens may be excluded from political participation, in the true aristocracy the class of actual and potential citizens is the same.[2] Offices in this regime are distributed strictly on the basis of merit, and those who rule do so not for private advantage but for the common good. Throughout the *Politics* Aristotle insists that the polis is a site for living well and acting nobly. The true aristocracy—composed of citizens who act well owing to their virtues and whose political practices and institutions promote, even as they depend on, concord, *homonoia*—seems uniquely able to reduce, indeed, to eliminate the conflict and dissensus, *stasis,* characteristic of other regimes. What makes the true aristocracy so free from stasis? According to most interpretations, there are no factions in the true aristocracy because, in the words of one commentator, "the diversity is missing of which faction is born."[3] This suggests that the true aristocracy is factionless because it is homogeneous. Its citizens—products of common habituation and instruction—share a way of life and common ends and are, therefore, of the same mind about the work of the polity.[4] The commonality attained by citizens owing to their ethical and political homogeneity frees the true aristocracy from faction and thus makes it the best.

    1. There are, strictly speaking, seven classes (*Pol.* VII.8). But these may be reduced to two: citizens and noncitizens. See also Coby, "Aristotle's Three Cities."
    2. Ober, *Political Dissent in Democratic Athens,* pp. 340–42, from whom I borrow the terms *actual* and *potential* regarding citizens.
    3. Coby, "Aristotle's Three Cities," p. 915.
    4. Klonoski, "*Homonoia* in Aristotle's Ethics and Politics," p. 316. I use *polity, regime,* and *constitution* to translate Aristotle's general use of *politeia.* To avoid confusion, I refer to the mixed constitution Aristotle calls politeia as a "constitutional polity."

Interpreting the true aristocracy in this way produces a sharp break between the final books of the *Politics* and the rest of Aristotle's ethical and political writings. In *Politics* IV–VI, Aristotle shows that most polities are characterized not by the consensus of the true aristocracy but by dissensus. His textured discussions in the *Nicomachean Ethics* demonstrate, especially in their astute explorations of human vice, the role of luck, and the human dependence on external goods, that most human beings are not fully virtuous but instead continually struggle with themselves and others as they strive, individually and collectively, to fulfill, as well as to discipline, their differentiated desires and ends. The virtue, unity, and homogeneity characteristic of the true aristocracy are, moreover, at odds with Aristotle's wariness of ethical and political mandates that refuse to take people as they are (*Pol.* 1289a1–3), his anti-utopian vigilance against presupposing the impossible in his discussions of regime formation and change (*Pol.* 1265a17–18, 1325b37–38), and his rejection of idealistic approaches to ethics and politics (*NE* I.3; *Pol.* II.2–6). They also render the true aristocracy—the culmination of Aristotle's contemplations about ethics and politics and, hence, his ethical and political philosophy itself—seemingly irrelevant for our pluralistic, diverse, and conflict-ridden times.[5]

In a manner more consistent with Aristotle's general philosophical approach and with the interpretations I have offered in the rest of this book, I read Aristotle's celebration of the true aristocracy not as a denial of complexity and conflict but as a way of inviting attention to the constitutional place of these features of ordinary ethical and political life and also of the means for managing them. This interpretation highlights the unity of Aristotle's *Politics* itself and of his ethical and political writings as a whole and insists on his continued relevance to those interested in these characteristic features of present-day political life as well. The point of departure for my reading is an interpretation of the true aristocracy as not an ideal but an Aristotelian *telos,* or end. Josiah Ober seems to offer a similar interpretation when he asks: "'What is the historical place of aristocracy in the political evolution of the polis?' The answer is, apparently, that aristocracy . . . does not (yet) exist."[6] That the true aristocracy "does not (yet) exist" suggests that, at some time in the future, it might. Unlike an ideal, which exists out of time, the tense of the true aristocracy, like all Aristotelian tele, is in time, in the future. To locate the true aristocracy in the future is not to turn it into a utopian regime.[7] Utopias may resemble

---

5. Ober, *Mass and Elite,* pp. 296 ff., argues, for example, that Aristotle's ultimate turn away from the real consigns him to irrelevance.

6. Ober, *Political Dissent in Democratic Athens,* p. 327.

7. On this point I agree with Ober, ibid., p. 347 ff.

140   CHAPTER FIVE

Aristotle's city of prayer in that they invite consideration of a future. But insofar as utopias actually (and literally) exist no place at all, they invite consideration of an unrealizable future. This means that impossibility is not an obstacle to utopia.[8]

At the beginning of his discussion of the city of prayer, by contrast, Aristotle excludes from consideration impossible presuppositions while admitting "ones to be prayed for, *euchomenoi*," in other words, imaginary ones (*Pol.* 1325b37–38).[9] Unlike the ideal or utopian, the imaginary, in Aristotle's epistemology, is limited by what we know and desire by virtue of our experiences, for, as Aristotle insists, there can be no imagination without perception (*DA* 429a1).[10] To treat the city of prayer as imaginable is to treat it as a possible future (*Pol.* 1325b39), a distant future, to be sure, perhaps even an unlikely future, but nonetheless an actualizable future (with good luck and hard work, *Pol.* 1331b21–22, 1332a30–31) insofar as it arises from an experienced past, or history.

Maintaining that Aristotle sees imperialism as providing the only opportunity for establishing polities like the city of prayer, Ober treats the city of prayer as a (not fully worked out) blueprint for a constitution, to be actualized "in the course of the expected Greco-Macedonian colonization of western Asia" and "established under the umbrella of a hegemonic international order."[11] Understanding the city of prayer in this way, however, as a creation ex nihilo, undermines Aristotle's insistence that the city of prayer be imaginable. Basing the city of prayer on human and material resources unavailable within the pasts or presents of any of the cities Aristotle examines turns it into a city that is not a possible future *for them*. Not in any sense an actualization of the practices and institutions of any existing polity or its

---

8. Indeed, premises not possible in the world in which they are presented are characteristic of some utopian literature. See, e.g., More, *Utopia.*

9. For some helpful comments about the Greek term *euche* and Aristotle's use of it, see Kraut, *Aristotle: Political Philosophy,* p. 192 n. 1.

10. For useful discussions of Aristotle on imagination, see Watson, "*Phantasia* in Aristotle," pp. 103, 108; Schofield, "Aristotle on the Imagination," pp. 122–23, 125; Labarrière, "Le rôle de la *phantasia* dans la recherche du bien pratique," pp. 234, 236–41, 246–52. Despite the differences among these treatments, all three commentators underscore the connection between imagination and actual perception, between imagination and action, and between imagination and language. These connections suggest the integral place of imagination for a politics concerned with the action of man as the being with speech *(zoon logon echon).* Note that though bound to actual perception, imagination is not a mere reproduction of what is experienced but can, rather, be generative.

11. Ober, *Political Dissent in Democratic Athens,* pp. 310, 327–28, 339, 347–51.

citizens, the city of prayer, as Ober envisages it, is not a telos but the product of design or artifice alone.

Aristotle, however, views the city of prayer as futural and actualizable insofar as it exists and continues to exist in the present as a possibility. This means that the city of prayer is a polity whose mode of being is one of continual becoming. This combination of future and present, of actuality (lying ahead) and potential (a current possibility), characterizes Aristotelian tele in general. Consider the most familiar of Aristotelian tele, *eudaimonia,* living well and happily. In the *Nicomachean Ethics,* Aristotle calls eudaimonia final and self-sufficient. It is that at which all things aim, the end of action (*NE* 1097b20). About eudaimonia Aristotle raises the following conundrum. On one hand, as the end of action (in two senses: as that at which activities aim and as that which, when achieved, is the termination of activity), it lies always and only ahead. A happy life is one that can truly be said to *have been* happy, and that judgment must wait until the life is over (*NE* I.10). At the same time, because eudaimonia is the ongoing practice of virtuous activity (*NE* 1098a17), Aristotle maintains that those who act well should also be called happy (*NE* 1101a15–18). Underscoring this interplay of present and future, he concludes, "We call happy those among living men in whom these conditions *are, and are to be,* fulfilled" (*NE* 1101a21, emphasis added), and he spends most of the rest of the *Nicomachean Ethics* exploring the ordinary virtuous activities that make possible a happy life. Aristotelian tele are temporally odd: although their tense is futural, their focus is not on the future but on the present, what is possible in the here and now. Aristotle's account of human eudaimonia concerns the practice of virtuous activities in the ongoing present of an individual life. His consideration of the eudaimonic constitution—the city of prayer—does the same, attending to the ongoing practices and institutions that condition the possibility of the best regime. Underscoring the similarities between the eudaimonic individual life and the eudaimonic constitution, Aristotle opens *Politics* VII with an analogy between soul and city (*Pol.* VII.1–2).

The ongoing present—what I called in chapter 1 the domain of ethics and politics—functions in relation not only to a future but to a past as well.[12] Whether a human being attains happiness will depend on her current activities, to be sure. In Aristotle's words, "it is the activity of the present that really counts" (*NE* 1168a6, 14–15). As we saw, current activities depend, in turn, on habits, that is, on who the

---

12. The future also functions in relation to the past, specifically, as we saw, by means of imagination, which projects a future on the basis of experiences.

agent has been. Similarly, whether a regime can have as its possible future the city of prayer will depend not only on its current practices and institutions but also on what sort of regime it has been. Although Aristotle explores many different cities in the *Politics*, the one of paramount importance to him is Athens, of which he is a harsh critic.[13] He calls the democratic regime governing the Athens he inhabits the "final" or worst form of democracy, arguing that it is not laws but the many who rule and, having "power in their hands, not as individuals, but collectively," they are, like a tyrant, "many in one" (*Pol.* 1292a10–12). In light of this criticism, and paralleling Aristotle's project in the *Nicomachean Ethics*, which is to investigate excellence so that human beings may become good (*NE* 1103b27), I take one of the key projects of the *Politics* to be Aristotle's investigation of how Athens can become a good regime.

Aristotle does not advocate transforming Athens as it currently is into the city of prayer. Given contemporary realities, that would not work.[14] Instead, he seeks a middle constitution that can emerge from Athens's current conditions (so that the democracy it is can become its past) and can also condition the possibility of the city of prayer, Athens's telos. This means that the *Politics*, like the *Nicomachean Ethics*, is most keenly focused on the present, the middle between past and future. To determine what sort of regime Aristotle takes to be the appropriate political present for Athens, I examine neither the futural city of prayer nor the final form of democracy that, according to Aristotle, Athens had achieved, but the sort of unity, friendship, and class relations that make possible, or operate as what Aristotle calls the "presuppositions" of, the city of prayer. Taking seriously his emphasis on difference in his account of political unity and his emphasis on conflict in his account of political friendship leads to the conclusion that the polity that best satisfies the presuppositions of the city of prayer is the polity Aristotle calls a "so-called" aristocracy ("so-called" because it combines aristocracy with democracy). To capture the political and ethical measures that combine to produce and preserve this mixed regime and to signal the political role of virtue as that which makes possible both the differences among citizens that can produce conflict as well as the mediation (but not elimination) of that conflict, I call this regime a democracy of distinction.

---

13. See, for discussion, B. Strauss, "On Aristotle's Critique of Athenian Democracy," who argues that Aristotle's critique rests on inaccuracies.

14. Kraut, *Aristotle: Political Philosophy,* p. 374, makes this point as well.

Unity and Difference

Criticizing the unity celebrated by Plato's Socrates in *Republic* V, Aristotle says: "As a polity goes on and becomes more of a unity, *hen*, it will not be a polity any longer. For a polity is by nature some sort of plurality, *plethos;* but as it becomes more of a unity, it will become first like a household instead of a polity, then like a man instead of a household. . . . So that even if we could attain this unity we should not do it. For it would be the destruction of the polity" (*Pol.* 1261a18–25).[15] Aristotle agrees with Socrates that a good polity must be a unity, but he insists that it must, at the same time, be some sort of plurality. How, against the backdrop of the homogeneity of the true aristocracy, might we make sense of Aristotle's commitment to plurality?

Aristotle explains the sort of unity he takes to be appropriate to a good polity in *Politics* II, where he contrasts political unity with the unity of an alliance and with that of an *ethnos,* or nation. An alliance, existing for the purposes of mutual assistance, is, he says, a multitude of persons all the same in kind (*Pol.* 1261a24). A polity is not. A nation such as the Arcadians (*Pol.* 1261a28–29), living a scattered village-based life without sufficient political organization to form effective coalitions, is rooted in a common ethnic identity.[16] A polity is not. Producing unison instead of harmony, not a rhythm but a single beat (*Pol.* 1263b35), the unities characteristic of alliances and nations, Aristotle insists, are not political. By claiming that alliances and nations lack harmony and insisting that harmony is a necessary component of political unity, Aristotle underscores that political harmony requires not homogeneity but difference. Indeed, he suggests that there can be no political harmony without difference. Against the usual interpretations of the well-constituted polity (attributed to Aristotle and advocated by Plato's Socrates), this means that a good polity is not a unity of the same but a unity of persons differing in kind (*Pol.* 1261a23). Moreover, the difference that conditions political harmony makes possible disharmony at the same time.[17]

---

15. Aristotle insists that a good polity must be "by nature" some sort of plurality. As I discussed in chapter 1, the nature of the polity is best understood by reference to the natures of the citizens who constitute it. See, for discussion, Yack, *Problems of a Political Animal,* chap. 3; F. Miller, *Nature, Justice, and Rights,* chap. 2.

16. There is controversy concerning the meaning of this passage. I take my guidance from Hornblower and Spawforth, *Oxford Classical Dictionary,* pp. 138–39; Pomeroy et al., *Ancient Greece,* p. 86.

17. Disharmony gives rise not only to conflict and divisiveness, i.e., the risk or bad side of difference. As a condition of political unity, disharmony is also positive. On the centrality of conflict to Aristotle's politics, see Yack, *Problems of a Political Animal.*

Arlene Saxonhouse similarly stresses Aristotle's emphasis on difference. Her Aristotle is "the hero" who, unlike earlier Greeks, is "able to . . . welcome the diverse."[18] Saxonhouse sees political unity not as a seamless and homogeneous whole but as a mode of "incorporation" constituted out of common ends that "raise [citizens] above the divisions that plague the city."[19] If the measure of political unity were the degree of devotion to a common end, however, then nations and alliances would exemplify political unity, and, as Bernard Yack points out, "bees and ants would be much more 'political' in their behaviour than human beings. But Aristotle argues precisely the opposite."[20] Like bees and ants, those who battle together or share an ethnic identity have a common end (mutual protection or identity preservation, respectively), to be sure. And yet, to Aristotle, the unity characteristic of alliances and nations is not genuinely political. This is because commonality, as such, is not the basis for political unity. A polity, he says, may require a site common to its citizens, but a common site alone will not produce political unity (*Pol.* 1260b39–41); nor will, for example, holding property in common (*Pol.* 1262b38–1263b29). Political unity is not a commonality that subsumes or transcends difference. It is, rather, a commonality that preserves difference.

If difference is important for genuine political unity, Aristotle also insists that differences can produce breaches in a city (*Pol.* 1303b14–15). Difference may be necessary to political harmony, but this suggests that, by itself, difference is neither sufficient nor constitutive of good politics. In Aristotle's words, a polity does not grow "out of a multitude brought together by accident" (*Pol.* 1303a27–28). Aristotle's comparison of political harmony to musical harmony is instructive in distinguishing the difference that is constitutive of harmony from mere dissonant or cacophonous difference. In music, harmony, *harmonia,* is a characteristic of notes in a melody, sounded one after the other and organized by a shared "mode."[21] The shared mode, in other words, supplies a commonality that itself depends on separate and distinct notes, or tones. In politics, likewise, different individuals organize into a harmony based on a commonality, which is less a common belief or a common plot of land than, as in music, a shared set of practices or a common mode of

18. Saxonhouse, *Fear of Diversity,* pp. 191, x.

19. Ibid., pp. xi, 195, 199.

20. Yack, "Community and Conflict," pp. 92, 95–97. Yack argues that the distinctive "sharing in which human beings surpass all other creatures," the sharing that defines human "politicality," is the capacity for "reasoned speech." I agree.

21. *Oxford Classical Dictionary,* s.v. "music."

interaction, itself dependent on differentiated and distinct activities. Discussing a well-constituted polity's system of education, Aristotle maintains that an education in music—not mere appreciation but learning to play—builds character and promotes, specifically, political virtue (*Pol.* 1340b40). Students must not be idle spectators or even theorists of music but must actually play, for it is only the activity itself that teaches the production of harmony appropriate to a political life and to music, namely, a harmony that depends on individual practices within a common mode. Harmony, so understood, is constituted of and preserves, but is not reducible to, difference.

If genuine political unity preserves difference, what difference might there be among the propertied, male Athenian citizens of the true aristocracy? Concerned precisely to emphasize Aristotle's distinction between a many of the same and a many of the different, Saxonhouse replaces "plurality" with "diversity." She explains: "I use the word 'diversity' rather than the word 'plurality' . . . because I want to emphasize that I am discussing not only many *similar* units that can be put together or separated like billiard balls, but also differences, e.g., differences between male and female rather than simply between many men."[22] Arguing that, for Aristotle, "it is differences in form *(ex eidei)* which are crucial to the existence of the polity," she maintains that "these in turn lead to differences in function" and that "it is in the realm of the family and human sexuality that the importance of difference of form is the most obvious and the unity that derives therefrom most evident."[23] Saxonhouse is right that the relevant difference for Aristotle is difference in form.[24] Parsing difference in form in terms of sex, however, is, I think, a mistake. As Saxonhouse notes, quoting Aristotle, "[the male] is marked off from his wife less by a difference in nature" than by "a difference in appearance, speech, and honors [1259b7–8]," socially constructed differences, in other words.[25] Saxonhouse concludes that this "suggests a congruity of souls between male and female in Aristotle which is seldom recognized."[26] Her conclusion is surely right. That

22. Saxonhouse, *Fear of Diversity,* p. 22 n. 2. See also Saxonhouse, "Family, Polity, and Unity."

23. Saxonhouse, "Family, Polity, and Unity," p. 211.

24. Note that unlike Plato, Aristotle, in his insistence on difference as a matter of form, refuses to form *all* transcendence of particularity. Indeed, for Aristotle, as I argued in chapter 1, differences in form are the same as differences in nature, and they involve particularity in the way a being's form involves its matter. As Aristotle explains in *De Anima,* the human soul is form, one of whose characteristic features is that it is embodied.

25. Saxonhouse, "Family, Polity, and Unity," p. 206.

26. Ibid., p. 207.

146   CHAPTER FIVE

there is such a congruity, however, implies that the differences in form that are constitutive of political plurality are determined and exemplified not by differences in sex but by something else.

If Aristotelian political plurality is not based on sexual identity, neither is it based on ethnic identity, for, as we have seen, ethnic or national identity depends on and produces a degree of unity that is inhospitable to genuine political difference.[27] Insofar as genuinely political difference is based on none of these, it is not properly understood as diversity.[28] Indeed, as we have seen, there is no diversity among the citizens of the true aristocracy and yet there must be difference, otherwise the true aristocracy would not be well constituted. If difference is a matter of neither ethnic nor sexual identity, it is also not a matter of the identity by virtue of which one gains membership in a class. For, although Aristotle, like Plato, takes the differentiation of function or interest among classes of individuals to be central to the cooperative activities he defines as political, differentiation of function no more satisfies Aristotle's quest for difference among the similar individuals of the true aristocracy than does differentiation based on gender or ethnic identity.[29]

All these varying treatments of difference pass too quickly over the kind of difference implicated in Aristotle's distinction between a polity, on one hand, and an alliance or a nation, on the other. Of concern to Aristotle is what difference there can be among the "many men" of a polity, in other words, among similar human beings. Underlying all of the differences of classification just mentioned is the difference that, in Saxonhouse's words, gives the "sense of oneself as an individual," the difference that makes each human being, in the words of Martha Nussbaum, "a 'this' and 'one in number'—i.e., a definite individual, countable as a single unit apart from others, and living a separate life."[30] It is not difference based on ascription or differentiation based on economic class but individual difference that, separating each

27. Political plurality and identity in the context of the constitutional polity may be based on devotion to the virtue of manliness and the ability to contribute to the practice of warcraft but, as I argued in chapter 4 regarding Sparta and return to below in the case of the constitutional polity, the presence of a pleonexia for conquest based on the celebration of manliness is, to Aristotle, a sign that a polity is not well constituted.

28. Aristotle's view of difference highlights the following paradox: diversity, suggesting some feature shared by many of the same gender, race, or class, connotes sameness, too. For a similar point in a very different context, see Mansfield, "Harvard Loves Diversity."

29. See Cooper, "Political Animals and Civic Friendship," p. 363, on the "politicality" of beings that are "regularly found taking part in cooperative activities involving differentiation of function."

30. Saxonhouse, "Family, Polity and Unity," p. 218; Nussbaum, "Aristotle, Feminism, and Needs for Functioning," p. 1023.

and every person from each and every other (notwithstanding similarities in such categories as class, gender, or ethnicity), marks the unique identity of a person.

This means that the difference in form or nature that defines political plurality in Aristotle's sense is ontological and nonessentialist. It is ontological in that, as Aristotle makes explicit in the *Metaphysics,* what is at stake in any discussion of plurality is the very identity of the being in question (*Meta.* IV.2). And it is non-essentialist in that, because plurality is, for Aristotle, a mode of not-being (*Meta.* 1004a10–20), there can be no static essence to the polity or, as we saw also in chapter 1, to its citizens. Saxonhouse captures the ontological nature of Aristotelian plurality in her treatment of difference in terms of form, but, by referring difference in form to sex and family, she essentializes it in a way that I think is inconsistent with the thrust of her own argument. It is worth underlining that individual difference, though prior to the other understandings of difference and, indeed, what makes sense of Aristotle's distinctive understanding of political plurality, can itself only come about in a context of plurality. I am countable as a single unity only in my contradistinction from others, that is, in my relation to them. It is only because there are others that I have a separate life to live. It is therefore only in the context of plurality that individual difference is possible.[31] For this reason, a polity must respect and preserve plurality, understood in terms of ontological and nonessentialist difference, if it is to be the properly political sort of unity. How is a polity, as a unity of the different, constituted and preserved? As we have seen so far, this is achieved via the prohairetic activities of a polity's citizens, specifically by their individual and shared practices of, among other things, property, justice, and law. These institutions—held by each citizen as a kind of property (as his own and for common use)—model the balance of difference and unity critical to the polity as a whole. Making these activities possible as shared practices, and simultaneously cultivated by them, is the ethical attitude citizens take to their practices, namely, one of friendliness.

Friendship and Faction

Aristotle calls friendship the bond of a polity: "Friendship seems too to hold polities together, and lawgivers to care more for it than for justice; for concord,

---

31. As is suggested by my accounts of Aristotelian property and reciprocity (chapters 2 and 3) and also by Aristotle's understanding of natural beings, discussed in chapter 1, that plurality conditions individual difference is true not only of human beings but of beings as such.

homonoia, seems to be something like friendship, and this they aim at most of all, and expel faction, *stasis,* as their worst enemy" (*NE* 1155a23–27).[32] Devoting a considerable amount of space to the dispositions, motives, and causes that give rise to factions and to the panoply of political ills that create cleavages that can undo a polity (*Pol.* V.2–7), Aristotle proposes concord or friendship among citizens, *homonoia,* as the remedy for these modes of discord (*NE* 1167b2–3). Aristotle's advocacy of political friendship as an antidote to faction seems obvious enough, indeed, tautological. Against the backdrop of the models of political friendship that prevailed in fifth-century Athens, however, it repays scrutiny.

Robert Connor identifies two such models: an "older and more traditional" model based on personal, familial, and social ties, and a newer model, arising late in the fifth century, that "stresse[d] the mass allegiance which skillful and eloquent leaders can win."[33] Rather than conducing to homonoia at Athens, these forms of political friendship proved, rather, to be sources of faction.[34] The traditional model of friendship was grounded in kinship relations among the wealthy, well-born, and powerful. Doing well by such friends (by, for example, granting special privileges) often created spheres of concentrated political influence that worked against the well-being of the polity as a whole. Indeed, Connor uses the term for faction, "stasis," to refer to the social clubs or hetairies that circumscribed the spheres of these relations.[35] If doing well by one's friends could lead to civic strife, the reverse was also true. In his itemization of the varying causes of strife, Aristotle includes cases of doing ill by one's kin (by means of, for example, insult or impiety, *Pol.* 1303b19–1304a17).

A new model of friendship seemed, at first, less divisive. Effecting, on the part of the wealthy, a "transfer of 'primary loyalties' from the *philia* group to the wider circle of the *polis* or the *demos*," it formed a civic bond that included the many. Unlike bonds of kinship, which concentrated political power in the wealthy and well-born, these bonds worked to the advantage of all members of the polity: the many gained political inclusion, and the wealthy were able to consolidate power with

---

32. For the difficulties translating *homonoia* and *stasis,* see Kalimtzis, *Aristotle on Political Enmity and Disease,* pp. 1–27.

33. See Connor, *New Politicians of Fifth-Century Athens.* Connor remarks on the artificiality of his division if held to too rigidly, noting traces of what he dubs the "new" model dating back to the sixth century and traces of the traditional model in the fourth (p. 135).

34. For a useful discussion of the divisiveness these political practices produced, see Balot, *Greed and Injustice in Classical Athens,* chaps. 3, 6.

35. Connor, *New Politicians of Fifth-Century Athens,* pp. 84, 136, 218.

support from the many in the name of service to the city as a whole.[36] Under the stresses of the later years of the Peloponnesian War, however, with Athens veering between oligarchic and democratic extremes, the strategic ties forged between the wealthy and the many could not be sustained.[37] Hetairies, now taking the form of ideological political clubs, primarily among the wealthy, emerged to displace earlier coalitions between the wealthy and the many. Directed at gaining political power at all costs, these clubs produced, as they had in their earlier form under the more traditional model of friendship, not concord but discord.[38]

Viewed in its historical and cultural context, Aristotle's claim that legislators should aim "most of all" at something like friendship to *expel* faction is surprising. That his account of political friendship shares features of these earlier practices makes his claim more surprising still. Aristotle treats the family, like the traditional mode of friendship, as an important source and model for political friendship (*NE* VIII.10–11).[39] He bases friendship among citizens, like the later mode, in no small part on strategic coalitions or mutual advantage (*NE* 1160a8–28, 1163b32–35; *EE* 1242a6–8, b23–28). Aristotelian political friendship also, however, differs in key ways from both of these earlier models. He distinguishes friendliness among citizens from relations among kin on the ground that the latter involve affection (*NE* 1161b17–20) but the former need not and, taking friendship among citizens to involve a coming to terms, *homonoia,* about "constitutional essentials" or "the fundamental terms of their cooperation" (*NE* 1167a27–b2), he treats political friendship as more enduring, especially in the face of conflict, than the strategic friendships between the wealthy and the many in the late fifth century proved to be.[40] Aristotle's account of political friendship shares features of the earlier practices, then, but he does not merely combine the two. Instead, he produces a mixed good with features of both and of neither. The feature he adds to the mix, absent from both earlier models but necessary if political friendship is to keep stasis at bay, is, we will see, virtue. Because Aristotle offers his most detailed account of

---

36. In Connor's words, this "new way of ordering loyalties" was also "a new technology of political power." If the new oligarchs presented themselves as the "truly devoted servants of the whole city," in fact, they were motivated by self-interest and the desire to consolidate a larger base of power than their competitors: see ibid., p. 107.

37. Ibid., p. 106.

38. Ibid., pp. 194–98.

39. For discussion, see Pangle, *Aristotle and the Philosophy of Friendship,* chap. 4.

40. For the phrase "constitutional essentials," see Schwarzenbach, "On Civic Friendship," p. 107. For "the fundamental terms of their cooperation," see Kraut, *Aristotle: Political Philosophy,* p. 468.

150   CHAPTER FIVE

homonoia among citizens in the context of his discussions of individual friendship in *Nicomachean Ethics* VIII–IX, I turn next to an exploration of the differing modes of individual friendship to determine which, if any, might best model political friendship.

Aristotle opens his investigation of friendship by distinguishing his approach from earlier ones that take friendship to rest either on similarity and kinship or on opposition and difference (*NE* 1155a32–b6). Aristotle rejects both approaches, turning instead to the place of virtue in friendship (*NE* 1155b10–11). He does this not to avoid the question of whether friendship rests on similarity or difference but to answer it, for, as we will see, it is the practice of virtue in friendships of all kinds that makes possible the unity *and* difference appropriate to each.

Aristotle introduces three kinds of individual friendship, based on virtue, use, and pleasure.[41] According to most contemporary political theorists, the balance of unity and difference appropriate to a political life is best modeled by use friendship, in which parties come together owing to the use or benefit each receives from the other (*NE* 1156a11–13). Rejecting virtue friendship on the ground that it demands a unity that is impossible to achieve among citizens and an intimacy that is, in any case, undesirable for political life, they argue that use friends are unified by virtue of the mutual gain of their association and that their difference is protected and preserved by the fact that they come together on the basis of their self-interest.[42] Aristotle is unambiguous regarding the matter, maintaining that "political friendship has been established mainly in accordance with advantage" (*EE* 1242a6–8, b23–28; *NE* 1160a8–28, 1163b32–35).

Modeling the unity and difference of political community on use friendship is not without its problems, however. If the paradigm of use friendship is a contract of exchange of goods and services based on self-interest and mutual gain, Aristotle describes the purpose of the polity differently. It exists not for the sake of trade and barter alone, or of meeting individual needs, but for the sake of noble actions, a virtuous life, and eudaimonia (*Pol.* III.9). Whereas the community formed by use

---

41. In the discussion that follows I focus on virtue and use friendships because these are generally treated as the best candidates on which to model political friendship.

42. See Yack, *Problems of a Political Animal,* chap. 4, esp. pp. 118–21; Bickford, *Dissonance of Democracy,* chap. 2; Price, *Love and Friendship in Plato and Aristotle;* Cooper, "Aristotle on the Forms of Friendship," pp. 645–48; Schwarzenbach, "On Civic Friendship"; Schofield, "Political Friendship and the Ideology of Reciprocity"; Stern-Gillet, *Aristotle's Philosophy of Friendship;* F. Miller, *Nature, Justice, and Rights,* p. 209; Pangle, *Aristotle and the Philosophy of Friendship,* p. 158; Kraut, *Aristotle: Political Philosophy,* pp. 466–70. There are, of course, differences among these accounts.

friends ends as soon as particular needs are satisfied and is, therefore, "fleeting," "impermanent," and "accidental" (*NE* 1157a35, 1156a17, 1156b11, 1157b5, 1156a23, 1157a14–15, 1158b5, 1164a11), a political community is enduring. If the "meeting of the minds" characteristic of a contract of exchange has to do with some matter of self-interest (my watch for your pen), the friendship that binds a political community concerns matters that pertain to the polity as a whole.

Advocates of use friendship as a model of political concord meet these objections by claiming that even if use friends do not themselves live the good life, their friendships nonetheless promote it.[43] They argue that impermanence and accident accurately characterize the coalitions that develop concerning political matters, that nothing prevents these alliances from becoming more lasting coalitions should they continue to benefit the parties, and, most important, that use friendship not only accommodates conflict, a not uncommon feature of a political life, but can also lead to greater cooperation.[44]

That use friendship is a source of conflict is evident. Aristotle says that "use friendship is full of complaints; for as they use each other for their own interest they always want to get the better of the bargain, and think they have got less than they should, and blame their friends because they do not get all they 'want and deserve'" (*NE* 1162b16–20). Use friends fight because each thinks that the other has gotten the better deal. This is usually why they come together in the first place. I agree to exchange my watch for your pen not only because I want the pen but also, perhaps, because I think I will get a pen that will be worth more than my watch. After the exchange I may worry that, in the end, you got the better deal. This means that conflict and cooperation both arise from the desire on the part of each party for more, *pleonexia*. How is cooperation achieved among use friends in the face of conflict? Yack claims that, lacking the resources within their relation to settle their conflict, use friends turn to law or a preexisting contract to settle it for them and that from the shared practice of settling disputes legally emerges a sense of justice.[45] Thus, if cooperation among use friends gives rise to conflict, it is also the case that conflict gives rise to cooperation, specifically, in the form of shared recourse to external measures to settle their differences.

Turning to external measures to settle differences, however, even if by agreement between the parties, generally spells the end of their *friendship*. It signifies

43. Yack, *Problems of a Political Animal,* p. 114; Cooper, "Political Animals and Civic Friendship," p. 373.

44. Yack, *Problems of a Political Animal,* p. 110.

45. Ibid., p. 112.

152   CHAPTER FIVE

that the friends could not themselves come to terms, something that friends, even quarrelsome ones, must be able to do if they are to remain friends. Are there truly no resources for mediating conflicts, in other words, no practices of justice *within* use friendship? To answer this question, consider Aristotle's paradigmatic case of use friendship: the exchange of goods and services (*NE* 1163b32–35). As we saw in chapter 3, such exchanges are governed by reciprocal justice and regulated, in the first instance, by an agreement reached by the parties to the exchange. This agreement, representing a just or fair exchange, is based on the parties' assessments of the relative worths of what they are exchanging as determined by their judgments with respect to use. The agreement itself thus reflects a shared practice of justice that emerges from within the use friendship itself. If one party breaches the agreement, the use friends may recur to law to meliorate their conflict. In the absence of fraud, however, Athenian law regulated contracts of exchange by enforcing the parties' own agreement (*Pol.* 1321b13–14; *AP* 51). The law, in other words, regulated the use friends' conflict by recourse to their own judgments about justice, as reflected in their agreement. Law, so understood, though more external to the use friendship than the use friends' agreement, is not itself a truly external measure either. Insofar as Aristotle treats law as a just force over and against a polity's citizens only when the law comes into being from those citizens' own just practices, as we saw in chapters 3 and 4, and insofar as both contract and law reflect and respect the friends' own judgments about fairness and, hence, their own practice of justice, both law and contract are better seen not as measures external to use friendship but as measures of self-regulation.

This reading of use friendship is consonant with the usual readings in that, like them, it takes use friendship to coalesce around self-interest, to require agreement not about a wide range of goods or the good itself but only about the particular goods that motivate the use friends' coalition, to produce an agreement about those goods to their mutual benefit, and to accommodate not only conflict but also the means for resolving conflict. Unlike the usual accounts, however, my interpretation finds resources for conflict resolution in the use friends' relation, specifically, in their mutually advantageous agreement. This is no small difference, for without such resources there can be no continued *friendship* in the face of conflict. Moreover, as I demonstrate next, cooperation can persist in and indeed grow out of conditions of conflict only when the mutually advantageous agreement between use friends, reflecting their shared sense of justice, is understood as more than a simple aggregation of their individual self-interests.

Consider again use friendships among commercial exchangers. These friends come together in the first instance exclusively for reasons of self-interest: one has a pen, wants a watch, and aims for the better deal so he can end up with more than he started with; the other has a watch and wants a pen and also aims for the better deal. Against the backdrop of their competition for more, use friends must, if they are to reach an agreement to their mutual benefit, that is, if they are to reach an agreement at all, negotiate and compromise and, to some small degree, trust one another (they must trust, for example, that neither is misrepresenting the item offered up for exchange).[46] As a result, the agreement they reach does not reflect their naked self-interests alone. It reflects, rather, an enlarged sense of their self-interests, one that takes into account the interests of both friends.[47] As we saw in chapter 3, the agreement takes into account the interests of both parties not because use friends are particularly other-regarding but because if it did not, there would be no agreement at all. Representing the use friends' *mutual* advantage, the agreement embodies, with respect to their exchange, a good that gives them both their due in accordance with their judgments about fairness, that is, it embodies their common good.

When Aristotle describes buyers and sellers as looking "to the thing" (*EE* 1242b33) for their mutual advantage, it is to their agreement that he is referring. He emphasizes not the persons involved but "the thing" (*NE* 1156a11–12) because, as we have seen, use friends need not be, and usually are not, particularly oriented toward one another: they need not particularly like one another nor need they be especially virtuous. Most important, perhaps, is that if their friendship is to continue *as friendship* in the face of conflict, use friends must be oriented not to their *own* persons in the form of their individual self-interest over and above the thing that represents their mutual advantage. Involving an initial coalition based on self-interest, to be sure, use friendship also orients the friends to their common good,

---

46. Aristotle distinguishes between legal and ethical use friendships. The difference is that whereas the former are based on agreement and are limited to the transaction at hand, the latter are based on trust. Aristotle is extremely skeptical about ethical use friendship and criticizes it by claiming that people who engage in such relations "wish to have it both ways at once." His complaint is against those who, while engaging in use friendship, act as if they are virtue friends (*NE* 1162b39–1163a2). By insisting on the place of trust in use friendship, I am not rehabilitating this suspect mode of friendship but rather underscoring that even use friendships of the legal sort depend on a minimal level of trust.

47. The game theory literature suggests that the need for trust emerges from the repeated iteration of games and thus over an extended time horizon: see Axelrod, *Evolution of Cooperation*. Aristotle, by contrast, argues that minimal trust is required from the get-go and forms the basis for an expanded sense of self-interest.

which is not simply determined by aggregating discrete self-interests and which, once determined, is not reducible to those interests.

If mutual advantage in the paradigmatic case of use friendship—commercial exchange—is reflected in the agreement between the parties to the exchange, what represents irreducible mutual advantage among sailors on a ship (*NE* 1160a15–16) or among members of an alliance (*NE* 1157a26–28), Aristotle's other examples of use friends? What, in other words, is the thing that makes it possible for these use friends to regulate their relations in cases of conflict? Richard Kraut provides the following answer: sailors, working together on a ship, collaborate "to make a profit or to promote each other's safety" and "cities form an alliance for the sake of mutual protection" because they "take it to be in their interest to cooperate with each other."[48] That is surely right, at least under cooperative conditions when what is mutually beneficial to use friends reflects what is in the self-interest of each. Among sailors and cities, as among commercial exchangers, however, this understanding of the mutual benefit of use friendship falters in the face of conflict, for then what is mutually beneficial to use friends often, if not always, involves not only self-interest but also compromise and even self-sacrifice.

What happens, for example, when promoting the safety of one sailor requires sailing into a port to procure medicine through waters that other sailors worry will put them at risk? To adjudicate such a conflict, the sailors look to the self-interest that got them aboard the ship in the first place, to be sure. They do so, however, not to perform a utilitarian calculus based on aggregating self-interests and to make a decision on the basis of majority rule. Following this course is the equivalent of terminating the friendship with the sick sailor rather than resolving their conflict as friends. If their friendship is to continue, the sailors must, like the commercial exchangers, look to the thing that represents their mutual benefit. Just as commercial exchangers look to their agreement, that without which they would not be buyers and sellers operating to *mutual* benefit, so do the sailors look to that without which they would not be sailors working to promote their own and each other's safety, namely, their ship. It is only by looking to the thing that makes their cooperation possible *as cooperation* that conflict management is possible.

If looking to the ship is the condition of the possibility of cooperation in the face of conflict, it does not, in itself, guarantee a successful coming to terms. Asking whether the ship can make the trip into port is only the point of departure for

---

48. Kraut, *Aristotle: Political Philosophy,* p. 466.

complex and difficult deliberations. This is because for the sailors to reach an agreement, they need to make the same sorts of judgments about the ship that, as we saw in chapter 3, buyers and sellers make (inchoately or explicitly) about the goods they exchange: What is this ship for? What is it made of? Has it been made well? Is it seaworthy? Can it tolerate the choppy waters? Deliberations about these matters will not be easy, nor will *they* necessarily be conflict-free. It is nonetheless *possible* for the sailors to come to terms on the basis of judgments oriented to the ship, and, if they are to come to terms *as friends,* they can do so only by orienting their self-interests in this way. Like the contractual arrangement between buyer and seller, the sailors' agreement will depend on some degree of good faith and trust. It might even involve sacrifice (if, for example, the sailors together judge the waters to be unsafe for passage and the ailing sailor suffers). The sailors' decision, arrived at from within the terms of the use friendship, although not necessarily happy for everyone, will nonetheless be just insofar as it is based on the mutual advantage of all the sailors (including the sick sailor) oriented to the thing. For this reason, it will sustain rather than destroy their friendship.

It is not difficult to imagine an analogous example in the case of an alliance, where, in the face of conflict, that form of use friendship requires an enlarged sense of self-interest, trust, and even sacrifice. Although not in the narrow self-interest of each soldier or city, sacrifices, when demanded fairly, that is, on the basis of the judgments of those whose self-interests are at stake, oriented toward the thing, will be justifiable even to those whose sacrifice is required. Such sacrifices are justifiable by virtue of the thing for the sake of which the members of the alliance coalesced in the first place, namely, their mutual preservation, which, though based on self-interest, is not reducible to it. Looking to the thing of mutual benefit thus makes it possible for use friends to resolve their conflicts *as use friends.* Indeed, looking to the thing offers use friends the only means available for resolving their conflicts *as friends,* that is, fairly and from within the terms of their relation. As we have seen, managing conflicts within use friendships is not without remainder or easy. It involves, instead, compromise and negotiation, sacrifice and trust.

Attending to the difficulties involved in sustaining cooperation in the face of conflict reveals the degree to which use friendships depend on the good judgment of the friends and on their capacities to moderate their orientations to their own self-interests with a view to their mutual benefit. That good judgment and moderation are necessary if use friends are to mediate their own conflicts suggests that

156   CHAPTER FIVE

use friendship depends on the exercise of virtue.[49] Aristotle implies as much at the very start of *Nicomachean Ethics* VIII when he explores the different modes of friendship from the perspective of virtue (*NE* 1155b10–11) and again when he describes use friendship as friendship by analogy, *kath' homoioteta*, to virtue friendship. This latter comment may signify Aristotle's degradation of use friendship relative to "the primary and proper meaning of the term" in virtue friendship (*NE* 1157a30–33). As discussed in chapter 3, however, Aristotle's use of analogy implies that use friendship not only differs from virtue friendship but also that they have similarities. One important similarity is that both involve virtue. To bring this similarity to the fore is not to claim that they involve virtue in the same way, nor is it to turn use friendship into virtue friendship. The differences between the two are hard to miss. In virtue friendships, the parties to the friendship look to one another. In use friendships, as we just saw, they look to the thing of mutual benefit (*NE* 1156a10–12, 1157a14–16). Virtue friends love, and wish to live with, one another. Use friends need feel no affection toward one another, and the coalitions they form demand no intimacy. Because insisting on the key place of virtue in use friendships may, nonetheless, appear to introduce into that relation a degree of unity undesirable and inappropriate to it, I turn next to Aristotle's account of the unity and difference characteristic of virtue friendship before bringing my insights about the virtues of use friendship to bear on political friendship.

Most accounts of Aristotelian virtue friendship privilege sharing, intimacy, and homogeneity rather than distinction, difference, and individuation. I offer instead an account of virtue friendship that depends not on the erasure but on the preservation of distinct selves and less on intimacy than on forbearance. Forbearance is what makes virtue friendship enduring, encouraging the work of a *modus vivendi* that "allows to each their own" (*NE* 1165a17).[50] If, for most commentators, virtue friends are of "the same mind" (*NE* 1167b5–7) owing to their homogeneity, I argue that concord among virtue friends, like musical and political harmony, requires not homogeneity but difference.

Consider the features that distinguish virtue friendship: equality, freedom, and

49. For others who reject the opposition between virtue and utility, see Pangle, *Aristotle and the Philosophy of Friendship;* Kalimtzis, *Aristotle on Political Enmity and Disease.*

50. Aristotle's stress on the important place of recognition, *anagnorisis,* in friendship, explained more fully in the *Poetics,* shows his interest in respecting rather than denying the limits of the possibility of identifying without remainder with another (*Po.* 1452a29–b8). For discussion, see Markell, *Bound by Recognition,* chap. 3; Hadreas, "*Eunoia,*" pp. 397–400.

mutual respect. Virtue friendships are most usually characterized by an equality in quantity, *poson,* or arithmetic equality that obtains among equals (*NE* 1158b28–34). Most commentators take this equality to require that virtue friends be as much as possible like one another.[51] In a sense, this is true. Virtue friends tend to resemble one another in virtue (*NE* 1159b4). There is, moreover, a sameness of mind among virtue friends (*NE* 1167b5–7). But it is a mistake to infer from these qualities a uniform identity between and among virtue friends. Aristotle, in the *Metaphysics,* offers a more complex picture of sameness, which, he maintains, always involves difference (*Meta.* 1004a10–15). When friends are equal in quantity, each party to the friendship, every friend, is a "one and a 'this'" (*Meta.* 1020a7). This means that virtue friends are homogeneous and unified only by virtue of their difference, that is, by virtue of their virtue, something particular to and different in each human being.

Virtue friends are similar, *homoioi,* to each other in virtue (*NE* 1156b7)[52] not by sharing a conception of virtue, for "as a condition of the possession of the virtues, knowledge has little or no weight" (*NE* 1105b3). Aristotle may call virtue a "habit concerned with choice, lying in a mean, this being determined by reason, *logos*" (*NE* 1106b35–1107a2), but the reason he refers to here is not a common or universal reason or theoretical knowledge but rather the right rule, *logos,* of the person with practical wisdom, *phronimos* (*NE* 1107a2), who, as we have seen, is virtuous not insofar as he knows what virtue is but insofar as he practices virtue, that is, acts prohairetically. Along similar lines, virtue friends resemble each other not by having virtue in common, for as we have seen in earlier chapters, the key to virtue is not its simple possession but its use. Finally, virtue friends do not possess identical virtues because no two people will hit the mean, which is to say, will act virtuously, by acting in the same way. Someone who is disposed to cowardice will need to act more bravely to hit the courageous mean than will someone who is already disposed to act bravely. If both hit the mean, however, they are both equally virtuous.

51. See, e.g., Aquinas, *Commentary on Aristotle's* Nicomachean Ethics, p. 501; Coby, "Aristotle's Three Cities," pp. 912–17; F. Miller, *Nature, Justice, and Rights,* chap. 6.

52. The *homo-* prefix appears throughout Aristotle's treatise on friendship. Signifying sameness, Aristotle uses it everywhere to mark not only sameness but also difference. As we saw, he speaks of *kath' homoioteta* with reference to the forms of friendship, indicating the ways in which pleasure and use resemble virtue friendships and the ways in which they differ (*NE* 1157a32, 1158b6). This suggests that without difference there can be no sameness. This Aristotelian insight is at the root of his accounts of friendship, good politics, and individual identity.

158   CHAPTER FIVE

All this suggests that virtue friends resemble each other in their differences. This is confirmed by Aristotle's insistence that, although virtue is to be used or exercised in the context of collective as well as individual activity and to achieve common as well as individual ends, to be used collectively it must be held as one's own.[53] Virtue is not a collective practice but a distributive or individuated one.[54]

This is not to deny that there is commonality or sharing in virtue friendship. But it is a different kind of sharing than is usually supposed. Consider just two examples. Although it is sometimes said that Aristotle takes friends' goods to be common goods,[55] he objects to common ownership as unjust not only for the well-constituted polity but for friendship as well. Common ownership makes impossible the free giving characteristic of liberality (*Pol.* 1263b6–14), the virtue that lies at the heart of friendship. With common ownership things are shared not because sharing is preferred but because it is required, so there is less friendship, not more, among those who hold everything in common (*Pol.* 1262b2).[56] Just as self-love is a condition of the possibility of the free love of another in friendship (*NE* IX.4), so too is holding as one's own a condition of the possibility of the free giving that is key to friendship. Consider as well the example Aristotle invokes to sum up his criticisms of the unity celebrated by Plato's Socrates. Aristotle maintains that "the unity [Plato's Socrates] commends would be like that of the lovers in the *Symposium*, who, as Aristophanes says, desire to grow together in the excess of their affection, and from being two become one, in which case one or both would surely perish" (*Pol.* 1262b10). Aristotle decries excessive unity between friends, between lovers, and, as we have seen, among members of political community. It is having and being an individual—remaining differentiated—that makes possible any relation of affiliation, private or political.

Virtue friends, then, do not resemble each other by being identical. Instead, they resemble each other in that "friends' actions are the same or similar for each acts well" (*NE* 1156b7–18).[57] Aristotle's understanding of friendly activity underscores

53. For discussion, see chapter 2.

54. Aristotle makes this plain in his discussion of the wisdom of the multitude (*Pol.* III.11). For the term *distributive* rather than *collective* as applied to Aristotelian virtue, see Ober, *Political Dissent in Democratic Athens,* p. 319.

55. Yack, *Problems of a Political Animal,* p. 118; Barker, *Politics of Aristotle,* p. 49, but see also p. 305.

56. Instead, as Aristotle puts it, friends' goods are, *for the purpose of use,* common goods, *pros to chresthai . . . koina ta philon* (*Pol.* 1263a30). This means that friends' goods are held as their own, but held in this way for use together.

57. See, for discussion, Cooper, "Aristotle on Friendship," pp. 310, 302.

the importance of differentiation among friends. Focusing on activities not conducive to friendship, such as acting selfishly by taking too large a share of things or overindulging one's passions and appetites, he insists that to act in these ways is to act as a slave to one's baser tendencies.[58] It is no less slavish, however, to act selflessly by considering a friend's interests only, while disregarding one's own (*NE* 1168a35), what we might call acting altruistically. To Aristotle, this is to live at another's beck and call and is, therefore, a form of unfreedom (*Rhet.* 1367a31–32). Appropriate to virtue friendship is living and acting as one's own person, which is to say, freely. A free man, like a virtuous friend, exists for himself and not for another (*Meta.* 982b26–27). Virtue friends come and stay together freely, each wishing to preserve the autonomy of himself and the other.[59] Freedom, for Aristotle, is not self-sufficiency or independence or an abstraction from or denial of the passions and desires that move us. Rather, what virtue friends have in their freedom is the capacity, *dunamis,* to be together and to share their particular lives and feelings without becoming enslaved to one another. This capacity is actualized among friends and indeed actualizes their friendship by means of their speaking and thinking together (*NE* 1170b10–11).

If acting well in friendship is acting freely, Aristotle takes a virtue friend to act freely when he treats his friend as what Aristotle variously calls "another self" (*NE* 1166a33), "a second self" (*MM* 1213a24), or "another me" (*NE* 1170b7). Most commentators take the emphasis in these phrases to be on the noun, "me" or "self," and so take Aristotle to be marking the degree to which a virtue friend must be assimilable to one's own self. In my view, the emphasis is better placed on the adjective, "*another* me" or "a *second* self." This suggests that a friend is a *separate* self.[60] Virtue friends, in other words, do not strive at every point to eradicate their differences but rather accept those differences by allowing to each his own (*NE* 1165a17).[61] In this way, they live in relation to one another as neither slaves of one another nor as

58. Buffoons, Aristotle says, are slaves to their sense of humor (*NE* 1128a34). Flatterers are slaves to the opinions of others (*NE* 1125a1). Boastful or falsely modest people are slaves to the question of whether their representations to others are believed. Gluttons are slaves to the pleasures of touch and taste in gastronomic matters (*NE* 1118a21–25). And one who is mean, either by being not liberal enough or by taking from others, is a slave to his greed (*NE* 1122a6).

59. The etymological roots of friendship and freedom confirm their connection to one another: see Onions, *Oxford Dictionary of English Etymology,* pp. 375–77; Pitkin, "Are Freedom and Liberty Twins?" p. 529; Weil, *Waiting for God,* pp. 204–5.

60. For discussion, see Sherman, *Fabric of Character,* pp. 138–44.

61. True friends consent "to be two and not one." Weil, *Waiting for God,* p. 205.

160   CHAPTER FIVE

slaves to their baser tendencies (*NE* 1124b31) but in accordance with their own respective and proper excellence (*NE* 1169a1).

Aristotle insists, however, that a friend wishes the same good for his friends as he wishes for himself, or "share[s] his friend's perception of his existence" (*NE* 1170b11), and so is of the same mind with him. How, in friendship so described, might friends retain their distinction? Aristotle explains the homonoia of virtue friendship in this way:

> If the virtuous man feels toward his friend in the same way as he feels toward himself (for his friend is a second self) then, just as a man's own existence is desirable for him, so, or nearly so, is his friend's existence also desirable. . . . It is the perception, *aisthesis,* of oneself as good that makes existence desirable, and such perception is pleasant in itself. Therefore a man ought also to share his friend's perception of his existence. (*NE* 1170b6–12)

This may read to some like the merging of minds characteristic of traditional understandings of virtue friendship. Aristotle's language, however, suggests otherwise. He says that friends share perception by living together and sharing their feelings and thoughts (*NE* 1170b10–13). Sharing feelings and thoughts distinguishes the human mode of living together from that of bees and other social animals (*Pol.* 1253a9) and from that of cattle, whose living together consists in grazing in the same pasture (*NE* 1170b13–14). Friends share their thoughts and feelings because they do not already know what one another's thoughts and feelings are. Aristotle's choice of the word *aisthesis,* perception, to describe what friends share is key. We perceive with our senses, and what we sense we perceive in its particularity or differences. Because we perceive in this way, one person cannot have another person's perception. To share a perception thus requires that the friend whose perception it is communicate it or make it common. This means that there can be no sharing of perception without speech. Indeed, Aristotle remarks that friends share their thoughts and feeling using speech, that which distinguishes the human mode of being from all other modes. Were the sign of virtue friendship the eradication of all difference, one friend would always already know what the other friend was thinking and feeling. Speech would be unnecessary.[62] But speech is necessary (*NE* 1170b12). Rather than a "primordial" sharing, concord among virtue friends is a sharing of perceptions or a coming to a shared perception via speech. As such, it

---

62. For common thinking or feeling absent speech, see Plato, *Symposium,* 192c.

depends on difference.[63] The harmony of virtue friendship, then, like the harmony of identity, as we saw in chapter 1, and properly political harmony, as we saw above, requires that there be difference in sameness.[64]

The harmony of virtue friends may be like political harmony but relations among citizens are not to be modeled on those among virtue friends. Aristotle insists that virtue friendships can exist only among a few people, the fully virtuous (*NE* 1170b30–71a12). They are rare and require time and intimacy (*NE* 1156b25–27). Virtue friends live together, share thoughts and feelings, and have a degree of affection for one another that political friends cannot have and most would surely not want. If, in all these ways, virtue friendship is to be distinguished from political friendship, the relative equality, freedom, and mutual respect found among virtue friends are nonetheless qualities to be prized among citizens of a polity as well. If the unity of virtue friendship is impossible and undesirable in a political life, the difference that makes that unity possible also makes possible political unity. Virtue friendship and political friendship, like virtue friendship and use friendship, are thus best understood analogically, that is, in their differences and their similarities.

Among political friends, as among virtue and use friends, there will be concord, *homonoia*, about the objects and ends of the friendship, which is to say, about that for the sake of which the friends act. This differs, however, for virtue, use, and political friends. Virtue friends, as we have seen, act for their own sake and for the sake of their friends. Use friends and, indeed, political friends also act for their own sake. Looking, however, to the thing that represents their mutual advantage or use, use friends act not for the sake of one another but with a view to the thing. The same is true of political friends. If among use friends in commercial transac-

---

63. *Contra* Klonoski, "*Homonoia* in Aristotle's Ethics and Politics," pp. 315, 316, 325, who argues that the sharing among virtue friends is "primordial."

64. Annas, "Self-Love in Plato and Aristotle," and Klonoski, "*Homonoia* in Aristotle's Ethics and Politics," pp. 318–19, understand Aristotle's insistence on self-love to show that he understands personal identity to be a matter of simple unity. They take the unity of the individual as expressed by proper self-love to be a condition of the possibility of the unity of two people in a friendship, and the unity of friendship to be a condition of the possibility of political unity. Though I agree that Aristotle builds these relations on one another, my argument is that the unity of the different of the polity depends on the unity of the different of friendship, which itself depends on the unity of the different of each individual soul, as demonstrated in chapter 1. This means that individual identity is not a simple unity but itself a unity of the different.

162 CHAPTER FIVE

tions, the thing is their contractual agreement to exchange items of immediate use and so their relation is generally fleeting, among political friends the thing, as we saw in chapter 4, is their constitution or way of life (*NE* 1167a27–b2). It is, therefore, a long-term and enduring project (*NE* 1160a22–23). In use friendships, as we saw, activity with a view to mutual advantage depends on and teaches good judgment and moderation. For this reason, use friendship, like virtue friendship, involves virtue. How exactly does political friendship involve virtue? Like use friends but unlike virtue friends, political friends do not need to be fully virtuous. Instead, they need to practice good judgment and moderation only with respect to the particular goods motivating their coalition, namely, in a political life, the fundamental terms of their cooperation. Just as good judgment about the particular goods motivating their coalition produces a contractual arrangement among use friends conducive to their common good, so too will judging well with respect to their constitution promote among political friends a life devoted to their common good. It is in this way that political friends, virtuous in the mode of use friends (that is, not fully virtuous), can promote the good life. The constitution, a result of cooperation among political friends based on self-interest and oriented also to their common good, is, as such, able to govern their relations not only under cooperative conditions but also in the face of conflict.

Modeled on use friendship and involving the practice of virtue, political friendship is best understood as a mixed good concerned with judging and acting well with a view to a polity's common good. What being a good political friend will amount to in any particular context—who will need to compromise, how, and with respect to what—is a priori unknowable.[65] Whether one has been a good political friend can always only be judged after the fact and by speech among the friends themselves. The coming to terms that constitutes homonoia among citizens, understood as a mixed good, depends neither on naked self-interest nor on primordial sharing. Among political friends, as among use and also virtue friends, homonoia is, rather, a continual project in action and in speech that, as ongoing and therefore vulnerable, is also always in question. Like use and virtue friendship,

---

65. The idea of indeterminacy at stake here is pervasive in Aristotle's ethical and political writings, most clearly in his formulations of the mean. Although he discusses at length the varying actions that would miss the mean, he never says exactly what acting with good judgment amounts to. This omission is necessary so as to respect the particularities of circumstance. Insofar as these are not static, proper action cannot be prescribed in advance.

political friendship involves compromise and sacrifice.[66] And, as we have seen, compromise and sacrifice require and build trust. What light does friendship understood in this way shed on the questions of class conflict and regime formation with which we began? These are the questions to which I turn next.

The Middle Class

Political science does not make men, but takes them from nature and uses them.
ARISTOTLE, *Politics*

Aristotle refers to the constitutional polity or timocracy as a model of friendship and describes the friendship among its citizens as one of equality *poson* and virtue (*NE* 1161a25–30), especially among the citizens belonging to the constitutional polity's distinctive middle class. The institutions and laws of the constitutional polity, designed to attenuate disparities between the wealthy and the many, produce this middle class "of quality." These laws include fining the rich if they refuse to serve as judges and paying the poor for their service, electing citizens to governmental offices rather than selecting them by lot, and electing from among citizens with property those who will deliberate about public affairs, hold magistracies, and exercise judicial power (*Pol.* 1298a36–40). Elected officials in the constitutional polity are accountable to the rest of the citizenry insofar as "affirmation of everything lies with the many" (*Pol.* 1298b5–11, 38–40). Accountability "secures that which is the greatest good in polities; the right persons rule and are prevented from doing wrong, and the people have their due" (*Pol.* 1319a1–4).

Aristotle describes the "ideal" constitutional polity, with its laws and institutions fostering equality, respect, and freedom, as one in which "all citizens shall be equal and shall be good, so that they all rule in turn and all have an equal share of power" (*NE* 1161a28–30). So described, the constitutional polity has substantial similarities with the city of prayer. As we saw at the start of this chapter, Aristotle divides the city of prayer into two broad classes: citizens and noncitizens. The citizens are property owners, with land both in the city and at its frontiers, because this property arrangement invites responsibility in regard to domestic issues—infrastructure and upkeep—as well as in regard to foreign policy and defense (*Pol.* 1330a15–25). Aristotle maintains that the territory of the city of prayer should be of

---

66. Guinier, *Tyranny of the Majority,* chap. 1; Allen, "Law's Necessary Forcefulness," pp. 860–68.

164 CHAPTER FIVE

a size that will enable the inhabitants "to live at once moderately and liberally" (*Pol.* 1326b31–32). The constitutional polity also has a large class of property holders: the middle class. The virtues of moderation and liberality distinguish the property holders of the constitutional polity, making the middle class less prone to faction, therefore stable (*Pol.* 1295b3–33).[67] Both regimes meet Aristotle's criteria for good constitutions: they distribute goods and offices on the basis of virtue, and those who hold political offices rule for the common advantage. The governments in both polities are "free." In the words of one commentator, "in their level of material prosperity, if not in their moral development, the middle class [of the constitutional polity] match the citizens of the ideal state."[68]

In the *Nicomachean Ethics* Aristotle states that there is only one constitution which is everywhere according to nature the best (*NE* 1135a5). Treating the constitutional polity and the city of prayer as substantially the same explains Aristotle's insistence on the singular. It also cuts against the grain of much Aristotle scholarship. For most commentators, the constitutional polity is only best given the limitations of the many. It is, in other words, the "best possible," "second-best," or "practicable" regime, but not the best simpliciter.[69] For these readers, this is both the flaw of the regime and its strength. It is a flaw because the constitutional polity will never be the city of prayer. It is a strength because, unlike the city of prayer, the constitutional polity is actualizable.

In my reading, the similarities between the constitutional polity and the city of prayer belie these purported differences. Most specifically, the alleged disparity between the two on the ground of possibility does not stand up to scrutiny. For, as it turns out, the constitutional polity is no more (or less) possible than the city of prayer. Aristotle may appear to characterize the constitutional polity as "according to nature" (*NE* 1135a5), that is to say, this regime may be found "always and for the most part," but he also claims that it has either not occurred or has not often existed (*Pol.* 1293a40–b1, 1296a36–38). This is because the middling citizens, *hoi mesoi*, like the truly virtuous, are relatively few (*Pol.* 1296a22–24). It is also because the constitutional polity's distinctive feature, its middle class, is exceedingly difficult to produce, requiring not simply a blending of institutions and laws but also friendliness, for, as we have seen repeatedly, these political and ethical measures

---

67. For discussion, see Nichols, *Citizens and Statesmen*, pp. 90–100.

68. Mulgan, *Aristotle's Political Theory*, p. 108. See also Kraut, *Aristotle: Political Philosophy*, p. 442.

69. For these formulations, see Kraut, *Aristotle: Political Philosophy*, p. 427; F. Miller, *Nature, Justice, and Rights*, p. 252; and Mulgan, *Aristotle's Political Theory*, p. 102, respectively.

depend on one another. When the constitutional polity simply combines oligarchy and democracy (*Pol.* 1293b33, 1294a40, 1294b14–19), the rich and the poor, and the distributive principles of wealth and freedom (*Pol.* 1294a16–17, 22–23, 1307a11–12), however, there can be no friendship in the polity and, in the absence of such friendship, a middle class cannot emerge.[70]

Consider once again the friendships between the wealthy and the many that characterized Athenian politics in the later part of the fifth century. These friendships arose because it was in each party's interest to cooperate: the wealthy benefited from the political support of the many and the many benefited by gaining inclusion in Athenian political life. The wealthy and the many were able to sustain their coalitions as long as the benefits of their cooperation outweighed their feelings of distrust and suspicion. When finding terms for cooperation was most necessary, however, as was the case in the later years of the Peloponnesian War, these coalitions could not be sustained. Instead, as we saw, they were displaced by mostly oligarchic but also democratic cabals that exacerbated the ongoing conflicts. This was not an isolated case of failure. Rather, as I demonstrate next, strategic coalitions between rich and poor are bound to falter in the face of conflict and, for this reason, cannot qualify as political friendships in Aristotle's sense at all.

Describing the conflicts between oligarchs and democrats in a way that echoes his account of the quarrelsome nature of use friendships, Aristotle maintains that each side worries that it has too little of what is properly due to it or that the other has too much (*Pol.* 1302a17–30). How might such conflicts be managed? The following passage from the *Nicomachean Ethics,* explaining how it is possible for there to be friendship among unequals (*NE* 1158b33–1159a5), is instructive: "Each party is justified in his claim . . . that each should get more out of the friendship than the other—not more of the same thing, however, but the superior more honor and the inferior more gain" (*NE* 1163b1–5). In this passage, Aristotle begins by speaking about unequal parties to an individual friendship and ends by discussing the possibilities for friendship among political unequals (*NE* 1163b4–13). Such friendships depend on the parties' wanting complementary things and on what he calls a "proportional equality." These criteria may be met by oligarchs and democrats under cooperative conditions, when the wealthy benefit from the political support of the many, the many benefit from inclusion in politics, and both accept that their arrangement depends on the inequality or hierarchy between

---

70. For a thorough and excellent discussion of the mixed constitution, see F. Miller, *Nature, Justice, and Rights,* chap. 7, esp. pp. 256–62.

166 CHAPTER FIVE

them.[71] Even under such conditions, however, these coalitions are fragile. This is because, as Aristotle points out, oligarchs tend to be dissatisfied with political support alone, demanding instead honor *and* profit (*Pol.* 1281a14–28), which, he explains, cannot be supported by the common property of the polity (*NE* 1163b7–9). Under conditions of political turmoil, when the terrain of conflict becomes political power itself, the complementarity that motivated and sustained their coalition disappears and, while the wealthy are prepared to uphold hierarchy, the many demand equality based on free birth (*Pol.* 1301a29–31).

Do the wealthy and the many, like use friends, have resources for managing their conflicts? Taking the relation between oligarchs and democrats to be paradigmatic of political friendship, Yack maintains that the wealthy and the many may moderate their conflicts by "broadening the one-sided views of justice that citizens ordinarily appeal to in political life."[72] In Aristotle's assessment, however, the prospects for public deliberation among the wealthy and the many when they are vying for political power are dismal. In language that mirrors the contentiousness of the relations he is examining, that is, with many "by Zeuses" and curses (*Pol.* III.10–11), Aristotle maintains that the "error common both to oligarchies and to democracies" is that rather than professing to maintain the cause of the rich, demagogues are always "cutting the city in two by quarrels with the rich," and, rather than professing to maintain the cause of the many, oligarchs swear, "I will be an enemy to the people and will devise all the harm against them which I can" (*Pol.* 1310a3–10). Such public professions do not promote deliberation, which, as Aristotle explains in the *Rhetoric*, depends on friendliness or trust between speaker and audience.[73] When the many and the wealthy hear the speeches just cited, no "recognition of another's worthiness" or "germ of friendliness," *eunoia*, can emerge to make possible a broadening of the one-sided views of justice held by each group.[74] The ill will that makes deliberative exchange between strife-ridden oligarchs and democrats impossible makes impossible any coming to terms between them on the question of the exchange of political power. Neither rich nor poor will consent to serve one another or to rule in turn because they mistrust one another (*Pol.* 1297a1–5). Instead, each side makes every attempt to grab all the political power for itself. As Aristotle puts it, the reason most governments are either

71. On hierarchy as a defining feature of proportional equality, see Schofield, "Political Friendship and the Ideology of Reciprocity," pp. 87–91.

72. Yack, *Problems of a Political Animal*, p. 235.

73. See, for discussion, Allen, "Intricate Democracy."

74. For these definitions of *eunoia*, see Hadreas, "*Eunoia*," p. 398.

democratic or oligarchic is that "the poor and the rich quarrel with one another, and whichever side gets the better, instead of establishing a just or popular government, regards political supremacy as the prize of victory, and the one party sets up a democracy and the other an oligarchy" (*Pol.* 1296a27–32).

Underscoring the characterological obstacles to cooperation among oligarchs and democrats, Aristotle notes that oligarchs know only how to be masters (*Pol.* 1295b21). Brought up with too much of the goods of fortune, they never learn the habit of obedience (*Pol.* 1295b13 ff.). Democrats, on the other hand, tend toward poverty, and being poor, tend to be slavish (*Pol.* 1295b19). Since conflicts between oligarchs and democrats exacerbate these dispositions, the only use they may be to one another in conditions of strife is as masters and slaves, respectively. This "resolution" to their conflict involves sacrifice and compromise, to be sure, but only on the part of the many, who, desiring equality, will not be happy slaves. This sort of "mutual advantage," then, will not meliorate conflict. Instead, it erases all possibility of political friendship (*AP* 2.1, 2.2, 2.3, 5.1), for, indeed, as Aristotle insists, there can be no friendship at all between master and slave (*NE* 1161b3). With no exchange of authority between democrats and oligarchs, there will be no mutual accountability and no sharing in practices to promote cooperation. Where there is nothing in common between ruler and ruled, which must be the case among oligarchs and democrats (for, as Aristotle notes, the statuses of wealth and poverty cannot, as such, be shared, *Pol.* 1291b7), there can be no friendship any more than there can be justice (*NE* 1161a33–34).[75]

When finding terms for cooperation is most necessary, in times of conflict, such is not possible between the wealthy and the many or poor. Unlike political friends, whose judgments produce an understanding of their mutual benefit that then regulates their relation in cases of conflict, among the wealthy and the many there is no such sharing in practices to produce a sense of political justice that can, in turn, promote greater cooperation. This is because when they conflict, as when they cooperate, the wealthy and the many look not to their mutual advantage or common good but only to their own advantage. Because their cooperative venture involves nothing conducive to their mutual advantage over and above what is in each side's discrete self-interest, the wealthy and the many can produce no agreements, laws, or constitution that will serve to govern their relation in cases of conflict. Instead,

---

75. Aristotle concludes his account of stasis between the wealthy and the many claiming that "this condition of affairs is very far removed from friendliness and from political commonality, for friendliness is an element of partnerships since men are not willing to be partners with their enemies, even on a journey" (*Pol.* 1295b23–27).

168   CHAPTER FIVE

when oligarchy and democracy do combine, the result is a constitution, like that of Sparta, discussed in chapter 4, that is captive to the excesses of both regimes and oriented toward the overreaching, *pleonexia,* characteristic of conquest. Against this backdrop, Aristotle's description of the constitutional polity in militaristic terms, with its leading citizens emerging from the hoplite classes (*Pol.* 1279b1–4, 1297b2–3), makes sense. When it combines oligarchy and democracy, the constitutional polity, like the Spartan constitution, can only be oriented toward war, not least within the ranks of the polity itself, where, in the absence of friendliness, laws must be enforced with might.

Few commentators speak to the obstacles to the emergence of political friendship from oligarchy and democracy or therefore to the obstacles to the production of the constitutional polity's distinctive middle class. Among those who do, some recommend that a lawgiver or legislator establish a middle class by persuading the conflict-ridden groups to cooperate.[76] It is true that Aristotle mentions a lawgiver in his discussion of the constitutional polity. But, unlike, say, Rousseau, Aristotle maintains that the lawgiver will come from within the existing ranks of a regime (unless he is founding an entirely new regime, *Pol.* II.11). The lawgiver who establishes the middle class of the constitutional polity from democracy and oligarchy will therefore be himself either a democrat or, more likely, an oligarch.[77] Unless graced, as in the case of Theramenes, by "outstanding judgment and intelligence" (*AP* 32.2), oligarchs are particularly ill-suited to meliorate the intractable distrust, disagreement, and enmity between rich and poor. And Theramenes, notwithstanding his good judgment (or, perhaps, because of it) was deemed a traitor. As we saw in chapter 4, among the nonpartisans who with Theramenes called for a return of the ancestral constitution, good judgment makes possible the first bonds of political friendship. It also depends on the hospitality of friendship. For this reason, Theramenes' treatment at the hands of Athens's democratic and, especially, oligarchic cabals (it was the Thirty, of whom he was a member, who orchestrated his execution) should come as no surprise. Where there is no political friendship, good judgment can be treacherous.

If no middle can emerge from a combination of oligarchy and democracy, from where, then, does the middle class come? Richard Mulgan offers the beginning of

---

76. F. Miller, *Nature, Justice, and Rights,* pp. 284 ff.; Mulgan, *Aristotle's Political Theory,* p. 112. Note that in his discussion of the deviant constitutions Miller recognizes the intractable divisiveness between rich and poor. He does not, however, read this back into his account of the constitutional polity.

77. F. Miller, *Nature, Justice, and Rights,* pp. 292 ff., notes this as well.

an answer when he points out that Aristotle seems to set them up as two main types of constitution "like the north and south wind" but then rejects this view. Oligarchy and democracy are, rather, "to be seen as perversions of the [constitutional] polity . . . ; that is, logically and analytically, the [constitutional] polity must be prior to oligarchy and democracy even if, when analyzing it, we have to use the previously identifiable characteristics of democracy and oligarchy as the elements of the mixture." Mulgan takes Aristotle's insistence on the priority of the constitutional polity to be an "unnecessary complication."[78] But it is not. Aristotle insists that the constitutional polity must, in some sense, supersede or precede its constituent parts and their institutions because, as we have just seen, the political fusion of oligarchy and democracy cannot on its own produce community from conflict. He maintains that to be able to create a middle class, the lawgiver must already be "from among the middle citizens": "a proof of the superiority of the middle class is that the best legislators have been of a middle condition" (*Pol.* 1296a18–21). As examples in this passage, Aristotle names Solon (of Athens), Lycurgus (of Sparta), and Charondas (of Catana), all of whom, in the seventh and sixth centuries, reformed laws in their respective cities to distribute power more evenly between the wealthy and the many and were themselves, like Theramenes, committed to moderating the excesses of democracy and oligarchy. The *ethos* or culture of friendship peculiar to the middle class must accompany a polity's blending of institutions if they are to be successfully blended. It is only in the presence of such an ethos, cultivated, as we have seen, by such practices of virtue as good judgment and moderation, that a polity can emerge in which there appear oligarchic and democratic elements and yet neither (*Pol.* 1294b13–15).

The answer to the question of how such an ethos, conducive to the constitutional polity and to the true aristocracy, may come about lies in another mixed regime: the "so-called" or attainable aristocracy. Most commentators pay little attention to the so-called aristocracy, claiming that they are following the lead of Aristotle, who, in the words of one writer, neglects this regime because "it upsets the theoretical symmetry and elegance of his account."[79] But it is a mistake to say that Aristotle neglects this regime, and for commentators to do so. First, as we will see, the so-called aristocracy appears, although not by name, in the *Nicomachean Ethics* as the regime that can both accommodate the friendship Aristotle prizes and promote the political homonoia he advocates (*NE* 1167b1–2). Second, al-

78. Mulgan, "Aristotle's Analysis of Oligarchy and Democracy," p. 312.
79. Mulgan, *Aristotle's Political Theory,* p. 103.

170 CHAPTER FIVE

though it is true that in his discussion of mixed and middling regimes in the *Politics* Aristotle devotes less space to so-called aristocracies than to constitutional polities, he does so because, insofar as they "approximate to the so-called constitutional polity, . . . [they] need no separate discussion" (*Pol.* 1295a32–34). Describing so-called or attainable aristocracies as bordering on constitutional polities (*Pol.* 1295a31–34), Aristotle maintains that these regimes "are not far from one another" (*Pol.* 1294a29–30) in that both depend on a certain "quality of character" among the citizens and, in both, citizens, having an equal share of political power, rule and are ruled in turn (*NE* 1161a27–31). Along similar lines, many of the institutions that Aristotle takes to be characteristic of the constitutional polity he claims are characteristic of the so-called aristocracy as well (*Pol.* 1300a30–b1). A key exception, to which I will return, is that in the former but not in the latter the poor are paid for their services.[80] Finally, Aristotle introduces so-called aristocracies against the backdrop of his description of the differing forms of democracy in *Politics* IV.6. Insofar as the so-called aristocracy and what Aristotle calls the "first and best" form of democracy are structurally the same—both combine aristocracy and democracy (*Pol.* 1308b38–39), are based on a proportionate equality between the many and the virtuous (*Pol.* 1291b30–34), and have similar rules regarding qualifications for office and accountability (*Pol.* 1318b27–1319a5, 1281b30–38, 1282a34–40)—we can learn about so-called aristocracies from Aristotle's discussions of that form of democracy: the democratic aristocracy.[81]

Josiah Ober condemns the democratic aristocracy on the ground that "with its property qualification for citizenship, its quiescent demos, and its ruling elite of office-holders [it] is so close to moderate oligarchy as to be virtually indistinguishable from it."[82] This is a mistake. The key difference between a democratic aristoc-

---

80. As in the constitutional polity, those occupying governmental offices in the so-called aristocracy expect (or hope) that the electing citizens will use the right criterion (political excellence, correctly understood and rightly perceived) to select the magistrates, and this in turn requires that the democratic citizens exercise the virtues of judgment and justice. As in the constitutional polity, the popular body is sovereign over the selection and evaluation of magistrates. See *Politics* 1281b30–38, 1282a34–40 for differences between strict and so-called aristocracies.

81. For discussions of the first form of democracy that reveal its similarities to the so-called aristocracy, see Ober, *Political Dissent in Democratic Athens*, pp. 332–39; F. Miller, *Nature, Justice, and Rights*, pp. 162–65.

82. Ober, *Political Dissent in Democratic Athens*, p. 337. Mulgan, "Aristotle's Analysis of Oligarchy and Democracy," pp. 309, 311, 316, says the same, claiming that the so-called aristocracy, by placing emphasis on noble birth and not on virtue, is really a mix of oligarchy and democracy.

racy and a moderate oligarchy is that it is not oligarchs who rule in the democratic aristocracy but *hoi epieikeis,* the virtuous. The aristocrats of the democratic aristocracy, like oligarchs, are wealthy in contradistinction to the many. There is, indeed, a property qualification for citizenship in the democratic aristocracy. This is so because, as we saw in chapter 2, moderate wealth is a necessary condition for ruling well in Aristotle's political philosophy. But, as we also saw, moderate wealth is necessary only insofar as it is bound to, is indeed the site of, virtue, which is a practice of those who rule the democratic aristocracy but not usually of oligarchs. It is not the wealth, then, of the aristocrats in the democratic aristocracy that qualifies them to rule. Nor is it their birth (*Rhet.* 1390b24), class, tribe, or tradition (*Pol.* 1283b15–30).[83] When Aristotle speaks of the so-called aristocracy, those who rule do so on the basis of their virtue alone.

How do the virtuous rule? Because, as Aristotle says (approving the saying of Bias), ruling well "shows the man" (*NE* 1130a2–3), the virtuous will rule in a way consistent with their virtue, which is to say, equitably and finely. This means, in the first instance, that they will rule in the interests of the polity as a whole and in a way that assures to each citizen his due (*NE* 1160b13, 1169a8–11; *Pol.* 1318b32–19a4). It also means that they will themselves not only rule but be ruled. This is because when virtue is a qualification for political office, the one with the best claim to rule is "he who is able and chooses *to be governed* and to govern with a view to the life of excellence" (*Pol.* 1284a2–3, emphasis added). As Aristotle explains, "it is impossible to become a good ruler without having been a subject" (*Pol.* 1277b14). Coupling these observations with his claim that the desire to rule continually is a sickness (*Pol.* 1279a10–16) produces the result that to actualize their virtue, those in office must willingly step down from rule. This is, indeed, precisely how Aristotle assesses the virtuous character: though the virtuous have the greatest justification for rising up to defend inegalitarian principles, they are the least likely to do so, he says, just as they are unwilling to stand on their rights (*Pol.* 1301a38–b2; *NE* 1138a1–3).

Ober is mistaken, then, to claim that democratic aristocracy is indistinguishable from oligarchy because in fact only the aristocrats will rule and the democrats will always only be ruled. A regime whose citizenry is divided into the best who rule (in perpetuity) and the many who do not initiates the processes by which citizens and rulers alike forget that everyone is capable of prohairetic activity. As we

---

83. When Aristotle refers to the notables or nobles in so-called aristocracies, he generally avoids language that refers to birth, tradition, tribe, and other status-based assignations. Kraut, similarly, claims that Aristotle has "contempt" for traditional elites: see *Aristotle: Political Philosophy,* p. 443.

172   CHAPTER FIVE

saw in chapter 1 and again in the relation between rich and poor treated in this chapter, this sort of forgetfulness leads to a polity of unfree masters and slaves, that is, to the destruction of the polity. There is a final important difference between the democratic aristocracy and a moderate oligarchy. Whereas in moderate oligarchies the demos is "quiescent," which is to say, subject to the rule of the few but not particularly happy about it, Ober's use of that word is misleading in the context of the democratic aristocracy, where, as we will see, the many actively acquiesce in the rule of others. As Aristotle often notes, acquiescence on the part of the members of a polity is a sign of a well-constituted regime, marking the absence of faction (*Pol.* 1272b30–32, 1294b34–40, 1320a14–17).[84] Aristotle's insistence on virtue as a criterion of office-holding produces a regime in which citizens actively acquiesce because "every man, whoever he is, can act best and live happily" (*Pol.* 1324a25).

How exactly can rule by rotation between the virtuous and the many be squared with Aristotle's claim that the criterion for the distribution of political offices in a democratic aristocracy is virtue? In my reading, the many will not be excluded, at least not necessarily. Aristotle describes the many in the democratic aristocracy as "of a certain quality" (*Pol.* 1319a5–6), which is to say, as possessing some virtue. What sort of virtue they have may be elucidated by unpacking the relation between the democratic principle of freedom (*Pol.* 1291b34–35) and the poverty of democratic citizens (*Pol.* 1317b40) using Aristotle's account of the virtue of liberality. Liberality, he says, is the proper use of useful things in regard to giving and taking, especially in regard to giving. As the etymological connections in English and Greek make plain, being liberal, *eleutheriotes,* is giving with liberty, *eleutheria.* Someone who gives too freely, that is, in excess, is prodigal. If someone gives too freely too much of the time, he becomes poor and, as we saw in chapter 2, may, by wasting his substance, lose himself (*NE* 1120a34). Short of that, however, Aristotle finds that giving too freely is not the worst vice because excessive giving shows a generous nature (*NE* 1121a19–30). Excessive generosity, then, may be a peculiarly democratic vice insofar as it leads to poverty, but generosity itself, as Aristotle notes in the *Constitution of Athens,* is also a peculiarly democratic virtue (22.4).[85] Whether the characteristic liberality of the poor develops into vice or virtue will depend on how this disposition is cultivated, and this, as we saw in chapter 1, will depend on the habits and activities of individual democrats and also on the com-

---

84. As F. Miller, *Nature, Justice, and Rights,* p. 273, puts it, "voluntary compliance of the subjects to political rule is evidence that the political rule is justified."

85. See Ober, *Political Dissent in Democratic Athens,* p. 356. Aristotle repeatedly finds democrats and democracies more praiseworthy than oligarchies, specifically regarding the

pany in which they find themselves and under whose rule. Where oligarchs, knowing only how to be masters, rule, for example, democratic liberality will tend to develop into the vice of slavishness. In a democratic aristocracy, by contrast, where the virtuous rule with a view to the good of the polity as a whole by giving to each his due, it is possible instead for democratic liberality to develop into virtue via the free and reciprocal giving that Aristotle locates at the heart of friendship (*NE* 1155a6–10, 1159a28).[86]

The sort of friendship that is possible between aristocrats and democrats in a democratic aristocracy is suggested by the passage in the *Nicomachean Ethics* already cited concerning friendship between unequals based on proportionate equality. For this friendship to work, the parties must want different things: the superior, a larger share of honor; the inferior, a larger share of profit (*NE* 1163b3). Unlike oligarchs, who want honor and profit (*Pol.* 1281a14–28), the virtuous will be satisfied with honor alone. The many, on the other hand, desire profit above honor (*Pol.* 1318b16–22). This means that complementary desires motivate cooperation between the virtuous and the many.[87]

Aristotle's discussion of Carthage offers a good case in point.[88] He says that Carthage is praiseworthy in that it is practically free from faction (*Pol.* 1272b29–32, 1316b6–7). This is because the notables, *gnorimoi,* at Carthage have acquired the friendship of the many by giving them one-time payments to buy land or set up a trade (*Pol.* 1320a35–b7). Aristotle endorses the practices of property in Tarentine as well, but his description of the class relations in the two cities differs. Between the notables and the many at Carthage there is friendship. Toward the notables at Tarentine, who make property communal for the purpose of use by the needy, the many have only goodwill, *eunoia* (*Pol.* 1320b11–12). Goodwill, though a necessary step on the way to friendship is, by itself, a passive and cognitive regard (*NE*

---

question of pleonexia (*Pol.* 1297a11–13); see also Aristotle's general ranking of democracies over oligarchies (*NE* 1160b19–21; *Pol.* 1289b3–5, 1290a27–28, 1296a9–21, 1302a8–9; *AP* 34–37).

86. Friends exact not what is due but what is possible (*NE* 1163b15). What is possible, in friendship, is what friends give freely.

87. Paul Millett underlines the reciprocity in relations between aristocrats and the demos in Athens in the fifth and fourth centuries in "Rhetoric of Reciprocity in Classical Athens," pp. 227–53. See also Millett, "Encounters in the Agora."

88. This is not a perfect case, however, because, as noted in chapters 2 and 4, Aristotle is also critical of Carthage. Specifically, he thinks that it tends toward oligarchy and avarice because it distributes offices on the basis of wealth and excellence rather than on the basis of excellence alone (*Pol.* 1273a5–6, 25–39).

1166b30–34). Resting on homonoia, friendship, by contrast, requires active involvement of both sides to the friendship. As Aristotle's preference for the property practices of Carthage's notables suggests, practices that help make the many well off (*Pol.* 1320b8), homonoia between classes depends on the capacity of the virtuous and the many to approach equality (*NE* 1159b2–3).

They do so on two fronts. Receiving profit, the many become wealthy enough to achieve relative economic independence (*Pol.* 1320b7) and, most important, to meet the property qualification for office-holding. In this way, the material inequalities between the virtuous and the many are reduced. Aristotle makes this point in a slightly different context when he maintains that "if office brought no profit, then and then only could aristocracy and democracy be combined" (*Pol.* 1308b39–1309a1). Aligning the democratic aristocracy with the Constitution of the Five Thousand discussed in chapter 4, and underscoring a key institutional difference between these constitutions and the constitutional polity, because in the latter pay for office is mandated, this passage may appear to confirm Ober's reading of the real agenda behind Aristotle's advocacy of the democratic aristocracy. When there is no pay for office-holding, even if the offices are nominally open to everyone (a democratic principle), only those not needing pay, namely, the wealthy, will hold office. The democratic aristocracy thus may appear to be no different from a moderate oligarchy. What Aristotle envisions happening to those thus excluded from holding office, however, is that they "will keep to their work and grow rich" (*Pol.* 1309a9). If the poor grow wealthier, the material gap between the virtuous and the many will decrease and the many will meet the property qualification for office-holding. If, alongside this narrowing of material differences, the virtuous follow the Carthaginian property practices that Aristotle commends, the result will be a dramatically expanded middle class of citizens.

The other key area of disparity among unequal friends that can vitiate friendship—inequalities based on virtue—will be lessened as well insofar as being ruled by the virtuous, unlike being ruled by oligarchs, allows the many to develop their own virtue. For some commentators, the development of virtue under such conditions is strictly one-sided. What is good for the common citizen in an aristocracy, says one author, is that the aristocrats are his aristocrats.[89] This formulation obscures the point that for the democratic citizen to benefit, he must be willing to benefit, and that presupposes and depends on a desire on his part to make use of his capacities for prohairetic activity. Moreover, although it is true that the good-

---

89. Cooper, "Politics and Civic Friendship," p. 374.

ness of the virtuous may bring benefit by modeling virtuous activity, this is hardly a one-sided relation. The virtuous have much to learn from the many as well. Specifically, they learn that their goodness belongs to them not by virtue of their status and not only by virtue of their moderation, but also, perhaps especially, in their emulation of the free giving characteristic of democratic liberality. A life of moderation alone, Aristotle insists, slips into a life of misery, distinguished only by restraint. A good polity requires both moderation and liberality (*Pol.* 1265a28– 40), a combination uniquely present in the democratic aristocracy by virtue of the characteristic activities of both the many and the virtuous.

As a unity of the different, based on respect, freedom, and relative equality, a democratic aristocracy appears to meet the "presuppositions" of Aristotle's city of prayer. That the many and the virtuous respect one another is evidenced by the fact that they give each other their due. Allowing to each their due, and giving of their own, they live freely. Although some argue that equalization between un- equals cannot occur, as we have seen, what begins as proportionate equality be- tween the many and the virtuous may, as disparities of wealth and virtue diminish, become equality *poson*, generating a large, stable, and virtuous middle class.[90] This can only happen if, by their individuated activities over time, the many and the virtuous come to perceive that in ways deeper than honor and profit, namely, in their capacities for prohairetic activity and, therefore, in the practices of the virtues that distinguish them, they are fundamentally equal and alike. The ex- change of honor for profit may initiate relations, but for these relations to con- tinue they must see and be actively committed to the ways in which they can, in their everyday practices, expand each other's capacities for prohairetic activity. Thus may proportional equality become, over time, equality *poson* (*NE* 1158b29– 33). And thus may the class of the virtuous and the class of the many become one large middle class of many virtuous citizens.

What happens in the relation between the virtuous and the many in cases of conflict? Do their self-governing practices of virtue regulate their relation from within? Does their relation, in other words, amount to political friendship, or *homonoia*? Aristotle maintains that there is homonoia among citizens when they agree about the objects and ends of political life, about the laws, the specifications of justice, and the other things—advantageous and harmful, right and wrong— that it is the business of the polity to address (*NE* 1167a22–b5). Offering his only example of homonoia in the political domain, he says that concord occurs when

90. For the claim that these disparities cannot be bridged, see Pangle, *Aristotle and the Philosophy of Friendship*, p. 62.

176 CHAPTER FIVE

"both the many, *demos,* and the virtuous, *hoi epieikeis,* wish that the best people shall rule" (*NE* 1167b1–2). That Aristotle refers to the relation between the many and the virtuous as one of homonoia signifies the active participation of both groups in their agreement about great political things and the cooperative nature of their venture. It is not that one class (the many) are mere spectators, as at an athletic event, having a good regard, *eunoia,* toward the virtuous. Such would betoken a kind of "idle friendship" (*NE* 1167a11). Homonoia signifies active participation on the part of both the many and the virtuous with a view to their mutual advantage, their common good, namely, as in Aristotle's example, their constitution.

In order to promote the common good when judging with respect to their constitution, the many and the virtuous will judge with a view to maximizing the prohairetic activity that the constitution and the polity itself depend on and make possible. By judging in this way, the many and the virtuous act for the sake of the polity as a whole and also (or therefore) for the sake of the thing that is to their mutual benefit: their constitution. In so acting, that is, by looking to the thing, all will wish that the best people will rule, that is, that the virtuous (whoever they may be) will rule. The many and the virtuous will thus be able to govern their relations in the face of conflict and will do so in a way that reproduces their mode of governance at the same time. As among virtue friends, homonoia among these citizens entails no primordial sharing about the positive content of the good life. As among use friends, homonoia among these citizens will emerge from the self-interests of the citizens seen through the lens of what is to their mutual advantage, namely, maximizing the prohairetic activity of every citizen. The ongoing coming to terms between the many and the virtuous that produces and reproduces their constitution as a mode of self-governance based on their self-interests and good judgment, moderation and liberality, is the homonoia characteristic of political friends and of the so-called aristocracy they inhabit.

Ober remarks that Aristotle consistently defers any direct confrontation between aristocracy and democracy.[91] In the reading I have offered, it is possible to see why. Aristocracy and democracy, unlike oligarchy and democracy, are not in opposition. Unlike wealth and poverty, which cannot be shared, Aristotle maintains that excellence and freedom temper one another (*Pol.* 1293b16). They temper one another not by relating to one another as practices that, once combined, remain discrete but rather, as in the virtue of generosity itself, combine to produce a mixed good. Like the opinions of the many and the wise that Aristotle consistently

---

91. Ober, *Political Dissent in Democratic Athens,* pp. 321, 326.

consults to come up with the middle, which, a combination of both and neither, is for him generally the true, so too does he combine democracy (freedom) and aristocracy (excellence) to generate the mixed good of political friendship that produces the middle class of virtuous citizens characteristic of both the constitutional polity and the city of prayer, but prior to them. This middle class emerges from an ongoing narrowing of the material and ethical differences that are inimical to political unity and a concomitant equalization and homogenization, of a sort. There is material equalization between the many and the virtuous not by forced redistribution but by virtue of the characteristic practices of property of the citizens themselves. This equalization by means of the exercise of moderation and liberality produces a homogenization along one axis of differentiation only: class. The equality and homogeneity characteristic of this middle class do not efface the difference on which its very unity and the unity of the polity as a whole depend. Rather, the equality, respect, and freedom distinctive of this expanded citizenry foster, even as they depend on, the differentiated practice of virtue, to both individual and collective ends, on the part of these self-same citizens. It is this crucial axis of difference, the practice of prohairetic activities informed by intellectual and moral virtue, what I earlier called ontological and nonessentialist difference, that produces and preserves the democratic or so-called aristocracy as a unity of the different.

Aristotle warns that "any change of government which has to be introduced should be one which men, starting from their existing constitutions, will be both willing and able to adopt, since there is quite as much trouble in the reformation of an old constitution as there is in the establishment of a new one" (*Pol.* 1289a1–5). A democratic aristocracy is a regime that the many and the virtuous will be "willing and able to adopt." Assured their due via the equitable distribution of goods and the opportunity to rule and be ruled in turn in a regime devoted to the common good, the many would have no reason not to acquiesce to so-called aristocratic governance. And, as Ober points out, although they might not "like democracy in general" and "even if they found many democratic practices and attitudes distasteful," many aristocrats "might [nonetheless] choose to be active citizens of a democracy."[92] This would hold, a fortiori, in the democratic aristocracy. The democratic aristocracy thus takes human beings as they are. It is, as such, a possible future for Aristotle's contemporary Athens. It is also a regime that uniquely meets the standards Aristotle formulates at the start of his discussion of

92. Ibid., p. 323.

178 CHAPTER FIVE

the city of prayer: it enables its members, considered individually, to attain the highest level of activity of which they are capable (*Pol.* 1324a23–25), and no citizens living in it would wish for another regime (*Pol.* 1294b38).[93] Indeed, in a democratic aristocracy, rotational rule is not merely a necessity demanded by equality (though it is that, too [*Pol.* 1261b1]) but also a virtue.[94] There may be exclusions from citizenship in this regime. As we saw in chapter 1, anyone who does not use his capacities for prohairetic activity to act well and, indeed, to meet the property qualification effectively excludes himself from citizenship. Aiming to maximize the possibilities for prohairetic activity for all the members of the polity, however, the constitution prohibits exclusions based on coercive institutions. These will be unjust and dangerous, not only to those who are subject to such measures but also to those who establish them. To protect against the unjust corruptions involved in mastery, the practice of prohairetic activity engages the citizens of this polity in ongoing and critical deliberations, informed by the democratic spirit of generosity, about the fundamental terms of their cooperation and conflict.

The Work of Politics

In his activity, the maker is, in a sense, the work produced.
ARISTOTLE, *Nicomachean Ethics*

The work reveals in actuality what the maker is in potentiality.
ARISTOTLE, *Nicomachean Ethics*

Aristotle's discussion of the democratic aristocracy offers the richest account of the possibilities for political friendship and the most textured description of the polity positioned both to imagine as its telos the city of prayer and to improve fourth-century Athenian democracy. With institutions appropriate to promoting homonoia, the political structures of the democratic aristocracy anticipate those of the city of prayer. By fulfilling the ethical requirements that open the possibility for the friendship which these institutions foster and on which they depend, the

---

93. F. Miller, *Nature, Justice, and Rights,* pp. 214, 269, calls this the principle of unanimity.

94. *Contra,* e.g., Lindsay, "Liberty, Equality, Power," who claims that Aristotle accepts rotational rule because democratic freedom leaves no room for the continual rule of one person or party.

As noted in chapter 3, of special import to Aristotle is the practice of initiation in an act of giving. In the political context, this suggests that the job of initiating the bond of friendship in a polity lies with those who have the most to give, namely, those whom the distribution of divisible goods in a polity initially favors.

citizens of such a polity are able to keep stasis at bay, to meliorate conflicts when they arise, and to promote and preserve the well-being of the polity as a whole. These ethical and political measures, taken together, produce what I call a democracy of distinction. It is mixed not only in that it combines regimes to produce an expanded middle class, combines forms of friendship, and is attainable, but also in that it occupies the temporal middle between the Athens that Aristotle would like to see become its past and the polity he hopes Athens will become in the future. Fourth-century Athens—the final form of democracy—is a regime governed by decrees, not laws, where all rule as one. Athens, as it has not yet existed, is the regime of the always already virtuous who rule and are ruled in turn. The democracy of distinction is the middle between the Athens Aristotle sees before him and abjures and the Athens he imagines, a middle that draws on Athens's past with a view to the future while recognizing the constitutional place of both faction and friendship. It is a middle that represents the ongoing coming to terms among human beings as they fulfill as well as discipline their differentiated desires and ends.

A democracy of distinction requires work, specifically, what I have called the work of politics. The work, *ergon*, in that polity is threefold. First there is the ergon of each citizen, whose job it is to actualize his virtue by means of his prohairetic activities. The ergon of the already virtuous is to continue to practice virtue. Otherwise, as we have seen repeatedly, they will lose their capacity. This is their ongoing work, for their virtue is not a possession held in reserve but something enacted and preserved by use. It is in this way that a "training in virtue arises from the company of the good" (*NE* 1170a12–13). The ergon of those who are not already virtuous, citizens and noncitizens alike, is to actualize their capacity for virtue and so their capacity not only for individual self-rule but for political rule as well.[95] They do this by emulating the prohairetic activities of the virtuous and by cultivating their own dispositions to generosity and virtue. Second, there is the ergon of all the citizens together, which is to produce, by their prohairetic activity, works, *erga*, in the way of practices and institutions, to facilitate an education to virtue and the equitable distribution of goods. Working in these ways, each citizen acting on behalf of his self-interest will contribute to the common good (*NE* 1169a9–11). Finally, there is the ergon of the constitution, which is to produce and continually reproduce the excellence of its citizens and to produce and reproduce itself as a site of excellence. The constitution, no less than the institutions that comprise it and the character of each citizen, is the work of the present from out of the past with a

---

95. Nichols, *Citizens and Statesmen,* pp. 81–84, makes a similar claim.

view to the future. Political science, so understood, is not the production and preservation of ideals but a consideration of political realities and possibilities. Perhaps paradoxically, it is an imaginary goal—the city of prayer—that offers the means for achieving a reasonable goal—a democracy of distinction—whose actualization, possible for polities everywhere, would be enough. Seen in this way, Aristotle's ethical and political lessons are no less timely for us than they were for fourth-century Athens.

WORKS CITED

Texts by Aristotle

Aristotle: Politics. Translated by C. D. C. Reeve. Indianapolis: Hackett, 1988.
Aristotle, Politics: Books I and II. Translated and with a commentary by Trevor J. Saunders. Oxford: Clarendon, 1995.
Aristotle, Politics: Books III and IV. Translated with introduction and comments by Richard Robinson. Oxford: Clarendon, 1995.
Aristotle: Nicomachean Ethics. Translated by Terence Irwin. Indianapolis: Hackett, 1985.
The Complete Works of Aristotle. Edited by Jonathan Barnes. Princeton: Princeton University Press, 1984.
De Anima. Translated by R. D. Hicks. Buffalo: Prometheus, 1991.
Metaphysics I–IX. Translated by Hugh Tredennick. Cambridge: Harvard University Press, 1980.
Nicomachean Ethics. Translated by David Ross, revised by J. L. Ackrill and J. O. Urmson. Oxford: Oxford University Press, 1980.
Nicomachean Ethics. Translated by H. Rackham. Cambridge: Harvard University Press, 1982.
Physics. Translated by Robin Waterfield with an introduction and notes by David Bostock. New York: Oxford University Press, 1996.
Politics. Translated by H. Rackham. Cambridge: Harvard University Press, 1977.
The Politics. Translated by Carnes Lord. Chicago: University of Chicago Press, 1984.
The Politics and the Constitution of Athens. Translated by Benjamin Jowett and J. M. Moore (respectively). Edited by Stephen Everson. Cambridge: Cambridge University Press, 1996.
The Politics of Aristotle. Translated by Ernest Barker. 1958; reprint, New York: Oxford University Press, 1969.

Other Texts

Allen, Danielle S. "A Democratic Theory of Judgment." Manuscript on file with author, 1997.
———. "Intricate Democracy." Ph.D. diss., Harvard University, 1999.
———. "Law's Necessary Forcefulness: Ralph Ellison vs. Hannah Arendt on the Battle of Little Rock." *Oklahoma City University Law Review* 26 (2001): 857–95.

182   WORKS CITED

———. *The World of Prometheus: The Politics of Punishing in Democratic Athens.* Princeton: Princeton University Press, 2000.

Ambler, Wayne. "Aristotle on Acquisition." *Canadian Journal of Political Science* 17 (1984): 487–502.

———. "Aristotle on Nature and Politics: The Case of Slavery." *Political Theory* 15 (1987): 390–410.

Annas, Julia. "Aristotle on Human Nature and Political Virtue." *Review of Metaphysics* 49 (1996): 731–53.

———. *The Morality of Happiness.* New York: Oxford University Press, 1993.

———. "Self-Love in Plato and Aristotle." *Southern Journal of Philosophy* 27 (1988): S1–S18.

Aquinas. *See* Thomas Aquinas

Arendt, Hannah. *Between Past and Future: Eight Exercises in Political Thought.* New York: Viking, 1961.

———. *The Human Condition.* Chicago: University of Chicago Press, 1958.

———. *Lectures on Kant's Political Philosophy.* Edited and with an interpretive essay by Ronald Beiner. Chicago: University of Chicago Press, 1982.

Arnhart, Larry. *Darwinian Natural Right: The Biological Ethics of Human Nature.* Albany: SUNY Press, 1998.

Austin, John. *The Province of Jurisprudence Determined and the Uses of the Study of Jurisprudence.* 3rd ed. Vol. 1. London: John Murray, 1869.

Axelrod, Robert. *The Evolution of Cooperation.* New York: Basic Books, 1984.

Balot, Ryan K. *Greed and Injustice in Classical Athens.* Princeton: Princeton University Press, 2001.

Bambrough, Renford. "Aristotle on Justice: A Paradigm of Philosophy." In *New Essays on Plato and Aristotle,* edited by Renford Bambrough, 159–74. London: Routledge & Kegan Paul, 1965.

Barber, Benjamin R. "Foundationalism and Democracy." In Benhabib, *Democracy and Difference,* 348–59.

Barker, Ernest. *The Political Thought of Plato and Aristotle.* New York: Dover, 1959.

Barnes, Jonathan. "Aristotle and the Methods of Ethics." *Revue internationale de philosophie* 34 (1980): 490–511.

Becker, Lawrence C. *Property Rights: Philosophic Foundations.* London: Routledge & Kegan Paul, 1977.

———. *Reciprocity.* Chicago: University of Chicago Press, 1990.

Beiner, Ronald. *Political Judgment.* Chicago: University of Chicago Press, 1983.

Bellemare, Pierre. "Note sur *l'oikonomia politike.*" In *Philosophy and Culture: Proceedings of the 17th World Congress in Philosophy,* edited by V. Cauchy, 3:755–61. Montreal: Montmorency, 1983.

Benhabib, Seyla, ed. *Democracy and Difference: Contesting the Boundaries of the Political.* Princeton: Princeton University Press, 1996.

Bentham, Jeremy. *An Introduction to the Principles of Morals and Legislation.* New York: Hafner, 1948.

Bickford, Susan. *The Dissonance of Democracy: Listening, Conflict, and Citizenship.* Ithaca: Cornell University Press, 1996.

Bodéüs, Richard. "Law and the Regime in Aristotle." In *Essays on the Foundations of Aristotelian Political Science,* edited by Carnes Lord and K. David O'Connor, 234–48. Berkeley: University of California Press, 1991.

Boegehold, Alan. "Resistance to Change in the Law at Athens." In Ober and Hedrick, *Demokratia,* 204–14.

Bolotin, David. *An Approach to Aristotle's* Physics *with Particular Attention to the Role of His Manner of Writing.* Albany: SUNY Press, 1997.

Booth, William J. *Households: On the Moral Architecture of the Economy.* Ithaca: Cornell University Press, 1993.

———. "Politics and the Household: A Commentary on Aristotle's *Politics* Book One." *History of Political Thought* 2 (1981): 203–26.

Broadie, Sarah. *Ethics with Aristotle.* New York: Oxford University Press, 1991.

Brunt, P. A. "Aristotle and Slavery." In *Studies in Greek History and Thought,* 343–88. Oxford: Clarendon, 1993.

Cartledge, Paul. *The Greeks: A Portrait of Self and Others.* New York: Oxford University Press, 1993.

Charney, Ann P. "Spiritedness and Piety in Aristotle." In *Understanding the Political Spirit: Philosophical Investigations from Socrates to Nietzsche,* edited by Catherine H. Zuckert, 67–87. New Haven: Yale University Press, 1988.

Coby, Patrick. "Aristotle's Three Cities and the Problem of Faction." *Journal of Politics* 50 (1988): 896–919.

Cohen, David. *Law, Sexuality, and Society: The Enforcement of Morals in Classical Athens.* New York: Cambridge University Press, 1991.

———. *Law, Violence, and Community in Classical Athens.* New York: Cambridge University Press, 1995.

Connor, W. Robert. *The New Politicians of Fifth-Century Athens.* Indianapolis: Hackett, 1992.

Cooper, John M. "Aristotle on Friendship." In *Essays on Aristotle's Ethics,* edited by Amélie Oksenberg Rorty, 301–40. Berkeley: University of California Press, 1980.

———. "Aristotle on the Forms of Friendship." *Review of Metaphysics* 30 (1997): 619–48.

———. "Aristotle on the Goods of Fortune." *Philosophical Review* 94 (1985): 173–96.

———, ed. *Plato: Complete Works.* Indianapolis: Hackett, 1997.

———. *Reason and Emotion: Essays on Ancient Moral Psychology and Ethical Theory.* Princeton: Princeton University Press, 1999.

Corcoran, Marlena G. "Aristotle's Poetic Justice." *Iowa Law Review* 77 (1992): 837–50.

Cover, Robert. "Nomos and Narrative." In *Narrative, Violence, and the Law: The Essays of Robert Cover,* edited by Martha Minow, Michael Ryan, and Austin Sarat, 95–172. Ann Arbor: University of Michigan Press, 1995.

Danzig, Gabriel. "The Political Character of Aristotelian Reciprocity." *Classical Philology* 95 (2000): 399–424.

Davis, Michael. *The Poetry of Philosophy: Aristotle's* Poetics. Lanham, MD: Rowman & Littlefield, 1992.

———. *The Politics of Philosophy: A Commentary on Aristotle's* Politics. Lanham, MD: Rowman & Littlefield, 1996.

184 WORKS CITED

Day, James, and Mortimer Chambers. *Aristotle's History of Athenian Democracy.* Berkeley: University of California Press, 1962.

Demsetz, Harold. "Toward a Theory of Property Rights." *American Economic Review, Papers and Proceedings of the Seventy-ninth Annual Meeting of the American Economic Association* 57 (1967): 347–59.

Derrida, Jacques. *Politics of Friendship.* Translated by George Collins. New York: Verso, 1997.

Diogenes Laertius. *Lives of Eminent Philosophers,* vol. 2. Translated by R. D. Hicks. Cambridge: Harvard University Press, 1972.

Dobbs, Darrell. "Aristotle's Anticommunism." *American Journal of Political Science* 29 (1985): 29–46.

Drucker, H. M. "Just Analogies? The Place of Analogies in Political Thinking." *Political Studies* 18 (1970): 448–60.

Dworkin, Ronald. *Law's Empire.* London: Fontana, 1986.

———. "What Is Equality? Part 2: Equality of Resources." *Philosophy and Public Affairs* 10 (1981): 283–345.

Engberg-Pedersen, Troels. "Discovering the Good: *Oikeiosis* and *kathekonta* in Stoic Ethics." In *The Norms of Nature: Studies in Hellenistic Ethics,* edited by Malcolm Schofield and Gisela Striker, 143–83. Cambridge: Cambridge University Press, 1986.

Finley, Moses I. "Aristotle and Economic Analysis." *Past & Present* 47 (1970): 3–25.

———. *Politics in the Ancient World.* Cambridge: Cambridge University Press, 1983.

———. *The Use and Abuse of History.* London: Chatto & Windus, 1975.

Finnis, John. *Natural Law and Natural Rights.* New York: Oxford University Press, 1980.

Foxhall, Lin. "Household, Gender, and Property in Classical Athens." *Classical Quarterly* 39 (1989): 22–44.

Frank, Jill. "Democracy and Distribution: Aristotle on Just Desert." *Political Theory* 26 (1998): 784–802.

———. "Integrating Public Good and Private Right: The Virtue of Property." In *Aristotle and Modern Politics: The Persistence of Political Philosophy,* edited by Aristide Tessitore, 258–77. Notre Dame: University of Notre Dame Press, 2002.

Frank, Jill, and S. Sara Monoson. "Aristotle's Theramenes at Athens: A Poetic History." *Parallax* 29 (2003): 29–40.

Frede, Dorothea. "Necessity, Chance, and 'What Happens for the Most Part' in Aristotle's *Poetics*." In *Essays on Aristotle's* Poetics, edited by Amélie Oksenberg Rorty, 197–219. Princeton: Princeton University Press, 1992.

Fuks, Alexander. *The Ancestral Constitution: Four Studies in Athenian Party Politics at the End of the Fifth Century B.C.* Westport: Greenwood, 1975.

Fuller, Lon L. *The Morality of Law.* New Haven: Yale University Press, 1969.

Gadamer, Hans-Georg. "Aristotle and the Ethics of Imperatives," translated by Joseph M. Knippenberg. In *Action and Contemplation: Studies in the Moral and Political Thought of Aristotle,* edited by Robert C. Bartlett and Susan D. Collins, 53–67. Albany: SUNY Press, 1999.

Garnsey, Peter. *Ideas of Slavery from Aristotle to Augustine.* Cambridge: Cambridge University Press, 1996.

Goodin, Robert E. *Reasons for Welfare: The Political Theory of the Welfare State.* Princeton: Princeton University Press, 1988.

Guinier, Lani. *The Tyranny of the Majority: Fundamental Fairness in Representative Democracy.* New York: Free Press, 1994.

Habermas, Jürgen. "Discourse Ethics: Notes on a Program of Philosophical Justification." In *Moral Consciousness and Communicative Action,* translated by Christian Lenhardt and Shierry Weber Nicholson, 43–115. Cambridge: MIT Press, 1990.

Hadreas, Peter. "*Eunoia:* Aristotle on the Beginning of Friendship." *Ancient Philosophy* 15 (1995): 393–402.

Hampshire, Stuart. *Justice Is Conflict.* Princeton: Princeton University Press, 2000.

Hansen, Mogens Herman. *The Athenian Assembly: In the Age of Demosthenes.* Oxford: Blackwell, 1987.

———. *The Athenian Democracy in the Age of Demosthenes: Structure, Principles, and Ideology.* Oxford: Blackwell, 1991.

——— *The Sovereignty of the People's Court in Athens in the Fourth Century B.C. and the Public Action against Unconstitutional Proposals.* Translated by Jorgen Raphaelsen and Sonja Holboll. Odense: Odense University Press, 1974.

Hare, John. "*Eleutheriotes* in Aristotle's *Ethics.*" *Ancient Philosophy* 8 (1988): 19–32.

Harrison, A. R. W. *The Law of Athens.* 2nd ed. Vol. 1. Indianapolis: Hackett, 1998.

Hart, H. L. A. *The Concept of Law.* Oxford: Oxford University Press, 1961.

Hayek, F. A. *The Road to Serfdom.* Chicago: University of Chicago Press, 1944.

Heidegger, Martin. *Aristotle's* Metaphysics *Theta 1–3: On the Essence and Actuality of Force.* Translated by Walter Brogan and Peter Warnek. Indianapolis: Indiana University Press, 1995.

———. *Being and Time.* Translated by John Macquarrie and Edward Robinson. New York: Harper & Row, 1962.

———. "The Origin of the Work of Art." In *Poetry, Language, Thought,* translated by Albert Hofstadter, 15–87. New York: Harper & Row, 1971.

———. *Plato's* Sophist. Translated by Richard Rojcewicz and André Schuwer. Indianapolis: Indiana University Press, 1997.

Heyman, Steven J. "Aristotle on Political Justice." *Iowa Law Review* 77 (1992): 851–63.

Hornblower, Simon, and Antony Spawforth. *The Oxford Classical Dictionary.* 3rd ed. New York: Oxford University Press, 1996.

Irwin, Terence. "Generosity and Property in Aristotle's *Politics.*" *Social Philosophy and Policy* 4 (1987): 37–54.

Joachim, H. H. *Aristotle: The* Nicomachean Ethics. Oxford: Clarendon, 1951.

Jones, J. Walter. *The Law and Legal Theory of the Greeks.* Oxford: Clarendon, 1956.

Kalimtzis, Kostas. *Aristotle on Political Enmity and Disease: An Inquiry into* Stasis. Albany: SUNY Press, 2000.

Kateb, George. "Democratic Individuality and the Claims of Politics." *Political Theory* 12 (1984): 331–60.

Keaney, John J. *The Composition of Aristotle's* Athenaion Politeia. New York: Oxford University Press, 1992.

Kelsen, Hans. *General Theory of Law and State.* New York: Russell & Russell, 1961.

Keyt, David. "Three Basic Theorems in Aristotle's *Politics.*" In *A Companion to Aristotle's Politics*, edited by David Keyt and Fred D. Miller Jr., 118–41. Cambridge, MA: Blackwell, 1991.

Keyt, David, and Fred D. Miller Jr., ed. *A Companion to Aristotle's* Politics. Cambridge, MA: Blackwell, 1991.

King, Desmond, and Jeremy Waldron. "Citizenship, Social Citizenship and the Defence of Welfare Provision." *British Journal of Political Science* 18 (1988): 415–43.

Kinsley, Michael. "The Ultimate Block Grant." *New Yorker,* May 29, 1995, 36–40.

Klonoski, Richard J. "*Homonoia* in Aristotle's Ethics and Politics." *History of Political Thought* 17 (1996): 313–25.

Koziak, Barbara. *Retrieving Political Emotion:* Thumos, *Aristotle, and Gender.* University Park: Pennsylvania State University Press, 2000.

Kraut, Richard. "Are There Natural Rights in Aristotle?" *Review of Metaphysics* 49 (1996): 755–74.

———. *Aristotle: Political Philosophy.* Oxford: Oxford University Press, 2002.

———. *Aristotle on the Human Good.* Princeton: Princeton University Press, 1989.

Labarrière, Jean-Louis. "Le rôle de la *phantasia* dans la recherche du bien pratique." In *Aristote Politique: Etudes sur la Politique d'Aristote,* edited by Pierre Aubenque, 231–52. Paris: Presses universitaires de France, 1993.

Laix, Roger A. "Aristotle's Conception of the Spartan Constitution." *Journal of the History of Philosophy* 12 (1974): 21–30.

Lane, Melissa. *Method and Politics in Plato's* Statesman. Cambridge: Cambridge University Press, 1998.

Lear, Gabriel Richardson. *Happy Lives and the Highest Good: An Essay on Aristotle's* Nicomachean Ethics. Princeton: Princeton University Press, 2004.

Lear, Jonathan. *Aristotle: The Desire to Understand.* New York: Cambridge University Press, 1988.

———. *Open Minded: Working out the Logic of the Soul.* Cambridge: Harvard University Press, 1998.

Lewis, Thomas J. "Acquisition and Anxiety: Aristotle's Case against the Market." *Canadian Journal of Economics* 11 (1978): 69–90.

Lindsay, Thomas K. "Liberty, Equality, Power: Aristotle's Critique of the Democratic 'Presupposition.'" *American Journal of Political Science* 36 (1992): 743–61.

Lord, Carnes, and David K. O'Connor, eds. *Essays on the Foundations of Aristotelian Political Science.* Berkeley: University of California Press, 1991.

Lummis, C. Douglas. *Radical Democracy.* Ithaca: Cornell University Press, 1996.

MacDowell, Douglas M. *The Law in Classical Athens.* Ithaca: Cornell University Press, 1978.

———. "The *Oikos* in Athenian Law." *Classical Quarterly* 39 (1989):10–21.

MacIntyre, Alasdair. *After Virtue: A Study in Moral Theory.* 2nd ed. Notre Dame: University of Notre Dame Press, 1984.

———. "*Sophrosune:* How a Virtue Can Become Socially Disruptive." Midwest Studies in Philosophy, vol. 13. Notre Dame: University of Notre Dame Press, 1988.

MacLachlan, Bonnie. *The Age of Grace: Charis in Early Greek Poetry*. Princeton: Princeton University Press, 1993.

Mansfield, Harvey. "Harvard Loves Diversity." *Weekly Standard*, March 25, 1996, 27–29.

Manville, Philip Brook. *The Origins of Citizenship in Ancient Athens*. Princeton: Princeton University Press, 1997.

Mara, Gerald. "The Culture of Democracy: Aristotle's *Athenaion Politeia* as Political Theory." In *Aristotle and Modern Politics: The Persistence of Political Philosophy*, edited by Aristide Tessitore, 307–41. Notre Dame: University of Notre Dame Press, 2002.

———. "Interrogating the Identities of Excellence: Liberal Education and Democratic Culture in Aristotle's *Nicomachean Ethics*." *Polity* 31 (1998): 301–29.

———. "The *Logos* of the Wise in the *Politeia* of the Many: Recent Books on Aristotle's Political Philosophy." *Political Theory* 28 (2000): 835–60.

———. "The Near Made Far Away: The Role of Cultural Criticism in Aristotle's Political Theory." *Political Theory* 23 (1995): 280–303.

Markell, Patchen. *Bound by Recognition*. Princeton: Princeton University Press, 2003.

Masters, Roger D. "Human Nature, Nature, and Political Thought." In *NOMOS: Human Nature in Politics*, edited by J. Roland Pennock and John W. Chapman, 69–110. New York: New York University Press, 1977.

Mathie, William. "Property in the Political Science of Aristotle." In *Theories of Property: Aristotle to the Present*, edited by Anthony Parel and Thomas Flanagan, 13–32. Ontario: Wilfred Laurier University Press, 1979.

Mayhew, Robert. *Aristotle's Criticism of Plato's Republic*. Lanham, MD: Rowman & Littlefield, 1997.

McDowell, John. "Virtue and Reason." *Monist* 62 (1979): 330–50.

———. *Mind, Value, and Reality*. Cambridge: Harvard University Press, 1998.

Meikle, Scott. *Aristotle's Economic Thought*. Oxford: Clarendon, 1995.

Mendelsohn, Daniel. "Theatres of War." *New Yorker*, 12 January 2004, 79–84.

Michelman, Frank. "Law's Republic." *Yale Law Journal* 97 (1988): 1493–1537.

Miller, Eugene. "Prudence and the Rule of Law." *American Journal of Jurisprudence* 24 (1979): 181–206.

Miller, Fred D., Jr. *Nature, Justice, and Rights in Aristotle's Politics*. Oxford: Clarendon, 1995.

Millett, Paul. "Encounters in the Agora." In *Kosmos: Essays in Order, Conflict, and Community in Classical Athens*, edited by Paul Cartledge, Paul Millett, and Sitta von Reden, 203–28. New York: Cambridge University Press, 1998.

———. "The Rhetoric of Reciprocity in Classical Athens." In *Reciprocity in Ancient Greece*, edited by Christopher Gill, Norman Postlethwaite, and Richard Seaford, 227–53. New York: Oxford University Press, 1998.

———. "Sale, Credit, and Exchange in Athenian Law and Society." In *NOMOS: Essays in Athenian Law, Politics, and Society*, edited by Paul Cartledge, Paul Millett, and Stephen Todd, 167–94. Cambridge: Cambridge University Press, 1990.

Moon, J. Donald. "The Moral Basis of the Democratic Welfare State." In *Democracy and the Welfare State*, edited by Amy Gutmann, 27–52. Princeton: Princeton University Press, 1988.

188 WORKS CITED

More, Thomas. *Utopia.* New Haven: Yale University Press, 2001.

Morrow, Glenn R. "Aristotle's Comments on Plato's *Laws.*" In *Aristotle and Plato in the Mid-Fourth Century,* edited by I. During and G. E. L. Owen, 145–62. N.p.: Goteburg, 1960.

Mulgan, Richard G. "Aristotle and the Value of Political Participation." *Political Theory* 18 (1990): 195–215.

———. "Aristotle's Analysis of Oligarchy and Democracy." In *A Companion to Aristotle's Politics,* edited by David Keyt and Fred Miller Jr., 307–22. Cambridge, MA: Blackwell, 1991.

———. *Aristotle's Political Theory: An Introduction for Students of Political Theory.* Oxford: Oxford University Press, 1977.

Munzer, Stephen R. *A Theory of Property.* New York: Cambridge University Press, 1990.

Nichols, Mary P. *Citizens and Statesmen: A Study of Aristotle's* Politics. Savage, MD: Rowman & Littlefield, 1992.

North, Helen. *Sophrosyne: Self-Knowledge and Self-Restraint in Greek Literature.* Ithaca: Cornell University Press, 1966.

Nozick, Robert. *Anarchy, State, and Utopia.* New York: Basic Books, 1974.

Nussbaum, Martha. "Aristotelian Social Democracy." In *Liberalism and the Good,* edited by R. Bruce Douglass, Gerald M. Mara, and Henry S. Richardson, 203–52. London: Routledge & Kegan Paul, 1990.

———. "Aristotle." In *Ancient Writers: Greece and Rome,* edited by T. James Luce, 1:377–416. New York: Charles Scribner's Sons, 1982.

———. "Aristotle, Feminism, and Needs for Functioning." *Texas Law Review* 70 (1992): 1019–28.

———. "Aristotle on Human Nature and the Foundations of Ethics." In *World, Mind, and Ethics: Essays on the Ethical Philosophy of Bernard Williams,* edited by J. E. J. Altham and Ross Harrison, 86–131. Cambridge: Cambridge University Press, 1995.

———. *The Fragility of Goodness: Luck and Ethics in Greek Tragedy and Philosophy.* New York: Cambridge University Press, 1986.

———. "Human Functioning and Social Justice: In Defense of Aristotelian Essentialism." *Political Theory* 20 (1992): 202–46.

———. "Nature, Function, and Capability: Aristotle on Political Distribution." *Oxford Studies in Ancient Philosophy,* supp. vol., 144–84. Oxford: Clarendon, 1988.

———. "Saving Aristotle's Appearances." In *Language and Logos: Studies in Ancient Greek Philosophy Presented to G. E. L. Owen,* edited by Malcolm Schofield and Martha Nussbaum, 267–93. New York: Cambridge University Press, 1982.

Nussbaum, Martha, and Hilary Putnam. "Changing Aristotle's Mind." In *Essays on Aristotle's* De Anima, edited by Martha C. Nussbaum and Amélie Oksenberg Rorty, 27–56. Oxford: Clarendon, 1992.

Ober, Josiah. *Athenian Revolution: Essays on Ancient Greek Democracy and Political Theory.* Princeton: Princeton University Press, 1996.

———. *Mass and Elite in Democratic Athens: Rhetoric, Ideology, and the Power of the People.* Princeton: Princeton University Press, 1989.

———. *Political Dissent in Democratic Athens.* Princeton: Princeton University Press, 1998.

Ober, Josiah, and Charles Hedrick, eds. *Demokratia: A Conversation on Democracies, Ancient and Modern.* Princeton: Princeton University Press, 1996.

O'Connor, David K. "The Aetiology of Justice." In *Essays on the Foundations of Aristotelian Political Science,* edited by Carnes Lord and David K. O'Connor, 136–64. Berkeley: University of California Press, 1991.

Onions, C. T., ed. *The Oxford Dictionary of English Etymology.* Oxford: Clarendon, 1966.

Ostwald, Martin. *From Popular Sovereignty to the Sovereignty of Law: Law, Society, and Politics in Fifth-Century Athens.* Berkeley: University of California Press, 1986.

———. *Nomos and the Beginnings of Athenian Democracy.* Oxford: Clarendon, 1969.

Pangle, Lorraine. *Aristotle and the Philosophy of Friendship.* New York: Cambridge University Press, 2003.

Park, David. *The Fire within the Eye: A Historical Essay on the Nature and Meaning of Light.* Princeton: Princeton University Press, 1997.

Pitkin, Hanna Fenichel. "Are Freedom and Liberty Twins?" *Political Theory* 16 (1988): 523–52.

———. "The Idea of a Constitution." *Journal of Legal Education* 37 (1987): 167–69.

Pomeroy, Sarah B., Stanley M. Burstein, Walter Donlan, and Jennifer Tolbert Roberts. *Ancient Greece: A Political, Social, and Cultural History.* New York: Oxford University Press, 1999.

Posner, Richard. *Economic Analysis of Law.* Boston: Little, Brown, 1977.

Price, A. W. *Love and Friendship in Plato and Aristotle.* Oxford: Clarendon, 1989.

Putnam, Robert D. "Bowling Alone: America's Declining Social Capital." *Journal of Democracy* 6 (1995): 65–78.

———. "The Strange Disappearance of Civic America." *American Prospect,* 1 December 1996, 34–48.

Radin, Margaret Jane. "Property and Personhood." *Stanford Law Review* 34 (1982): 957–1015.

———. "Reconsidering the Rule of Law." *Boston University Law Review* 69 (1989): 781–819.

Rasmussen, Douglas B., and Douglas J. Den Uyl. *Liberty and Nature: An Aristotelian Defense of Liberal Order.* Lasalle, IL: Open Court, 1991.

Rawls, John. *A Theory of Justice.* Cambridge: Harvard University Press, 1971.

Reden, Sitta von. *Exchange in Ancient Greece.* London: Duckworth, 1995.

Rhodes, P. J. *A Commentary on the Aristotelian* Athenaion Politeia. New York: Oxford University Press, 1993.

Ritchie, D. H. "Aristotle's Subdivisions of 'Particular Justice.'" *Classical Review* 8 (1894): 185–92.

Rose, Carol M. *Property and Persuasion: Essays on the History, Theory, and Rhetoric of Ownership.* Boulder: Westview, 1994.

Rosen, Stanley H. "A Note on Aristotle's *De Anima.*" *Phronesis* 6 (1961): 127–37.

Rousseau, Jean-Jacques. *On the Social Contract.* In *The Basic Political Writings.* Translated by Donald A. Cress. Indianapolis: Hackett, 1987.

Salkever, Stephen. "Aristotle's Social Science." In *Essays on the Foundations of Aristotelian Political Science,* edited by Carnes Lord and David O'Connor, 11–48. Berkeley: University of California Press, 1991.

190   WORKS CITED

———. *Finding the Mean: Theory and Practice in Aristotelian Political Philosophy.* Princeton: Princeton University Press, 1990.

———. "'Lopp'd and Bound': How Liberal Theory Obscures the Goods of Liberal Practices." In *Liberalism and the Good,* edited by R. Bruce Douglass, Gerald M. Mara, and Henry S. Richardson, 167–202. London: Routledge & Kegan Paul, 1990.

———. "Women, Soldiers, Citizens: Plato and Aristotle on the Politics of Virility." In *Essays on the Foundations of Aristotelian Political Science,* edited by Carnes Lord and David O'Connor, 165–90. Berkeley: University of California Press, 1991.

Saxonhouse, Arlene W. "Family, Polity and Unity: Aristotle on Socrates' Community of Wives." *Polity* 15 (1982): 202–19.

———. *Fear of Diversity: The Birth of Political Science in Ancient Greek Thought.* Chicago: University of Chicago Press, 1992.

———. *Women in the History of Political Thought: Ancient Greece to Machiavelli.* New York: Praeger, 1985.

Scalia, Antonin. "The Rule of Law as a Law of Rules." *University of Chicago Law Review* 56 (1989): 1175–88.

Schlaifer, Robert. "Greek Theories of Slavery from Homer to Aristotle." In *Slavery in Classical Antiquity: Views and Controversies,* edited by M. I. Finley, 120–27. Cambridge, U.K.: Heffer, 1960.

Schlatter, Richard. *Private Property: The History of an Idea.* New York: Russell & Russell, 1951.

Schofield, Malcolm. "Aristotle on the Imagination." In *Articles on Aristotle,* vol. 4, *Psychology and Aesthetics,* edited by Jonathan Barnes, Malcolm Schofield, and Richard Sorabji, 103–32. New York: St. Martin's, 1978.

———. "Equality and Hierarchy in Aristotle's Political Thought," in Schofield, *Saving the City,* 100–114.

———. "Ideology and Philosophy in Aristotle's Theory of Slavery," in Schofield, *Saving the City,* 115–40.

———. "Political Friendship and the Ideology of Reciprocity," in Schofield, *Saving the City,* 82–99.

———. *Saving the City: Philosopher-Kings and Other Classical Paradigms.* New York: Routledge, 1999.

———. "Sharing in the Constitution," in Schofield, *Saving the City,* 141–59.

Schwarzenbach, Sibyl A. "On Civic Friendship." *Ethics* 107 (1996): 97–128.

Sherman, Nancy. *The Fabric of Character: Aristotle's Theory of Virtue.* Oxford: Clarendon, 1989.

Shklar, Judith. *Political Thought and Political Thinkers.* Chicago: University of Chicago Press, 1998.

Simmel, Georg. *The Philosophy of Money.* 2nd ed. Translated by Tom Bottomore and David Frisby. New York: Routledge, 1990.

Singer, Kurt. "*Oikonomia:* An Inquiry into Beginnings of Economic Thought and Language." *Kyklos* 11 (1958): 29–57.

Skocpol, Theda. "Unravelling from Above." *American Prospect,* March–April 1996, 20–25.

Smith, Nicholas. "Aristotle's Theory of Natural Slavery." In *A Companion to Aristotle's Politics*, edited by David Keyt and Fred Miller Jr., 142–55. Oxford: Blackwell, 1991.

Smith, Thomas W. *Revaluing Ethics: Aristotle's Dialectical Pedagogy.* Albany: SUNY Press, 2001.

Ste. Croix, G. E. M. de. *The Origins of the Peloponnesian War.* Ithaca: Cornell University Press, 1972.

Stern-Gillet, Suzanne. *Aristotle's Philosophy of Friendship.* Albany: SUNY Press, 1995.

Stillman, Peter. "Hegel's Analysis of Property in the *Philosophy of Right.*" *Cardozo Law Review* 10 (1989): 1031–72.

Strassler, Robert. *The Landmark Thucydides: A Comprehensive Guide to the Peloponnesian War.* New York: Touchstone, 1998.

Strauss, Barry S. "On Aristotle's Critique of Athenian Democracy." In *Essays on the Foundations of Aristotelian Political Science,* edited by Carnes Lord and David K. O'Connor, 212–33. Berkeley: University of California Press, 1991.

Strauss, Leo. *The City and Man.* Chicago: University of Chicago Press, 1964.

———. *Natural Right and History.* Chicago: University of Chicago Press, 1953.

Swanson, Judith A. "Aristotle on Nature, Human Nature, and Justice: A Consideration of the Natural Functions of Men and Women in the City." In *Action and Contemplation: Studies in the Moral and Political Thought of Aristotle,* edited by Robert C. Bartlett and Susan D. Collins, 225–47. Albany: SUNY Press, 1999.

———. *The Public and the Private in Aristotle's Political Philosophy.* Ithaca: Cornell University Press, 1992.

Tessitore, Aristide, ed. *Aristotle and Modern Politics: The Persistence of Political Philosophy.* Notre Dame: University of Notre Dame Press, 2002.

———. *Reading Aristotle's Ethics: Virtue, Rhetoric, and Political Philosophy.* Albany: SUNY Press, 1996.

Thomas Aquinas. *Commentary on Aristotle's* Nicomachean Ethics. Translated by C. I. Litzinger. Notre Dame: Dumb Ox, 1993.

———. *Summa Theologica,* Questions 90–97. In A. P. d'Entrèves, *Aquinas: Selected Political Writings.* Oxford: Blackwell, 1954.

Veyne, Paul. *Bread and Circuses: Historical Sociology and Political Pluralism.* London: Butler & Tanner, 1980.

Villa, Dana. *Arendt and Heidegger: The Fate of the Political.* Princeton: Princeton University Press, 1996.

Waldron, Jeremy. "On the Objectivity of Morals: Thoughts on Gilbert's *Democratic Individuality.*" *California Law Review* 80 (October 1992): 1361–1411.

———. *The Right to Private Property.* Oxford: Clarendon, 1988.

———. "The Wisdom of the Multitude: Some Reflections on Book III, Chapter 11 of Aristotle's *Politics.*" *Political Theory* 23 (1995): 563–84.

Wallach, John. "Contemporary Aristotelianism." *Political Theory* 20 (1992): 613–42.

Waltz, Kenneth N. *Man, the State, and War: A Theoretical Analysis.* New York: Columbia University Press, 1959.

Walzer, Michael. *Just and Unjust Wars: A Moral Argument with Historical Illustrations.* New York: Basic Books, 1977.

Watson, Gerard. "*Phantasia* in Aristotle, *De Anima* 3.3." *Classical Quarterly* 32 (1982): 100–113.

Weil, Simone. *Waiting for God*. Translated by Emma Craufurd. New York: Harper & Row, 1951.

Weinrib, Ernest J. "Aristotle's Forms of Justice." *Ratio Juris* 2 (1989): 211–26.

White, Stephen K. "Three Conceptions of the Political: The Real World of Late Modern Democracy." In *Democracy and Vision: Sheldon Wolin and the Vicissitudes of the Political*, edited by Aryeh Botwinick and William E. Connolly, 173–92. Princeton: Princeton University Press, 2001.

Williams, Bernard. *Ethics and the Limits of Philosophy*. Cambridge: Harvard University Press, 1985.

———. "Replies." In *World, Mind, and Ethics: Essays on the Ethical Philosophy of Bernard Williams*, edited by J. E. J. Altham and Ross Harrison, 185–224. Cambridge: Cambridge University Press, 1995.

———. *Shame and Necessity*. Berkeley: University of California Press, 1993.

Wilson, Peter. *The Athenian Institution of the Khoregia: The Chorus, the City and the Stage*. Cambridge: Cambridge University Press, 2000.

Winthrop, Delba. "Aristotle and Political Responsibility." *Political Theory* 3 (1975): 406–22.

———. "Aristotle and Theories of Justice." *American Political Science Review* 72 (1978): 1201–16.

Wittgenstein, Ludwig. *Philosophical Investigations*. 2nd ed. Translated by G. E. M. Anscombe. Oxford: Blackwell, 1978.

Wolin, Sheldon. "Fugitive Democracy." In Benhabib, *Democracy and Difference*, 31–45.

———. "Norm and Form: The Constitutionalizing of Democracy." In *Athenian Political Thought and the Reconstruction of American Democracy*, edited by J. Peter Euben, John R. Wallach, and Josiah Ober, 29–58. Ithaca: Cornell University Press, 1994.

———. "Transgression, Equality, and Voice." In Ober and Hedrick, *Demokratia*, 63–90.

Wormuth, Francis D. "Aristotle on Law." In *Essays in Law and Politics*, 14–26. Port Washington, NY: National University Publications, 1978.

Yack, Bernard. "Community and Conflict in Aristotle's Political Philosophy." *Review of Politics* 47 (1985): 92–112.

———. "Natural Right and Aristotle's Understanding of Justice." *Political Theory* 18 (1990): 216–37.

———. *The Problems of a Political Animal: Community, Justice, and Conflict in Aristotelian Political Thought*. Berkeley: University of California Press, 1993.

Zashin, Elliott, and Phillip C. Chapman. "The Uses of Metaphor and Analogy: Toward a Renewal of Political Language." *Journal of Politics* 36 (1974): 290–326.

INDEX

accident: as bond of use friendship, 151; and citizen identity, 23–24, 51; independent of human agency, 40; and nature, 38, 39–40, 44–45; and slavery, 26, 27–28, 37

action, *praxis:* and activity, 10, 34–36; and character, 10; and choice, 33; and habit, 10, 34–37, 70–71, 108–11, 122–26; popular, 9; and property, 61–62; as self-governing, 9–10, 121; stable and unpredictable, 10; as work, 35

activity, *energeia:* and action, 9–10, 12, 34–36; and agency, 10; and capacity, 46–51; centrality to Aristotle's ethical and political philosophy, 8–9; and character, 10–12, 35–36, 47; characteristically human, 33–38 (*see also* prohairetic activity); circularity of, 22; and citizenship, 22–25; collective, 24–25, 91; defined, 3, 22; and habit, 10, 12, 34–37, 108–9; law as, 114, 123–26; and nature, 21–25, 26–38, 42, 45–46; and political institutions, 10–12, 50–51; property as, 56–69; singularity of, 12; as site of change, 12, 36, 41, 45–49; and slavery, 26–28, 33; virtue as, 13, 34–37, 109; as work, 1

affirmative action, 2–3

agency: and accident, 40; and activity, 10; and character, 10, 13; and force, 39, 43

Allen, Danielle, 88n13, 120n32

analogy, 38–39n53, 68n33, 70–71, 107, 129–30, 156, 161; phronetic judgment as, 95–98

ancestral constitution, 132–33, 136

Annas, Julia, 41n59, 42n61, 48n70, 50, 161n64

aporia, 8; as poverty, 79; as puzzle, 79

Archinus, 133

Arendt, Hannah, 1, 120

arete. See virtue

aristocracy, as exclusionary, 5, 17. *See also* so-called aristocracy; true aristocracy

arithmetic equality, 78, 85, 97, 110, 157, 175

art, *techne,* 44–45, 64, 121, 126

artisans, 92n21

Barber, Benjamin, 9n19

barter. *See* not proper use

Becker, Lawrence, 100

Benhabib, Seyla, 8n18

bipartisanship, 5, 133

capability. *See* capacity

capacity, *dunamis:* and activity, 46–51; habit as, 35–38; and justice, 107–8

Carthage, 75, 127n48, 173–74

certainty, Aristotle's rejection of, 9, 41

chance. *See* accident

character, individual: and activity, 8, 10, 11, 47; and agency, 10, 13; and choice, 1–3; and habit, 72; and political institutions, 1–4, 11–12, 15; and prohairetic activity, 34, 121–22; and property, 71–73, 79–80; and slavery, 30–31; and talents, 2–3; and virtue, 2–3; as work, 1, 12. *See also* soul

choice, *prohairesis,* 1, 33–34, 102. *See also* prohairetic activity

choregia: defined, 54–55n4; as life's sustenance, 59–64; as a political institution, 59–64; and proper use, 59–64; and the virtue of magnificence, 62–64. *See also under* proper use

193

194 INDEX

chreia. See use

citizens, 1, 15, 21–25; and accident, 23; and activity, 22–25; dangers of slavery to, 20–21; defined, 22; and force, 23; and political institutions, 11, 23–25, 91, 114, 123–26, 135–37; and regime, 22–23

citizenship: exclusions from, 8, 122; good, 116–17; as sharing in ruling and judging, 118, 120–26

city of prayer. *See* true aristocracy

civil strife, *stasis:* and friendship, 148–49; and property, 55, 65, 76; between rich and poor, 165–69. *See also* conflict

Cohen, David, 112–13n4, 119–21

commensurability, 66, 85, 86–92

commercial exchange. *See* not proper use

common good: and constitution, 162, 176; defined, 106; and law, 105; as maximizing prohairetic activity, 176, 180; and property, 58; and regime classification, 75; in so-called aristocracy, 171; in use friendship, 152–56

common ownership, Aristotle's rejection of, 54, 55, 58, 73–74

communism. *See* common ownership

communitarians, and liberals, 12, 14, 24

compulsion. *See* force

concord, *homonoia:* acquiescence as sign of, 172, 177–78; distinguished from goodwill, 174–75, 176; among political friends, 149–50, 161–63, 174, 175–80; and property, 56, 76; among use friends, 153–56; among virtue friends, 156–61. *See also* harmony

conflict, 13, 50, 139, 143; between aristocrats and democrats, 175–76; between oligarchs and democrats, 165–69; in use friendship, 151–56. *See also* civil strife

Connor, Robert, 148–49

conservatives, on welfare reform, 2

constitution: democratic-oligarchic, 127–28, 130–31, 165; as measure of law, 126–28, 135; as a practice of citizenship, 135–37, 162, 176; preserved by law, 128, 135; preserved by moderation, 130–37; and property, 74–76; of Sparta, 127–31

constitutional polity, *politeia:* compared to

so-called aristocracy, 170, 174; compared to true aristocracy, 163–65; as model of friendship, 163, 169

Constitution of the Five Thousand, 131–32, 136, 174

corrective justice: as arithmetic equality, 85, 97–98, 110; defined, 82, 85, 109–10; and impartiality, 104–6; in oligarchies and democracies, 103–4; and virtue, 109–10

craftsmen. *See* artisans

Danzig, Gabriel, 82n3

Davis, Michael, 30n39

decrees, *psephima,* 78, 112, 118

democracy, contemporary: Aristotle's relevance to, 4, 5–9, 16, 25, 52, 139, 180; challenges for, 4

democracy, fourth-century: Aristotle's criticisms of, 6, 8, 142; and freedom, 76; and poverty, 76, 167

democracy of distinction, 5, 9–11, 15, 16, 142, 179–80. *See also* so-called aristocracy

democratic aristocracy. *See* so-called aristocracy

democratic sovereignty, 6, 15, 52; and the rule of law, 118–26, 135–37. *See also* self-governance

desert. *See* merit

desire, 34, 72–73, 87, 112–15, 121, 173

despotism, 20–21, 28. *See also* tyranny

difference: distinguished from diversity, 145–147; in distribution of property, 78; and equality, 84, 86, 88–89, 101; and identity, 14, 80, 85; and justice, 98; as plurality, 4, 78; in practice of property, 64, 73; in the soul, 50; and unity, 7, 12–13, 16, 64, 143–47, 177; among virtue friends, 156–61

distinction. *See* difference

distributive justice: and affirmative action, 2; and citizenship, 21–22; defined, 82, 85, 107; as geometric equality, 78, 85, 97; and impartiality, 104–6; in oligarchies and democracies, 103–4; and phronetic judgment, 106–9; and punishment, 3; and slavery, 26; and virtue, 108–9

dunamis. See capacity

energeia. See activity

episteme. See scientific knowledge

equality: between aristocrats and democrats, 173–75; before the law, 13, 117; fourth-century democratic, 8; and property, 75, 76, 77–79; in reciprocal justice, 83–84, 85, 86, 88–89, 101; in so-called aristocracy, 177; among virtue friends, 157. *See also* arithmetic equality; geometric equality

equipment. See *choregia*

equity, 51, 81, 105, 111, 114–15, 171

ergon. See work

ethics, 3, 8, 13–15, 130, 137, 179

eudaimonia. See happiness

excellence. *See* virtue

exploitation. *See* improper use

faction. *See* civil strife

first-level capacity, 28–29, 33, 37

force, 23–24, 26, 27–28, 30, 37; law as, 22–23n20, 26–28, 81, 115; and necessity, 38, 43–44

foreigners: and climate, 31; as natural slaves 29–32; and tyranny, 31–32

formal cause, 28–29

freedom, 5; characteristic of virtue friendship, 158–59; democratic, 8, 76, 130; distinguished from independence, 159; among political friends, 175; and politics, 19, 20, 27, 28; and poverty, 172–73; and reciprocal justice, 100–101; and spirit, 31, 128; and virtue, 177

friendship, 16, 27; as bond of polity, 101, 147–48; property arrangement in, 55, 58, 158; as source of civil strife, 148–49; and virtue, 150. *See also* political friendship; use friendship; virtue friendship

geometric equality, 78, 85, 97–98, 107, 165–66, 173

goodwill, *eunoia*, 166; distinguished from concord, 174–75, 176

Habermas, Jurgen, 8n18

habit: and action, 10, 34–36, 70–71, 108–11, 122–26; and activity, 12, 34–37, 51; and character, 10; and choice, 33–34; of obedi-ence, 115–17; as property, 70–72; and virtue, 7, 34–37, 51

happiness, *eudaimonia*, 14, 141; and property, 55–57, 72

harmony: musical, 16, 144–45; political, 52, 143; of the soul, 49–50, 52. *See also* concord

Heidegger, Martin, 44–45

hierarchy: and politics, 19–21, 165–66; and property, 77

Hippocrates, 31n42

Hobbes, Thomas, 19

homonoia. See concord

identity: and action, 24, 40; of citizens, 21–25; and difference, 14, 85, 143–47; ethnic, 143, 144, 146; personal, 7, 15; and property, 79–80; sexual, 145–47; of slaves 26–30

impartiality, Aristotle's challenges to, 104–6

improper use: distinguished from not proper use, 65–66, 88; and money, 66–67, 90–91; of people, 74; of property, 64–69

independence: from government, 2; and property, 55–56, 59; and self-sufficiency, 2

instrumentality, and property, 56–57, 59, 61, 62, 64–70

judgment. *See* phronetic judgment

justice: and affirmative action, 2–3; contemporary approaches to, 81–82; and equality, 4, 97; and impartiality, 104–6; and law, 81, 110–11, 114–15; and phronetic judgment, 16, 84, 155; and politics, 102–6; of slavery, 26, 30–31; among use friends, 151–56; and virtue, 15–16, 84–85, 91–92, 101–11. *See also* corrective justice; distributive justice; reciprocal justice

Kant, Immanuel, 11, 102 (Kantian)

Klonoski, Richard J., 161n64

Kraut, Richard, 33n43, 37nn49–50, 81, 133n61, 154

law, *nomos*: contemporary approaches to, 115, 117, 125–26, 136–37; defined, 113; and equality, 4, 117; and equity, 114–15; as force, 22–23n20, 26, 81, 115; and generality, 13, 16,

law, *nomos* (*continued*)
114, 117, 124; and impartiality, 13, 105, 117; and justice, 81, 110–11, 114–15; and phronetic judgment, 116–26; and practical wisdom, 117–18, 120–26; as a practice of citizenship, 11, 114, 123–26, 135–37, 152; as regime-dependent, 16; as regulation, 13, 113, 130, 151; and virtue, 15, 110–11, 117–26
law, rule of: compared to rule of men, 7, 112–15, 118–26, 135–37; as habit of obedience, 115–17, 126; and overreaching, 112–15, 135–36
Lear, Jonathan, 41n58, 49
liberality, virtue of, 71–72, 76, 77, 158, 172, 175, 178
liberals: and communitarians, 12, 14, 24; and property, 78; on welfare reform, 2
liberty. *See* freedom
Locke, John, 19
Lummis, Douglas, 9n19

MacIntyre, Alasdair, 7n16, 93n22
magnificence, virtue of, 62–64, 76
majority rule, Aristotle's rejection of, 6, 118–19, 154
Mara, Gerald, 113n6
masters, 5, 8, 20; distinguished from citizen-rulers, 20–21; oligarchs as, 167; and unfreedom, 28, 128
material cause, 28, 29, 48–49
Mathie, William, 67
mean: Aristotle's doctrine of the, 4–5, 50, 157; distinguished from mediocrity, 5; as a middle or common term, 4–5, 6; money as a, 66; property as a, 54–55
mediocrity, 5
Meikle, Scott, 66, 86, 87n11, 90
merit: as criterion of citizenship, 22; as criterion of distributive justice, 107–9; as criterion of slavery, 26, 30–31, 37–38
Midas, 64
middle class, the: Aristotle's celebration of, 4, 163–78; as a mean, 4–5; and property, 16, 77
Mill, John Stuart, 11
Miller, Eugene, 119–21

Miller, Fred, Jr., 54n3
moderation, 50; as a constitutional virtue, 130–37; and law, 114, 130; among political friends, 162–63, 175; and property, 72–74, 77, 130; and self-knowledge, 93–94; among use friends, 155–56
money, 65–69, 86, 89–91
Mulgan, Richard, 168–69

nature, *phusis:* and accident, 38, 39–40, 44–45; and activity, 21–25, 26–38, 42, 45–49; of citizens, 21–25; distinguished from *natura,* 19–20; duality of, 40, 48–49; as form, 28–29, 48–49; and freedom, 18; and imprecision, 40–41; as matter, 28, 48; and necessity, 17, 19, 32, 38–40, 41–44; and phronetic judgment, 122; and politics, 15, 17–21, 52–53; and property, 64; and regime, 31–32; of slaves, 26–38; as what happens usually and for the most part, 40–45
necessity: as force, 38, 43–44; independent of human agency, 39, 43–44; and nature, 17, 19, 32, 38–40, 41–44; and scientific knowledge, 39; as subsistence, 57–58, 59, 99, 60–61, 62, 64; war as, 129
Nichols, Mary, 6n13
nomos. See law
nonpartisanship, 5, 132–33
notables, *gnorimoi,* distinguished from oligarchs, 132–33, 170–75
not proper use (of property): as commercial exchange, 88–90, 152–54; distinguished from improper use, 65–66, 88
numerical equality. *See* arithmetic equality
Nussbaum, Martha, 18n7, 21n15, 146

Ober, Josiah, 9, 25, 112–13n4, 113n8, 120n31, 139–41, 170–72, 174, 176, 177
oligarchy, 76; justice in, 103–4; as a regime of mastery, 130, 167
ousia, 21–22n15, 54–55n4, 72, 79–80
overreaching, *pleonexia:* as characteristic of fundamentalisms, 4; as characteristic of oligarchic-democratic regime, 130–31, 168; and justice, 84; and law, 112–15, 135–

36; and material gain, 64–69, 90–91, 129–30; as motive for use friendship, 151, 153; as unmoderated desire, 90, 112–15; and war, 129–31

partiality: characteristic of judges, 104–5; characteristic of oligarchy and democracy, 104; and moderation, 93–94; and phronetic judgment, 92–97, 106, 121

Pericles, 128–29

Phaleas, 75, 77

philosophical method, Aristotle's, 6–7, 9–10; as anti-idealist, 139–40; circularity of, 51–52, 137; whole and part relation in, 24–25, 82

philosophy, *theoria:* and money, 67–69; and necessity, 39, 67–68

phronesis. See practical wisdom

phronetic judgment: defined, 94, 96, 98; in distributive justice, 106–9; and law, 116–26; and partiality, 92–97, 106; among political friends, 162–63, 168; and practical wisdom, 84, 94, 121; and reciprocal justice, 16, 84, 94–100; and rotational rule, 99, 101; as thinking analogically, 95–98; among use friends, 155–56; and using well, 61; and virtue, 34, 35, 51, 84, 101–3

phusis. See nature

Plato, 49, 93, 124, 136, 145n24, 146

pleasure, 72, 87

pleonexia. See overreaching

plurality, and unity, 12, 143–47. *See also* difference

politeia. See constitutional polity

political clubs, *hetairies,* 132–33, 148–49

political friendship, 149–50; between aristocrats and democrats, 173–80; and concord, 175–80; and conflict, 175–76; and moderation, 162–63; between oligarchs and democrats, 165–69; and phronetic judgment, 162–63, 168; and use friendship, 161–63, 165–68; and virtue friendship, 161–63

political institutions: and activity, 8, 11–12, 51, 91; and character formation, 1–4, 15; and citizenship, 22–25; and slavery, 27–28.

See also constitution; justice; law; property

political participation, 25, 107

political rule: distinguished from mastery, 21, 28; as rotational rule, 101, 120

political wisdom, *politike,* 99, 135; and practical wisdom, 109, 124–26

politics: and character, 3, 11; distinguished from despotism, 20–21, 28, 128; and economics, 82–83, 86–92; and ethics, 3, 8, 13–15, 130, 137, 179; and freedom, 19, 20–21; and hierarchy, 19–21; and justice, 102–6; and nature, 15, 17–21, 52–53; and property, 56, 58–59, 69, 74–79; as a unity of the different, 4, 7, 12, 16, 52, 143–47, 175, 177; and virtue, 6, 14–15, 170–80; as work, 1, 12, 179–80

poverty: and freedom, 172–73; and regime classification, 75–76, 165–69. See also *aporia*

power. *See* capacity

practical wisdom, *phronesis:* and law, 113–15, 117–19, 121–26, 135–37; and moderation, 93–94; and partiality, 92–97; and political wisdom, 109; and reciprocal justice, 84, 92, 94; in slaves, 28–29; and true opinion, 98, 135. *See also* phronetic judgment

practice, defined, 7n16. *See* activity

praxis. See action

prohairetic activity, 33–38; as the common good, 162, 176; constitution as, 137; and money, 90–92; and nature, 34, 44–45, 47; among political friends, 137, 175; and politics, 45, 52; and property, 64, 67; reciprocity as, 84–85, 99; and virtue, 34–38, 51, 52, 84, 91, 122, 157; as work, 179–80

property: and action, 61–62; as an activity of use, 16, 56–69, 70–71; as a characterological good, 71–73; constitutionality of, 75–76; contemporary theories of, 54–56, 75; defined, 7, 16, 54–57; duality of, 55–56, 71–73, 79–80; and equality, 4, 75, 77–79; as an external good, 69, 71; among friends, 55, 58, 158; and instrumentality, 56–57, 59, 61, 62, 64–70; and nature, 64; and necessity, 57–58, 59, 60–61, 62; and politics, 56, 69,

property (*continued*)
74–79, 171; as a practice of the home, 55, 57–58; private and public character of, 55–56, 58–59, 60; and virtue, 15, 56–57, 62–64, 69–74, 76, 78–79. See also *choregia; improper use; not proper use; ousia; proper use; wealth*

proper use: as immediate, 87–88; as non-instrumental, 60–64; and phronetic judgment, 100; and property, 16, 56–64, 76, 70; and virtue, 13, 70–71. See also *choregia*

proportional equality. *See* geometric equality

punishment, 3

Putnam, Robert, 2

Rackham, H., 59

Rawls, John, 11

reason. *See* practical wisdom

reciprocal justice, 82–94; as bond of polity, 16, 82–83, 99–101; defined, 82; equality in, 83–84, 85, 97–98; in oligarchies and democracies, 103–4; and phronetic judgment, 16, 84, 98–99; and practical wisdom, 84, 92, 94; return and initiation in, 100; rotational rule as, 83; and virtue, 91–92. *See also* not proper use

regime: Aristotle's classification of, 75–76, 112; and citizenship, 22, 24–25; mixed and middling, 4, 142, 169–80; and slavery, 31–32. *See also* constitutional polity; democracy; oligarchy; so-called aristocracy; true aristocracy; tyranny

responsibility: criminal, 3, 43–44; individual, 2, 45, 50; political, 2, 18, 114–15

retail commerce. *See* improper use

Rhodes, P. J., 133n59–60, 134

Ritchie, D. G., 99

rotational rule: and hierarchy, 20; in office-holding, 120, 171–78; as reciprocal justice, 83, 99, 101; as work, 1

Rousseau, Jean-Jacques, 11, 19, 168

Salkever, Stephen, 14, 17n4, 40n57, 129n52, 130

Saxonhouse, Arlene, 144–46, 147

Schofield, Malcolm, 22

scientific knowledge, *episteme*, 39, 121, 126

self-governance: action as, 9–11; political, 15, 24–25, 52, 130; among political friends, 175–80; and property, 79; rule of law as, 135–37; and slavery, 29; among use friends, 152–56; virtue as individual, 11, 13, 52, 121–23, 130

self-interest, 5; and partiality, 92–94; in political friendship, 176, 179–80; and regime classification, 75; in use friendship, 150–55

self-rule. *See* self-governance

Skocpol, Theda, 2

slavery, 5, 15; and activity, 26–28, 32–38; and climate, 31; dangers of, 20–21; and hierarchy, 20–21; and justice, 20, 26, 30–31, 37; natural, 17, 26–38; and political institutions, 27–28; and self-governance, 29; and tyranny, 31–32

Smith, Adam, 11

so-called aristocracy, 142, 169–80; compared to constitutional polity, 170; concord in, 176–80; conflict in, 175–76; distinguished from moderate oligarchy, 170–72

social capital, 2

Socrates, 54, 71n38, 74, 93, 105n47, 143, 158

soul: as formal cause of nature, 28–29; invisibility of, 29, 31, 33; and prohairetic activity, 33; as source of motion, 47; unity of, 49–50, 52

Sparta, 75, 127–31, 168

speech, 33, 144n20, 160–63

spirit, *thumos*, 31, 128

stasis. See civil strife

Strauss, Leo, 114

Swanson, Judith, 20n11, 91

Tarentine, 173

techne. See art

teleology, 10, 48–49, 139–42

temporality, 39–40, 48–49, 50, 139–42, 179–80

Tessitore, Aristide, 103n44

Thales, 68

Theramenes, 22n20, 115–17, 123, 125, 129, 131–34, 136, 137, 168

timocracy. *See* constitutional polity

touch, sense of, 72–74

true aristocracy, 138–42, 175, 178; and constitutional polity, 163–65

trust: among citizens, 76, 89, 166; among friends, 58, 153n46, 155, 163

tyranny: elective, 32; hereditary and legal, 31–32; lawlessness of, 112, 133

unity: of Aristotle's writings, 4, 139; and difference, 4, 12–13, 16, 64, 143–47; political, 7, 177; and property, 64–65, 67, 73; of the soul, 49–50, 52; among virtue friends, 156–61

use, *chreia:* as a common measure, 86–89; distinguished from utilitarian conception, 87. *See also* improper use; not proper use; proper use

use friendship: and conflict, 151–55; justice in, 152–55; and moderation, 155–56; mutual advantage in, 150, 152–56; and phronetic judgment, 155–56; political friendship, compared to, 150–51, 161–63; and self-interest, 150–55

utopianism, Aristotle's rejection of, 139–40

vice, 3, 13, 43–44, 131, 172–73

Villa, Dana, 49n72

virtue: and character, 2–3; characteristic of Sparta's constitution, 128; as constituted by habits and actions, 7, 34–37, 108–10, 122–26; as criterion of distribution, 3, 36–37; and freedom, 177; in friendship, 150, 156; and justice, 84–85, 91–92, 98, 101–11; and law, 15, 110–11, 117–26; and partiality,

13, 93–94; as personal responsibility, 2, 43–44; and politics, 6, 13–15, 170–80, 173; and prohairetic activity, 34–38, 91, 157; and property, 56–57, 69–74, 76, 78–79; and rotational rule, 171–78; as self-governing activity, 13, 14, 109; and slavery, 28–29, 30–31, 37–38. *See also* liberality; magnificence; moderation; phronetic judgment; practical wisdom

virtue friendship: equality in, 157; freedom in, 158–59; and political friendship, 150, 161–63; as unity of the different, 156–61

Waltz, Kenneth, 15n30

war, 128–29, 130–31, 168

wealth, *plutos:* 56–57, 58, 62–64; as criterion for office-holding, 171, 174; and regime classification, 75–77, 165–69

wealth-getting. *See* improper use

welfare reform, 1–2

White, Stephen, 4

Williams, Bernard, 13n27, 36n48, 49

Wilson, Peter, 61–63

Winthrop, Delba, 23n22, 103n44, 104

work, *ergon:* action as, 35; activity as, 1; of capacity, 46–47; of democracy, 15; of humans, 1, 34–35, 49–52, 179–80; of politics, 3, 12, 179–80; politics as, 1, 11; and virtue, 34–35, 50, 179–80; of wealth, 62–64. *See also specific political institutions*

Yack, Bernard, 12n25, 113n6, 115n15, 118, 119, 121, 144, 151, 166